CORPORATE GOVERNANCE IN GOVERNMENT CORPORATIONS

To Shelley,
more familiar with Government than I ever wish to be

Corporate Governance in Government Corporations

MICHAEL J. WHINCOP
*Key Centre for Ethics, Law, Justice and Governance,
Griffith University, Australia*

LONDON AND NEW YORK

First published 2005 by Ashgate Publishing

2 Park Square, Milton Park, Abingdon, Oxon OX14 4RN
711 Third Avenue, New York, NY 10017, USA

Routledge is an imprint of the Taylor & Francis Group, an informa business

First issued in paperback 2016

Copyright © Michael J. Whincop 2005

The author hereby asserts his moral right to be identified as the author of the work in accordance with the Copyright Designs and Patents Act, 1988.

All rights reserved. No part of this book may be reprinted or reproduced or utilised in any form or by any electronic, mechanical, or other means, now known or hereafter invented, including photocopying and recording, or in any information storage or retrieval system, without permission in writing from the publishers.

Notice:
Product or corporate names may be trademarks or registered trademarks, and are used only for identification and explanation without intent to infringe.

British Library Cataloguing in Publication Data
Whincop, Michael J.
  Corporate governance in government corporations. - (Law,
  ethics and governance)
  1.Corporations, Government - Management 2.Corporate
  governance - Law and legislation 3.Corporations, Government
  - Queensland - Management 4.Corporate governance - Law and
  legislation - Queensland
  I.Title
  346'.067

Library of Congress Cataloging-in-Publication Data
Whincop, Michael J.
  Corporate governance in government corporations / by Michael J. Whincop.
        p. cm. -- (Law, ethics and governance)
  Includes bibliographical references and index.
  ISBN 0-7546-2276-2
  1. Government business enterprises--Management. 2. Corporations, Government--
Management. 3. Corporate governance. I. Title. II. Series.

  HD62.35.W45 2004
  352.2'66--dc22

2004020206

ISBN 13: 978-0-7546-2276-5 (hbk)
ISBN 13: 978-1-138-27783-0 (pbk)

Contents

List of Tables and Figures		*vi*
Preface		*x*
Acknowledgements		*v*
1	Introduction	1
2	Historical and Comparative Issues	22
3	The Management of the Government Corporation	63
4	The Government as Shareholder	112
5	Stakeholders and Corporate Governance	162
6	Reforming Government Corporations	187
Bibliography		*229*
Index		*243*

List of Tables and Figures

Table 1.1	Population and Sample	20
Table 1.2	Breakdown of Sample	20
Table 2.1	Initial Equity Shares in Privatisations in Poland	48
Figure 2.1	Total Agency Costs in Government Corporations as a Function of Ministerial Discretion	58
Table 3.1	Overcompensation of the CEO (by Portfolio)	75
Table 3.2	Effects of Undercompensating the CEO (by Portfolio)	76
Table 3.3	Experience in Corporate Governance	80
Table 3.4	Experience and Qualifications (by Portfolio)	81
Table 3.5	Agreement with Propositions to Improve Board Composition and Functioning (by Portfolio)	83
Table 3.6	Cross-tabulation of Remuneration Perceptions and Listed Company Experience	85
Table 3.7	Cross-tabulation of Perception of Adequacy of Remuneration and Effects of Legal Liability	86
Table 3.8	Relation between Effect on Reputation and Public Company Experience	88
Table 3.9	Perceptions of Directors' Duties	89
Table 3.10	Means by which a Conflict Would and Should be Handled	91
Table 3.11	Crosstabulation of Responses to how the Conflict in the Enterprise Bargain Transaction Would and Should be Handled	92
Table 3.12	Crosstabulation of Responses to how the Conflict in the Enterprise Bargain Transaction and the Country Services Transaction Would be Handled	93
Table 3.13	How the Conflict in the Enterprise Bargain Transaction Would be Handled (by Portfolio)	94
Table 3.14	Summary Statistics of Director Terms	95
Table 3.15	Completed Director Terms in Continuing GCs Associated with Change of Government and Party	96
Table 3.16	Directors Reappointed at the End of their Terms (by Portfolio)	96
Table 3.17	Relation of Experience in Listed Companies to Reappointment	97
Table 3.18	Relation of Experience in Listed Companies to Reappointment (by Portfolio)	97
Table 3.19	Relation of Change of Government to Reappointment	98
Table 3.20	Relation of Change of Party Forming Government to Reappointment	98
Table 3.21	Relation of Change of Party Forming Government to Reappointment (by Portfolio)	98
Table 3.22	Econometric Model of Reappointment (Logit Regression)	100

List of Figures and Tables

Table 3.23 Early Termination of Directorships (by Portfolio)	100
Table 3.24 Early Termination of Directorships (by Portfolio)	101
Table 3.25 Relation of Experience in Listed Companies to Early Termination	102
Table 3.26 Relation of Experience in Listed Companies to Early Termination (by Portfolio)	102
Table 3.27 Relation of Change of Government to Early Termination	102
Table 3.28 Relation of Change of Government to Early Termination (by Portfolio)	103
Table 3.29 Relation of Change of Party Forming Government to Early Termination	103
Table 3.30 Relation of Change of Party Forming Government to Early Termination (by Portfolio)	104
Table 3.31 Econometric Model of Reappointment (Logit Regression)	104
Table 3.32 Factors Likely to Result in Termination or Non-reappointment (Means by Portfolio)	106
Table 3.33 Factors Likely to Result in Termination or Non-reappointment (comparison between current and former directors)	107
Table 3.34 Reasons for Non-reappointment (by Portfolio)	108
Table 3.35 Reason for Non-reappointment (by Portfolio)	109
Figure 4.1 Total Agency Costs in Government Corporations as a Function of Ministerial Discretion	121
Table 4.1 Basis for Consideration as an Appointment	123
Table 4.2 Major Contact Regarding Appointment	124
Table 4.3 Circumstances of Ministerial Involvement in Management	125
Table 4.4 Relation between Expectations of Political Intervention in the GC and Public Company Experience	125
Table 4.5 Relation between Expectations of the Effect of Change of Government and Public Company Experience	128
Table 4.6 Nature of SCI and Corporate Plan Formulation	130
Table 4.7 Monitoring of SCI Goal Achievement (by Portfolio)	131
Table 4.8 Relationship between Minister's Active Negotiation of SCIs and Board Monitoring of SCI goals	132
Table 4.9 Consequences of not Meeting SCIs	132
Table 4.10 Relationship between Active Negotiation of SCIs and Consequences of not Meeting SCI Goals	133
Table 4.11 Frequency of Using Particular Means of Communication	135
Table 4.12 Frequency with which Ministers Raise Particular Issues	136
Table 4.13 Frequency with which Portfolio Ministers Raise Particular Issues (Means by Portfolio and ANOVA)	137
Table 4.14 Frequency with which Treasurers Raise Particular Issues (Means by Portfolio and ANOVA)	137

viii   *Corporate Governance in Government Corporations*

Table 4.15 Circumstances Where the Board would Initiate Communications with a Minister Regarding Particular Issues   138

Table 4.16 Effect of Ministerial Involvement in the Business of the GC   139

Table 4.17 Effect of Portfolio Minister's Involvement in the Business of the GC (Means by Portfolio and ANOVA)   139

Table 4.18 Ministerial Intervention in GC Management or Governance (broken down by Director Status and Portfolio)   140

Table 4.19 Motivations and Circumstances in which a Minister Will Intervene in Management under Particular Circumstances   141

Table 4.20 Circumstances where Intervention by the Portfolio Minister is Political Interference   142

Table 4.21 Attribution of Minister's Credibility to Particular Sources of Power   143

Table 4.22 Differences in Objectives between the Portfolio Minister and the Treasurer   144

Table 4.23 Resolution of Conflicting Objectives by the Portfolio Minister and the Treasurer   144

Table 4.24 Aspects of the Working Relationship between GCs and the Portfolio Department (Means by Portfolio)   148

Table 4.25 Aspects of the Working Relationship between GCs and Treasury (Means by Portfolio)   149

Table 4.26 Differences Between the Working Relationship with the Portfolio Department and Treasury (Means by Portfolio)   150

Table 4.27 Difference in the Perception of Directors with Listed Public Company Experience of the Working Relationship between GCs and the Portfolio Department (Means by Portfolio)   152

Table 4.28 Freedom in Relation to Services and Prices (by Portfolio)   154

Table 4.29 Effect of Government Policies (by Portfolio)   155

Table 4.30 Effect of Government Policies (by Director Status)   156

Table 4.31 Effect of Government Policies (by Portfolio and Director Status)   156

Table 4.32 Response to Government Policies (by Portfolio)   157

Table 4.33 Relation Between Effect of and Response to Government Policies   158

Table 5.1 Lobbying of Board Members or Management by Customers (by Portfolio)   166

Table 5.2 Advocacy by Board Members for Customers or Users (by Portfolio)   167

Table 5.3 Relation between Lobbying and Advocacy by Directors   168

Table 5.4 Political Pressure on Services (by Portfolio)   169

Table 5.5 Relation between Political Pressure on Services and Lobbying of Board Members   170

Table 5.6 Relation between Political Pressure on Services and Directors Advocating Interest Groups   170

List of Figures and Tables

Table 5.7	Relation between Sufficient Freedom on Service Levels and Directors Advocating Interest Groups	171
Table 5.8	Relation between Political Pressure on Services and Sufficient Freedom on Service Levels	171
Table 5.9	Relation between Political Pressure on Services and Expectations Regarding Inefficient Constraints by Government	172
Table 5.10	Relation between Sufficient Freedom on Service Levels and Expectations Regarding Inefficient Constraints by Government	172
Table 5.11	Relation between Political Pressure on Services and Incidence of Informal Intervention by Ministers in Management and Governance	173
Table 5.12	Relation between Political Pressure on Services and Incidence of Informal Intervention by Ministers in Management and Governance (by Portfolio)	173
Table 5.13	Relation between Sufficient Freedom on Pricing and Services and Incidence of Informal Intervention by Ministers in Management and Governance	174
Table 5.14	Liberty to Maximise Workforce Productivity (by Portfolio)	175
Table 5.15	Liberty to Maximise Workforce Productivity Related to Corporate Governance Experience in a Listed Public Company	175
Table 5.16	Liberty to Maximise Workforce Productivity Related to Corporate Governance Experience in a Listed Public Company (by Portfolio)	176
Table 5.17	Crosstabulation of Liberty on Pricing and Services and Freedom to Maximise Workforce Productivity	177
Table 5.18	Efficiency of Staff Productivity (by Portfolio)	178
Table 5.19	Labour Representative on the Board (by Portfolio)	178
Table 5.20	Over- or Underpricing of CSOs (by Portfolio)	180
Figure 6.1	Costs of Financial Distress and Agency Costs with respect to Leverage	189
Figure 6.2	Changes in Agency Costs and Costs of Financial Distress in a GC	190
Table 6.1	Time and Remuneration of Non-executive Directors (by Company Type)	199
Table 6.2	The Chairman and the Government as Sources of Advice	202
Table 6.3	Increase in Performance-related Pay and Portfolio	206
Figure 6.3	Representation of Political and Pecuniary Conflicts	210
Figure 6.4	Strategic Incentives with respect to Required Returns in SCIs	219

Preface

Over the last two decades, governments across the world have responded to the need for greater efficiency in the delivery of government services in different ways. These means range across privatisation, competitive tendering, outsourcing, and the reorganisation of bureaucracies in ways designed to subject them to incentives to operate efficiently. A common theme in this transformation has been to expose service delivery to market incentives, or to attempt to emulate these incentives by organisational structure and contracts. Research on the effects of market incentives on efficiency is, of course, fundamental to microeconomics. Rather more neglected, however, is a study of the role that governance processes serve in the delivery of the economic and social objectives of the modern state. This neglect is surprising, as a major theme of modern economics, and also of contemporary legal and public administration scholarship, is that governance is fundamental.

I pursue the study of governance in this book in the context of government corporations. Even after the wave of privatisations in the 1980s and 1990s, government corporations continue to manage highly important utilities, infrastructure, and businesses worldwide. The governance arrangements in these organisations, to which competitive market forces apply weakly, are of particular importance. However, scholarly attention has scarcely been directed to them. In this book, besides reviewing and synthesising the theoretical literature on corporate and public governance, I provide empirical evidence on these questions, based on a study of government corporations in Queensland, Australia. The research was funded by Queensland Treasury, and the Australian Research Council under a SPIRT grant. The views expressed in this book do not necessarily represent the views or policies of either of those bodies.

I want to acknowledge my gratitude to David Skeel and Maxwell Stearns for their substantial contribution to this research project; A.J. Brown and Jon Leckie for their research assistance; Jackie Martin, Andrew McMicking, Bruce Macallum, and Jeff Lassan for Treasury's contributions and input; and my mother and sister for love and support.

Michael J. Whincop
Brisbane, Australia

Acknowledgements

This book reproduces parts of material previously published by me. Chapter 3 includes material previously published in my article, 'Another Side of Accountability: The Fiduciary Concept and Rent-Seeking in the Governance of Government Corporations' (2002) 25 *University of New South Wales Law Journal* forthcoming. Chapter 4 includes material previously published in my essay, 'The Role of Ministerial Shareholders in the Governance of Government Owned Corporations', which is published as chapter 6 of Michael Whincop (ed.), *From Bureaucracy to Business Enterprise: Legal and Policy Issues in the Transformation of Government Services* (Ashgate, 2002).

Chapter 1

Introduction

In the 1980s and 1990s, governments across the world sought to roll back the borders of the state, and to pursue, to the extent possible, the satisfaction of demands for essential services and utilities by way of competitive markets. It is common to analyse this transition in terms of the economic theory of public choice. In this theory, the behaviour of governments is best explained by the idea that political actors selfishly seek to maximise their own welfare, rather than selflessly furthering the public interest (*e.g.*, Buchanan and Tullock 1965; Niskanen 1968, 1971). Because of the different parameters of markets to those of governments, the selfishness that is a virtue in the former becomes a vice in the latter. The normative thrust of most public choice theory is the desirability of smaller government. Public choice theory therefore provided a theoretical pedigree for the roll-back of the modern state over the last two decades, even though it was hard-pushed to explain why selfish politicians would behave in this uncharacteristic welfare-increasing manner.

Although the public choice explanation is important, particularly in its emphasis on comparative efficiency of public and private provision, there is something incomplete about it. Greater attention to history beyond the last two decades suggests that the questions of which services governments should provide, and the means by which it provides them, are only ever answered provisionally and are revisited at turns of political and economic cycles. The enthusiasm demonstrated in the 1980s and 1990s for neoliberal economic reform was not a permanent move away from public provision. Rather, it was a step best comprehended (without the distraction of its ideology) as a response, in part, to budgetary pressures, political agendas, and organisational crises within bureaucracies. Similar explanations apply to the signs of retreat from these principles at turn of the twenty-first century. Consider two examples. One is the quasi-nationalisation inherent in a number of government bailouts of airlines, such as Air New Zealand and Swissair (see generally Dirmeyer *et al.* 2002), and of the \$15 billion bailout of the airline industry in the US.[1] The other occurs in the wake of the chaotic conditions of the electricity market in the United States, especially in California (Business Week 2001). Here, there is a move towards 'community choice' in the provision of electricity, which involves municipal governments becoming buyers of electricity on behalf of communities.[2] These developments need to be understood by reference to distributional concerns, politics, and the insolvency of private firms providing essential services. Historical evidence confirms that this is not merely a one-off cycle.

In an environment that behaves cyclically, there is a risk that even the more public-regarding policy aspirations that guide restructuring and reform will fall by the wayside. For one example, the price regulation that accompanies privatisation may be used to advance the interests of incumbent firms, rather than consumers. For another, governments may refuse to allow privatised firms providing essential services or infrastructure to face the full wrath of the marketplace. They may willingly bail them out, or subsidise others to do so. Finally, governments may renege on their commitments to free public bureaucracies from political micro-management. Thus, these forms of restructuring simply shift the boundaries, and alter the forms, of the opportunism that economists call 'rent-seeking' in the political process.[3]

This scenario suggests that the governance arrangements of private firms and public bureaucracies supplying essential services, infrastructure and utilities are of prime importance. These governance arrangements determine the extent to which these hierarchies are protected against rent-seeking and political opportunism, and reflect the commitment of the government, now and in the future, to the goals declared at the time of its reform program.

This may appear to be self-evident. The study of governance in economics, law and public administration is of course well-established. However, the literature on governance of arrangements for service provision in the modern state is only beginning to emerge. Much of the analysis of privatisation consists of comparative static analysis of the economic efficiency of firms in public and private ownership (Megginson and Netter [2001] reviews these studies in detail). Many of these comparisons, however, tell us relatively little. It is doubtful that the managers of private and public owners both seek to maximise the same objective functions, or that the function that one maximises is more closely aligned with social welfare than the other.

In this context, the difficulty of equating the objectives that motivate governance structures complicates the extrapolation of the apparently concrete conclusions of much economic analysis of governance in corporations. The economic literature generally assumes that the goal of governance is to maximise the value of the firm's assets. The entitlements of parties with claims on those assets are restricted to the extent that they are likely to induce post-contractual opportunism, such as moral hazard or hold-out behaviour (Jensen and Meckling 1976; Williamson 1985). By contrast, where the state continues to have some involvement in the provision of goods and services, the efficiency objective must compete with a 'representational' objective. That is, the governance process must be capable of allowing community concerns to be brought to bear upon the provision of services that are thought to be integral to community welfare. The difficulty associated with trading off these different objectives makes the governance of these processes more complex, and complicates the extrapolation of normative conclusions reached regarding private firms.

Despite these problems, a literature on the governance issues associated with privatisation and partial privatisation is emerging, which focuses microanalytically on institutions and their limitations (*e.g.*, Graham and Prosser 1991; D'Souza *et al.* 2000; Boubakri *et al.* 2001). By contrast, what is almost entirely absent is a sustained, general analysis of the governance of public firms organised and expected to be managed as business corporations (*cf.* Prichard 1983; Stevens 1993), except in the *sui generis* context of transitional economies (*e.g.*, Shirley 1999). Even after the wave of privatisations and divestments of the 1980s and 1990s, government corporations (GCs) continue to serve vital functions in many economies throughout the world. In Western economies, GCs continue to have a pervasive role in markets that tend towards natural monopoly. In emerging economies, where markets lack equivalent sophistication, GCs will serve even more important roles, especially since privatisation has had limited success in some parts of the world (*e.g.*, Kuznetsov and Kuznetsova 1999; McCarthy *et al.* 2000; Pagoulatos 2001).

To be sure, the GC has attracted its share of attention — in particular, the process of *corporatisation*, by which a government department is transformed into a substantially autonomous entity embracing the praxis and disciplines of a business corporation (see generally Collier and Pitkin 1999). However, much of that literature suffers from three serious flaws. The first is that the literature explicitly or implicitly proceeds from the premise that corporatisation is a process lacking 'closure'. That is, the corporatised entity awaits privatisation, the ultimate *coup de grâce*; or that corporatisation is somehow the 'wimp's' privatisation, awaiting a government of stronger will and conviction. That premise is unhelpful. In the first instance, its factual merit is debatable. There are a sufficiently large number of GCs that have not been privatised that the GC has every right to be analysed in its own terms. Further, analysis that begins by asserting the superiority of privatisation is unlikely to be helpful.

The second flaw is that where the literature analyses governance issues, it starts with the claim that the closer the parameters of the governance

4 *Corporate Governance in Government Corporations*

environment are to those of the business corporation, the better for all concerned. This, however, is overgeneralised. To see this fallacy, we may briefly turn our attention to the general theory of the second best in welfare economics (Lipsey and Lancaster 1956). There are a number of market imperfections which cause market equilibria to diverge from the social optimum. The theory asserts that the serial correction of these imperfections is just as likely to move an economy *away* from the optimum as it is to move it in the opposite and presumably desired direction. In much the same way, one cannot assert that emulating *aspects* of a governance institution that may be useful to business corporations will necessarily be desirable in a GC. The governance environment is different in a number of important respects, so the ideal governance equilibrium may look different as well (Stevens 1993).

The third flaw is that, despite its normative gravity, the literature is based on relatively little empirical evidence of governance institutions in corporatised organisations. Normative claims are usually based on intuition, experience in business corporations, and comparative public-private efficiency analyses. We lack solid evidence of governance processes in GCs, and in particular the role served by the government in its place as the shareholder. Because governments differ from the normal shareholding body of a business corporation in regards both to objectives and powers, the analysis of the behaviour of government shareholders is a subject of particular interest. It presents an opportunity for us to examine economic theories of political behaviour, and to gauge their application in particular institutional conditions.

In light of this hiatus in the literature, and the analytical flaws in most considerations of GCs, this book has several objectives. The first is to develop a more general theorisation of the governance of these entities, which does not begin with any presuppositions regarding the desirability of privatising the GC. In order to do that, we need to begin from the bottom and work up. Specifically, rather than being misled by the corporate form of the GC, which might narrow our inquiry undesirably, we must start by identifying each of the constituencies associated with GCs and analyse the interests that each has which might appropriately be protected by the governance process.

My second objective is to examine empirical evidence associated with governance processes in the GC. As noted above, the empirical analysis of corporatisation is often tendentious in its assumptions regarding the objective function that GC managers are supposed to be maximising. To compensate for these deficiencies, it is necessary to examine these issues microanalytically at the level of the relation between the various constituencies that governance processes supposedly protect.

Introduction 5

Although my theoretical analysis is general, the empirical evidence is much more specific. More fully described below, it arises from a consideration of GCs in a specific jurisdiction, namely the Government Owned Corporations of the State of Queensland, Australia. Obviously, that evidence is only susceptible of imperfect generalisation to other systems. However, taken as a case study, its contribution outweighs its limitations. It shows some of the dilemmas developed in the theoretical analysis, and it illustrates a fundamental governance problem of *commitment*. That is, how is it possible for a government to commit to a governance environment in which managers attempt to pursue efficiency, even to the extent of enforcing that commitment against itself? I consider various answers to this question in the final chapter of this book.

My third objective is to make some tentative suggestions regarding the means of improving governance processes in GCs. Particularly if civil society is turning away from the dogmatic commitment to markets that characterised the 1980s and 1990s, it is necessary that public provision be accompanied by a strong commitment to governance. Otherwise, one simply sows the seeds for future cycling, with its attendant instability, waste, and rent-seeking. Weak governance will, at the margin, empower constituencies that advocate radical change, either towards or away from markets. There seems to be anecdotal evidence for the proposition that the weaker the economy of a state, the more its state-owned enterprises and GCs will be used for non-commercial, political objectives, especially employment creation (*e.g.*, Stevens [1993], comparing the experience in Manitoba and Alberta, Canada). This in turn exacerbates the case for privatisation further along the political cycle. For that reason, at least, the strength of the commitment to governance is imperative.

Even if the perception that there is a move away from markets is a false or overstated one, substantial and important assets remain in the ownership of GCs and similar state-owned monopolies. It is important to ensure that those assets are subject to appropriate governance, however 'appropriateness' in either representation or efficiency is defined.

The remainder of this chapter is devoted to the following tasks. The first task is to develop the basic framework used in this book to analyse the principal governance problems that GCs experience. Whereas the business corporation (BC) essentially needs only to solve a single governance problem — how to align the interests of investors and managers — there are at least three distinct problems in the GC. These are, first, and as in a BC, the alignment of the interests of the GC's managers with those of its ultimate owners. Unlike the BC, however, the interests of the ultimate owners of the GC are much more heterogeneous than those in the BC, which can be described without distortion in terms of the desire for wealth

6   *Corporate Governance in Government Corporations*

maximisation. Next, there is the problem associated with the alignment of the interests of those wielding delegated governance power over managers with those of its ultimate owners. Governance powers will often be delegated to members of the executive government. As actors in the political process, questions arise regarding the extent to which these persons are inclined to use those governance powers for political advantage. The final governance problem is the reduction of social costs associated with anti-competitive behaviour by the GC. This links back to the first governance problem, since it is an aspect of the relation between managerial behaviour and the interests of the ultimate owners. However, the first governance problem relates to the 'agency costs' of management (Jensen and Meckling 1976), and the moral hazard problems arising from delegated power; whereas this governance problem involves the social costs associated with monopoly.

Second, a brief description of the governance structure of a GC is provided. The representative model is taken from the Queensland corporatisation regime. This provides a primer on organisational form, a point of departure for the GCs in other jurisdictions, and a reference to understand the empirical analysis. In chapter 2, this sketch is placed in perspective by evaluating both its historical antecedents and modern comparisons in other jurisdictions. Third, I outline the remaining chapters of the book.

Governance Problems in GCs

It is useful first to examine the logic of governance in a BC, in order to understand the necessary points of departure in the GC. The essential governance problem experienced in a private firm is associated with the arrangement between an investing principal and a managerial agent. The principal must find the optimal contract (defining that term widely to include all the incentives and governance processes applying to that contract) to encourage the agent to maximise the value of the principal's investment in the firm. The principal's incentives in choosing the contract, and the governance mechanisms it requires, correspond closely to social welfare. The principal bears the residual wealth effects of the contract chosen, and by maximising his wealth he should maximise social welfare (Jensen and Meckling 1976).

The notion that the governance problem in a BC is bilateral is a simplification, but it is often a workable one. First, all but the smallest BCs have multiple shareholders. Since Berle and Means (1932), it has been recognised that the existence of a large number of small shareholders can distort the incentive of those shareholders to choose an optimal contract, to monitor, and to exercise powers against managerial derelictions when required. However, combining the fungibility of the returns to shareholders with the operation of capital markets allows differences between shareholders to be finessed into a single objective to which all shareholders agree (De Angelo 1981).

The second and greater complication to the bilateral governance problem in the BC is the existence of non-shareholder constituencies, and their potential claims to protection through governance processes. This question has formed, and still forms, a dividing line between corporate law scholars on the left from those on the right. Economically-minded scholars conventionally dismiss the relevance of these constituencies by emphasising that their interests can be protected through the contracting process that occurs when they become part of the firm, which is renegotiated at intervals thereafter (*e.g.*, Macey 1991). However, economic analysis has also been used to argue that governance processes in corporations afford the corporation's peak governance body, the board of directors, the discretion to make adjustments between the interests of the shareholders and other constituencies (Blair and Stout 1999). One issue that transcends this somewhat intractable debate is to ask to what extent those who control the firm are likely to side with shareholders over other constituencies. Coffee (1990) suggests that the takeovers wave of the 1980s tended to realign managers with shareholders, in maximising value. By contrast, they had previously tended to be more sympathetic to creditors and employees through a shared preference for decreased volatility and increased corporate size.[4] The balance, however, is never a completely stable equilibrium, and shifts may occur over time.

Through the lens of these two complications of the bilateral governance model, we can examine some of the governance singularities of the GC. In the first instance, it is much harder to identify a single constituency with a single common objective in a GC. This is because the constituency to whom the GC's agents are ultimately accountable — the people — stands in a dual relation to the GC. On the one hand, they are the GC's residual claimants, as shareholders are in a BC. Although there is little or no opportunity for them to trade their interests, as the shareholders of a traded BC can, members of the public bear the residual returns of the corporation after all its fixed claimants, including creditors and employees, are paid off. On the other hand, they are also frequently the principal recipients of the goods and services the GC provides. In this context, the GC will often have a monopolistic relation to the members of the public; its situation in public ownership typically reflects elements of natural monopoly. This dualistic relation between the GC and the public makes it difficult to concretise the

8   *Corporate Governance in Government Corporations*

meaning of acting in the best interests of the public. This complicates the evaluation of both the actions of the managers, as well as the exercise of governance powers by the government or government officials. One commentator argues that GCs do *not* belong to the public, but to the managers and public officials who can appropriate the GCs surpluses (Walker 1998).

To make this discussion more specific, consider that one of the ways by which the advocates of modern corporatisation programs have tried to resolve the tensions between the public as residual claimant and the public as beneficiary is by means of the 'community service obligation' (CSO).[5] The CSO purports to enable the managers of the corporation to maximise the value of the GC by allowing the executive government to mandate and pay for any activities insupportable by the object of value maximisation. Although that mechanism does reduce some of the conflict, for the most part it simply relocates it. The mandated CSO raises a series of questions regarding its interpretation and its effect when there is a change in the state of the world between the time the CSO was mandated and the time it is to be performed (Quiggin 2003). The CSO may become inflexible and costly to reverse (Trebilcock and Prichard 1983). Questions also arise regarding the appropriate measure for the funding of the CSO, in a world where the GC lacks a key response in bargaining with the government — to walk away — and in the absence of market prices that might proxy for marginal cost.

The problem with non-shareholder constituencies that we observe is similar to the BC. That is, a GC must respond to demands by these constituencies for representation in the governance processes of the firm. However, unlike the BC, where that issue is normally resolved by bargaining between the corporation and the constituency, the risk in GCs is that these issues may be resolved by the exercise of governance power by the executive government in response to political self-seeking by the constituency. This also reveals the more general problem of conflict between the management of the GC, and the executive government with governance power over the GC in relation to the conduct of the business. It is true that interest groups in BCs may also seek to achieve aims legislatively that they could not further by negotiated contract. However, the key difference in GCs is that the management is rarely independent of the legislative arm of the government (especially in the Westminster system). Its incentive to resist private-interest-serving legislation limited to GCs is much more limited.

Because of these complications, it becomes very difficult to maintain that the governance processes of the GC will have the economy of purpose that characterises the bilateral relations of the BC. In particular, we must ask whether or not the governance processes in the GC should attempt to serve purposes other than, and possibly inconsistent with, the control of management agents.

The first of these questions is the extent to which the governance processes should attempt to serve the purpose of regulating competition, either by furthering it or protecting it. In the BC, there is never any suggestion that corporate governance processes serve the purpose of responding to concerns about monopoly. Antitrust law performs that task; it represents a constraint, within which managers attempt to maximise the value of the corporation. Why should matters be any different for a GC? The answer begins with the recognition that a GC's business often partakes of elements of natural monopoly — the sort of consideration that caused it to be publicly owned in the first place. Thus, the greater proximity of monopoly is relevant.

In addition, the government officers who have governance power over the firm experience an inescapable conflict arising from several distinct areas of interest that they are expected to further. The government's interest as *shareholder* is to maximise the value of the corporation (which requires the firm to maximise its monopoly rents, including raising barriers to entry). By contrast, its duty as *guardian of the public interest* is to maximise social welfare. This may require, at times, the charging of 'equitable' prices which undercut market competition. Finally, politicians may have interests in controlling the GC in a manner which indirectly creates anti-competitive effects — such as achieving outcomes with high political payoffs or distributing monopoly rents so as to maximise political support. As such, it may sometimes be desirable to design the governance structure to pre-commit the means by which these dilemmas are to be resolved.

Second, the governance structure may need to accommodate the fact that the governance game is played 'outside the square' of the formal governance apparatus. In order to understand this, bear in mind that the relationship between the government and the GC is multi-faceted. The government is the shareholder of the GC. However, it is also typically the regulator of the GC, and it determines the parameters of the legal environment in which the GC exists and does business. It may be the principal customer of the GC, and the principal lender to it. The capacity to use power associated with these other relations may enable the government to circumvent the established governance processes that limit its power in the management of the firm. For example, managerial decisions may be fixed by legislation as the fief of management alone, in which the executive government will not take part. However, the incidence of power arising from a relationship outside the formal governance apparatus enables the government to make credible threats to managers that enable it to influence

Corporate Governance in Government Corporations

or control management. For that reason, the governance structure may need reinforcement to protect *managers* from collateral forms of power, in a way that is unthinkable in a BC.

Third, and relatedly, the governance structure may need protection against political abuse. In the classical firm, the shareholder is the principal, who owns the firm's residual income. In the modern exchange-traded corporation, however, the shareholders who often exert the greatest governance leverage are the financial institutions with substantial blocks of equity in the firm. Although it has been customary to encourage institutional investors to take a more active and demanding role in the GC, there is evidence that the representatives of some institutional investors sometimes engage in substantial sub-goal pursuit (*e.g.*, Romano 1999), such as the furtherance of political agendas. An institutional investor, however, will always be monitored on portfolio returns, and competes with other institutions on that basis, so the need for governance processes to be buttressed against political behaviour is limited. By contrast, maximising the value of GCs will rarely win many votes in the electorate given free-rider problems (cf. Trebilcock and Prichard 1983). Politicians, by contrast, are likely to seek to maximise electoral support, by responding to the demands of well-organised interest groups (Buchanan and Tullock 1965; Peltzman 1976). Interest group politics may affect governance.

Besides the politician with the ultimate responsibility for governance, such as a Minister in the Westminster system, the governance environment is also complicated by the presence of government departments. A department bureaucracy will have its own unique interests, such as maximising its budget, or maximising its role in the determination of policy and the application of discretionary funding (Niskanen 1971; Dunleavy 1991). Strategic planning in GCs may often be distorted by the need to form (or to counter) issue-specific coalitions designed to further self-interested aims, formed between the Minister and the department, the GC and the department, or the Minister and the GC (Trebilcock and Prichard 1983; Langford 1979).

To summarise the issues reviewed so far, we have seen that the bilateral nature of governance in the BC breaks down in the GC, by virtue of the fact that members of the public are both the customers and the residual claimants of the GC. The existence of a single objective function — the maximisation of profits — simply disappears. In addition, corporate governance processes may need to deal with a range of issues that are foreign to the BC. These are the need to respond appropriately to market competition; the complex interactions between the government's governance power over a GC, and other forms of power; and the incidence of political or strategic behaviour by government shareholders (or their

Introduction　　11

departments). Although these complexities may well rule out the existence of a single 'first-best' governance equilibrium, it nonetheless remains possible to identify a short-list of governance objectives. These objectives can be used to show how different governance structures represent compromises in the extent to which they achieve one or the other of these objectives.

The first objective, which is familiar from the BC, is to economise on the agency costs of management. Overreaching and expropriation continue to be as undesirable in GCs as in BCs. The governance processes applicable to the BC can be adapted to address this objective to some extent. Examples are the use of fiduciary prohibitions to deter overreaching and compensation packages to encourage value to be added. However, the peculiarities of the GC's governance environment create complications here. The proximity of interest groups and political activity to GCs creates a new category of 'political' conflicts of interest that challenge traditional fiduciary norms (Whincop 2002a). Likewise, compensation packages are complicated by the absence of stock prices and the need to rely on proxy measures of value (King 2003). Further, there are no market mechanisms that signal the GC's success in reducing these costs.

The second objective arises from the role of politicians in mediating the conflict between the public's interest as the consumers of the GC's output and as the residual claimant on the GC's income stream. We may describe this objective as the minimisation of the agency costs of *governance*. Politicians or other senior members of the executive government exercise governance powers in GCs. Although objectives in the GC are more confused than in private firms, Ministerial shareholders should exercise their power for public-regarding purposes, not for political gain.

In relation to this objective, in particular, it may be appropriate not to endorse the norms and precepts associated with governance in BCs. There is no analogous norm limiting the shareholder's governance power in private corporations (cf. Romano 1999). There is considerable tension between this and the first objective. Greater governance power ought *in principle* reduce the agency costs of management. However, it would be expected to increase the agency costs of governance. Conversely, giving greater power to management might be thought to increase the agency costs of management, but it may also reduce the capacity of politicians to misuse their power.

The source of the trade-off between the two can be thought of as a consequence of positive transaction costs. As we saw with the CSO, one of the difficulties associated with it is that a CSO is likely to be insufficiently state-contingent — it is not specified with sufficient particularity to respond to many changes in the outside world. This problem is well-known in the

12   *Corporate Governance in Government Corporations*

economics of contracts. Contracts cannot anticipate every state the world might take in the future because of transaction costs associated with such a bargain and the difficulties of verifying which states of the world actually occur (Ayres and Gertner 1992; Schwartz 1992). Accordingly, governance power must be conferred in an all-or-nothing manner. Of itself, this is characteristic of most forms of governance in the real world (Hart 1995), and these relatively simple arrangements can be quite effective. The problem, however, is that the effectiveness of these simpler allocations of 'self-enforcing' rights depends on strong incentives to maximise the value of one's share of the exchange surplus. That incentive, however, is harder to replicate in GCs, especially for politicians whose welfare may be no more than weakly tied to the value of the exchange surplus. What is needed, then, are governance mechanisms in GCs where the parties have incentives to self-enforce appropriate, welfare-increasing behaviour. Finding these mechanisms, however, remains a considerable challenge in an environment where property rights are hard to develop.

The third objective is the need to constrain the GC from acting anti-competitively, particularly in situations where the GC operates a natural monopoly. The literature is divided in its assessment of whether or not 'corporatising' a government function increases or decreases the incidence of anti-competitive behaviour (Sappington and Sidak 1999; *cf.* King 2003). On the one hand, removing direct Ministerial interference may eliminate the impetus to engage in projects that have high political payoffs but which harm private competitors. On the other hand, the means by which GCs are compensated may encourage managers to maximise the *size* of the firm rather than its value, with consequent cross-subsidised expansions into areas which a competitive market would adequately service. As we saw above, anti-competitive effects can arise from a number of discrete incentives — maximising value, distributional objectives, and political self-seeking. It is therefore appropriate for governance to reduce the incidence of anti-competitive behaviour. There may be other instruments for doing this, such as utilities regulation of the kind familiar from the United States. However, that form of regulation is often a *substitute* for government-ownership and a complement of private monopolies. Therefore, this objective should be regarded as important.

The relation between this objective and the other two is unclear, although it is less obviously antagonistic to either than the relationship between the two forms of agency cost. Whether controlling anti-competitive behaviour increases or decreases the agency costs of management depends on management's incentive to act anti-competitively. We have seen that this incentive is an empirical question. The relation between the agency costs of governance and the costs of anti-competitive behaviour is similarly open. The appropriate question to examine, therefore, when tailoring governance mechanisms in order to respond to anti-competitive behaviour is to examine the incentives that management and the government as shareholder will have in relation to that behaviour. That will reveal the frictions such a measure will create and the degree of reinforcement such a measure is likely to need in order to be effective.

In light of the unclear and at times inconsistent relation between these objectives, relatively few governance measures will serve all three purposes simultaneously. Measures are likely to involve compromises and constrained inefficiencies. As observed above, this environment is one where the practice of corporate governance in private firms can only be applied to GCs with care. Those practices are usually directed to minimising the agency costs of management only.

We may compare the dilemmas of the governance of the GC with what Oliver Williamson (1996) describes as the *impossibility of selective intervention*. Williamson argues that alternative means of organising and governing productive activity are associated with qualitatively different incentives which are not susceptible of calculated emulation. Thus, market activity preserves strong incentives to maximise value, but also exposes parties to opportunism, where parties make investments that depend on future cooperation for their value. By contrast, organising activity within a firm weakens incentives, but does afford greater protection against opportunism. The strength of one cannot be duplicated by the other — one can only choose between discrete alternatives. The GC stands in a similar situation. The BC transacts in a number of discrete markets and faces the incentives these markets create. The GC is not subject to these incentives. It follows that it may be both impossible and unproductive to attempt to emulate selectively the governance environment of the BC.

The following chapters of this book explore how the governance of the GC can be evaluated in terms of these three objectives. To do this, I evaluate matters from a 'constituency' perspective — I examine the major active players whose interests may be affected by the governance of the GC, and their relation to the ultimate principal, the public at large. These principal players are the managers, the empowered political agents, and a group of active stakeholders including customers and employees. In the next section, we briefly describe some of the essential features of the governance structures and processes used in GCs. This allows us to see the extent to which these processes reflect the objectives postulated in this section above, and also to provide a point of reference for the comparative and historical analyses in Chapter 2, the critical analyses in Chapters 3, 4 and 5, and the normative analysis in Chapter 6.

14   *Corporate Governance in Government Corporations*

A Brief Primer on Governance Practices in Government Corporations

GCs have been used in the delivery of government functions for many years. Until the advent of a corporatisation agenda in New Zealand, Australia and elsewhere in the 1980s and 1990s, GCs were commonly structured pragmatically, to suit the needs associated with the specific enterprise it managed. That meant that the overall distribution of governance parameters in these organisations was highly idiosyncratic. This is still true of GCs in the United States, where a corporatisation agenda was largely absent (Froomkin 1995). By contrast, the corporatisation platform pursued in the 1980s, initially in New Zealand, and then in Australia as part of a combined federal-state microeconomic reform initiative, was rather different in its character — it proposed a structure that was more uniform in its governance parameters. This tendency to adopt a standardised structure was often conditioned by the expectation that corporatisation was an interim process occurring before privatisation. The imperative was therefore to develop a formal vehicle that would allow equity in the GC to be sold, which in turn dictated a governance structure that would need a minimum of changes when it came under private ownership.

To situate our analysis, it is appropriate to discuss aspects of the extant corporatisation model in Australia and New Zealand. It is useful to discuss its basic features here for several reasons. First, it remains arguably the state-of-the-art model used for the organisation and governance of GCs in those Western economies that have systematically pursued a corporatisation agenda. It therefore helps to set it down here. Second, the historical and comparative analyses in Chapter 2 make more sense once we outline the current model. Third, it is useful to set that model down before we discuss aspects of the GCs comprised in the sample from which we draw our empirical evidence. By contrast, in Chapter 2, we discuss how the model emerged from the political environment of the time and some of the variations in its adoption between jurisdictions. We also consider the experience of corporatisation and the governance of GCs in emerging economies making the transition from central planning. Chapter 2 also draws comparisons with thinking and policy on corporate governance in GCs prior to the adoption of the extant model in those jurisdictions where it is used.

The Extant Corporatisation Model

Long before the reform movements of the 1980s, it was accepted wisdom that government functions varied in the extent to which they required independence and insulation from hands-on, day-to-day control by the

Introduction 15

executive. That principle underlay, for example, many of the governmental reforms in the New Deal (Sunstein 1987). As we shall see in Chapter 2, those parts of government providing goods and services typically came to be run as commissions or statutory corporations under a supervisory board, the members of which were appointed by and accountable to the executive government, but empowered to exercise independent managerial discretion. This supposedly gave both the requisite autonomy required for management to pursue long-term objectives, while also enabling management to be monitored on their performance of those functions for which they were directly responsible.

Much the same principles were central to the corporatisation of government functions in the 1980s. We can recognise three objectives that drove this process. The first was to establish an entity that was capable of having clear and achievable objectives. This is a necessary condition if the GC is to have management autonomy, because clear and achievable objectives are required if the managers of the GC are to be held accountable for the discharge of that autonomy. That required the partitioning of the corporatised assets so that the managers of the new entity are able to operate independently of both the government and other entities. Thus, the entities are established with independent legal personality. Government is not the principal, in law, of the GCs and not bound by their actions. It is, instead, a shareholder of the corporation via the agency of shareholding Ministers, who are entrusted with governance power. The GCs have no regulatory responsibilities to occlude the managerial task. Regulatory responsibilities would also enhance the risk of moral hazard that would arise where managers seek to achieve performance targets by regulatory means rather than good management. Obviously, where the GC is intended to be privatised in due course, it is essential that the business enterprise has the ability and autonomy to achieve objectives after its divestment.

Connecting closely with these objectives are two other central themes in corporatisation — independent, accountable management, and competitive neutrality. The former principle asserts the need for the executive government to have only limited powers in relation to the management of the GC. Management has authority to manage the GC, but must ultimately account for its performance (relative to its efined objectives) to the relevant part of the executive government. This is designed to create the appropriate incentives both for management to perform, and for government to reward good performance and punish bad performance.

Competitive neutrality, on the other hand, is designed to create appropriate incentives for the conduct of the GC's business — in particular, to minimise the extent of its competitive advantages, and their possible use against private competitors or in relation to new lines of business. This responds both to the likely presence of market power on the part of the GC, and of regulatory advantages, such as barriers to entry that generate rents.

Given these aspirations, we can now study how the corporatisation process has attempted to resolve these three objectives. The first, and perhaps most important, is the existence of a process for the *ex ante specification of performance targets*. This is important for several reasons. Although the targets specified may be on the soft side, the targets at least allows for some scope to evaluate the quality of management's performance ex post. Once these targets are specified, they provide some scope for limiting or resisting attempts at governmental interference, to the extent these would undercut the ability to achieve performance targets. As we shall see later, ex ante specification is a good response to the inefficient incentives arising from inequalities in the objectives of two or more members of the executive government with governance power.

In the extant model, this establishment of targets is accomplished by a formal planning process and the use of a contract-like performance agreement. These usually require annual renegotiation between the board of the GC and the shareholding Ministers. The specific consequences of not achieving specified performance targets are not, however, formally articulated. As we shall see, there may be *no* consequences in practice.

A second essential parameter of the extant corporatisation model is the existence of independent management, subject to the authority of an independent board of directors. This parameter is inextricably linked to the first parameter. A process by which targets are defined, and management held accountable for their performance, only really makes sense when there is an arm's length relationship between the party setting targets, and the parties held accountable for them. Where that relation doesn't exist, the accountability will achieve nothing. As we shall see below, the lack of independence of management from government has been the bane of state-owned enterprise — Ministers have often intervened liberally in the management of GC business. Creating the conditions under which government *can't* intervene (as opposed to *aren't supposed* to do so) is difficult, because Ministers may have other forms of leverage over the GC, beyond the formal governance processes. Negativing these is very difficult.

A third parameter is the reservation to government of a series of defined powers. These reserved powers do two things. First, they permit the government to enforce the stewardship obligations of management. That is, they enable the government to set goals to monitor their achievement, and to enforce consequences for failure to achieve them. It is also possible and almost always observed that government has power to appoint the board members, much as shareholders do in BCs. Second, reserved powers enable

Introduction 17

governments to respond to distinctively public objectives, such as equity, community development, and so on. Because these are objectives at odds with management incentives to maximise value, the reserve powers are created by qualifying authority in the GC in specific respects. This could, and can, be done in both an 'ex ante' sense (enabling government to impose targets and objectives for achievement as part of the planning process) and an 'ex post' sense (enabling government to issue specific directions for immediate action).

In the extant model, these parameters are achieved by specific allocations of authority between a board of directors and the shareholding Ministers. The board is conferred with managerial authority and the power to supervise the managerial hierarchy and the CEO. The shareholding Ministers have power to appoint and terminate the appointment of directors, and also have a series of explicit reserve powers. These include ex ante reserve powers affording a power of fiat in the imposition of objectives in the planning process where agreement on these objectives fails to materialise; a capacity to mandate community service obligations (CSOs), that is, decisions in relation to production, investment or pricing that are not supportable by the commercial objectives of management; and a more general power of direction ex post. In general, the extant model requires that the exercise of the CSO or general directive powers be conditional on government funding the incremental costs imposed by the exercise of the power. This allows management to pursue its commercial objectives with less distortion.

In chapter 2, we expand on this picture somewhat, by analysing its historical antecedents and contemporary counterparts in other jurisdictions. This enables us to see the extent to which the motivations and objectives behind the parameters, as well as the parameters themselves, recur across time and jurisdictional boundaries. What we find is that the demand for corporatisation, and for movements in and out of public ownership tend to move in political cycles over time. However, issues of governance represent a crucial qualification on the cycle, as its volatility, and the social costs associated with radical changes, are tied to its integrity. This can be most vividly seen in the contrasting experiences in Australia, on the one hand, and England, on the other. We also examine some of the governance practices employed in other jurisdictions, and the extent to which earlier generations succeeded in identifying the principal challenges in a way that later generations failed to do.

Chapters 3 to 5 explore the extent to which these parameters achieve those objectives, and the integrity of the governance that occurs in their context. Chapter 3 examines the issues associated with the management of the GC. It reviews, initially, the motivations and objectives that managers might be expected to have in a government-owned but autonomously managed organisation. A major focus in chapter 3 is on the interaction between the board of directors and the executive management. This relationship is one of pivotal importance in the BC and has invariably been a focus for those seeking to improve corporate governance practice, such as institutional investors, law reformers, and other bodies.

Chapter 4 addresses issues associated with the exercise of governance power by the executive government. It considers the effectiveness of the parameters which are established to regulate the involvement of the executive government, and how, if at all, the government is able to surpass those parameters. In addition, it analyses the motivations of members of government, how they interact with the board, and particular priorities they are likely to seek to attempt to further.

Chapter 5 analyses the interaction between 'non-investing' constituencies of the firm and its corporate governance. Do these constituencies have any theoretical claim to a privileged position in the corporate governance of the GC, as opposed to the BC? The arguments here are less clear in the GC than in the BC, especially to the extent that GCs are involved in regional development. One question is the extent to which the political process itself enables affected constituencies' interests to be addressed, and thus diminishes their need to be specifically represented in the corporate governance processes of the GC. Accordingly, Chapter 5 examines the role of lobbying by interest groups of management and the directors of the GC, the influence of political pressure on goods and services, the operation of CSO mechanisms, and the application of government policy to GCs.

The final chapter, Chapter 6, concludes by examining ways in which the corporate governance of the GC could be improved. Various possibilities are open to limit inefficient forms of political interference with the management of the GC and to provide stronger incentives for management to decrease costs and increase the value of the firm. One focus is on the extent to which the financing of the GC can be used as a device by which government can credibly commit to defined domains of authority for itself and for management. In general, these devices can be effective, provided that one accepts the appropriateness of requiring the GC to maximise value as its primary objective, and allowing any other appropriate social objectives to be furthered by other supplementary means. This is an example of relying on the existence of substitute mechanisms for non-efficiency objectives; separate governance processes are required to ensure that these are effective.

A Note on Data

The empirical evidence studied in this book comes from an examination of the governance arrangements employed in those entities in the State of Queensland, Australia which fall under the Government Owned Corporations Act 1993 enacted in that state. All of the Australian States undertook extensive microeconomic reforms, of which corporatisation was one part, in the late 1980s and early 1990s. These were associated with the larger microeconomic reform process put in place as part of the National Competition Policy agreed in 1993 between all state and federal governments. The implementation of microeconomic reform was substantially dependent on the financial circumstances of each state. Thus, the states with the worst budgetary positions, such as Victoria and South Australia, were most likely to privatise state assets, whereas the states with better positions, including Queensland, typically retained their assets but corporatised them. Nonetheless, there are similarities between the corporatisation legislation adopted by the States. The Queensland legislation adopts a model which confers management authority over a government-owned corporation on a CEO and a board of directors. Governance discretion is conferred on two Ministers of the Crown, one of whom is the Minister whose portfolio concerns the services the corporation provides, and the other of whom is the Treasurer (as part of whole-of-government financial responsibility).

In Queensland, at the time of our research, there were 22 GCs under this scheme, all but four of which are divided between the portfolios of transport (ports and railways) and electricity (generation and distribution). Those outside the transport and electricity portfolios are mostly within the portfolio of the Treasurer, and for the purposes of empirical analysis are treated as forming a single amalgamated portfolio. Much of our research is taken from a survey in the form of a structured written questionnaire. It was sent to all past and current directors of Government Owned Corporations in Queensland. This was undertaken as part of a project funded by the Australian Research Council and Queensland Treasury into corporate governance arrangements in GCs. The evident participation of Treasury imposed a selection bias on our results, but it very likely boosted our response rate (43%) compared to a 'cold call' survey.[6]

Table 1.1 summarises the population of directors, the number of directors whom we were able to send surveys to, and the reasons why directors could not be reached in other cases.

20   *Corporate Governance in Government Corporations*

Table 1.1   Population and Sample

Directors identified as serving or having served on Queensland GCs	307
Number of directors for whom addresses were not found	13
Number of surveys 'returned to sender' for wrong addresses	7
Number of deceased directors	4
Maximum possible responses	283
Number of completed surveys	121

Table 1.2 summarises the breakdown of present and past directors, and information about the GCs they came from. We do not identify which portfolio is which, given confidentiality undertakings.

Table 1.2   Breakdown of Sample

	Past directors	Current directors	Total
Portfolio A	32	22	54
Portfolio B	28	24	52
Portfolio C	6	9	15
Total	66	55	121

Some background in relation to the political context of GCs in Queensland is appropriate. Queensland has a unicameral legislature. The three major political parties represented in parliament are the Australian Labour Party (ALP), the National Party and the Liberal Party. The National and Liberal parties, which represent conservative politics in Queensland, have been in and out of coalition. They were in coalition until 1983, and between 1989 and 2001. The corporatisation legislation was introduced in 1993 by an ALP government (which had been in power since 1989). It lost government in 1995 to a National-Liberal coalition, which formed a minority government with an independent member's support until 1998, when it was displaced by a minority ALP government. The ALP gained a bare parliamentary majority in 1999 after a by-election, and was returned to office with a huge parliamentary majority in 2001. There have been no substantial changes in the GC regime since its enactment.

In Chapters 3 and 4, we undertake analysis of other empirical evidence associated with these GCs. This evidence will be introduced in due order.

Notes

1. Air Transportation Safety and System Stabilization Act, 115 Stat. 229; Public Law 107-42.
2. Massachusetts and Ohio have adopted community choice legislation allowing local authorities to become suppliers (see, *e.g.*, the Northeast Ohio Public Energy Council, http://www.nopecinfo.org/index.html). It is notable that electricity deregulation in American States was accompanied, for example, in California and Massachusetts by multi-billion dollar bailouts for privately-owned energy companies (Weisman 1997).
3. Rent-seeking refers specifically to behaviour designed to increase one's share of the distribution of economic surplus.
4. On the other hand, court-sanctioned barriers to takeovers, such as the poison pill (a device that boards may adopt unilaterally, which triggers a ruinous wealth transfer away from hostile acquirers) undoubtedly insulate the management once again. For a popular review of the issue, see Deutsch (2003).
5. See Chapter 2, p. 36 and Chapter 5, pp. 179–180 *infra*.
6. The selection bias would be expected to manifest itself in defensive responses to questions regarding Ministerial involvement and interference. Directors would be expected to understate the incidence of such behaviour.

Chapter 2

Historical and Comparative Issues[*]

In the 1990s, the literature on corporate governance began to compare the governance structures of business corporations in different parts of the world, and to examine their evolution across time. This literature debated the extent to which corporate governance processes were *path dependent*, that is, influenced by local, and often temporary, conditions during formative periods (Bebchuk and Roe 1999). Closely related to that question was whether or not increased global competition in products and security markets would lead to convergence in corporate governance, as all corporations attempt to minimise the costs of debt and equity capital attributable to agency costs (Hansmann and Kraakman 2000). The likelihood of convergence depends, amongst other things, on the extent to which local institutions provide comparative advantages that are incapable of transplantation or emulation (Gilson 1996).

A similar undertaking, in relation to the history and comparative analysis of the governance of state owned enterprises ('SOEs') is also important. It reveals, first, the enduring importance of the governance questions we have identified by illustrating their pervasiveness over time and across jurisdictions. Second, we can examine the relative success of different approaches to these governance problems. Third, we can compare the relative prevalence of, and relation between, corporatisation and privatisation in resolving these governance problems.

As with the corporate governance of BCs, the governance equilibria for SOEs will also be affected by both considerations. On the one hand, there are factors that feature in a narrow efficiency calculus, such as the agency costs of management and governance and the social costs of public monopolies. On the other hand, a range of other factors can also be relevant. One of these may be idiosyncratic and historically derived preferences for the involvement of government in the economy. As we shall

---

[*] This chapter was co-authored with Jonathan Leckie.

see, the Australian approach has differed from that in the United States and England. Ideology is also relevant, as can be seen in the advocacy of privatisation by conservative governments. Fiscal considerations also matter enormously, as the incentive to privatise has been strong for governments with large budgetary deficits.

Path dependency is likely to feature strongly in these governance equilibria because there are much greater frictions associated with the transition from public to private ownership, compared to those associated with governance changes in firms that have remained in private ownership at all times. A BC might go through important transitions — it may begin life as a venture-capital-funded startup, proceed to an initial public offering after which its equity can be publicly traded, be the subject of a spin off into a new public company, go private in a leveraged buy-out by management, and restructure its claims as part of a work-out or arrangement with its creditors. There are non-trivial transaction costs at each point but the transitions occur relatively often, and the property rights of shareholders and creditors encourage them to occur in situations where the reorganisation of claims adds value to the enterprise.

The governance of SOEs, by contrast, is unlikely to be ruled by similar incentives. A government may choose to privatise a SOE, but rarely in response to change in the relative value of the enterprise in public and private ownership. Indeed, the tendency to corporatise as a prelude to privatisation in New Zealand and Australia in the 1980s and 1990s demonstrates this. Corporatisation should add value to the SOE in public ownership, by altering managerial incentives and ministerial opportunities. However, corporatisation adds little, if anything, to the value of the SOE once transferred to *private* ownership, because the government lacks comparative advantage in resolving the subset of governance problems common to public and private ownership (*cf.* Gibbon 1997; Kikeri *et al.* 1992; Lopez de Silanes 1997). In much the same way, the nationalisation of private enterprises has hardly ever coincided with any kind of comparative advantage on the part of the government in running such a business. Far more important to this decision is the relevance of liquidity constraints on the government's budget. Liquidity constraints encourage privatisation (since privatisation proceeds decrease budgetary deficits) and discourage nationalisation. Even when the budget is in surplus, governments rarely nationalise viable industries, since policy objectives can be achieved in other ways, in the absence of committed socialist economic policy. This asymmetry, in which privatisation is more likely than nationalisation lends governance of these assets a path dependent quality: mistaken nationalisations will be rare but easy enough to correct, but mistaken privatisations will usually remain unchanged.

24   *Corporate Governance in Government Corporations*

This chapter begins by comparing the experience of SOEs in three countries — the United Kingdom, Australia and New Zealand. Given the ubiquity of the United Kingdom in the colonisation of Australia and the New Zealand, we might expect a relatively common development of policy regarding SOE governance. However, this is not the case. Autochthonous responses mirrored local circumstances until largely irreversible decisions were made to privatise. In this section, we also discuss the form of the 'trans-Tasman' GC, foreshadowed in Chapter 1, which represents a state-of-the-art standard form response to GC governance problems and is the context for much of the analysis in the following chapters. We then compare the experience in these Commonwealth jurisdictions to the United States, where there has been a long-standing antipathy to SOEs and a preference for regulated private enterprise. Finally, we compare the experience in economies recently emerging from central economic planning and control.

The Commonwealth Experience

United Kingdom

The government of the United Kingdom extensively nationalised major sections of British industry after the end of the Second World War. This was done in the expectation, championed by Herbert Morrison (Minister of Transport, 1929–31, Lord President, London County Council, 1945), that public ownership could be managed in a way that would allow the realisation of public goals, for the benefit of Britain (Ashworth 1991, p. 62). This involved a separation of day-to-day management from political interference. As such, it recognised the concerns associated with the agency costs of governance. It is accepted, however, that interference continued unchanged, and damaged the efficiency of British public industry.

According to Tivey (1966), post-war nationalisations took place according to four general principles. First, industries were nationalised on a non-profit making basis — breakeven point was the principal financial objective. Second, management was unified in monopolistic entities — competition was not considered a useful instrumental value. Third, nationalised industries were to serve the public interest. Finally, the nationalised entities were to be subordinate to the government. This would allow the operation of these industries to be coordinated with other government initiatives to manage the economy to smooth out fluctuations in the economic cycle, a policy approach derived from Keynes (Tivey 1966, pp. 144–145; Barry 1965, p. 295). This latter desire rationalises the

Historical and Comparative Issues

pervasiveness of the informal control British Ministers of the era exercised over their portfolio industries.

The governance structures of post-war British nationalised industries was set out in specific industry statutes, such as the *Coal Industry Nationalisation Act* 1946. Formally, such structures were restricted to a Ministerial power to give mandatory directions (which was qualified by a requirement to consult with the board). Further powers related to the appointment and dismissal of directors. Despite the magnitude of these powers, and in keeping with British traditions of government, they were exercised only infrequently. Ministers and directors instead relied on informal interaction, consisting of lengthy conversations, often going to great detail on the specifics of a particular industry. Tivey (1966) describes this as a two-way process of information sharing, with directors having influence on Ministerial views in addition to Ministers influencing management. However, in the event a negotiated agreement was not possible, the Minister's best alternative was very strong, as he could simply dictate by fiat. This informal interaction meant that Ministerial input pervaded the smallest detail of operations, such as education and training, research, investment, management of reserve and surplus funds, pricing levels, and even wage negotiations. Treasury was to be consulted on such issues as the disposal of reserves, salaries of board members, stock issues, and the form of company accounts. Tivey suggests that the informality and casualness of interactions between Ministers and board members, against the backdrop of significant legal powers, made it very difficult for boards to operate with any independence.

The result was that a Minister often interacted with the board in the same manner as he would interact with his own department. At the close of the 1970s 'the principle that the nationalised industries should operate independently of the government had been replaced with one premised on comprehensive and detailed regulation of their activities' (Veljanovsky 1991, p. 60). Managerial independence was sacrificed in the name of far-reaching political control over commercial decision-making, in line with the contemporary view of government as the necessary Keynesian regulator of economic cycles. This had important constitutional implications:

> The Minister had certain powers over the corporations. For the exercise of these powers he was answerable to Parliament, just as he was answerable for all his other powers. On those matters where the Minister exercised no powers, there was no accountability. This would correspond with the extent of the corporation's managerial independence. ... In practice, this was expected to mean that Parliament could discuss 'broad policy', but not 'day-to-day management' (Tivey 1966, p. 121).

26   *Corporate Governance in Government Corporations*

In practice, the pervasive extent of informal Ministerial interactions, outside the formal powers for which he was accountable to Parliament, led to a breakdown in managerial independence, and ultimately, in parliamentary accountability.

At the same time that the Minister's unaccountable interactions with the GC increased the agency costs of governance, the weak break-even financial criterion would also be expected to increase the agency costs of management. Management had little incentive to reduce waste or the funding of unproductive research or investments (especially where these could be justified as having value to society — or could be given Ministerial imprimatur). Even though Treasury provided continuing monitoring of prices and the like, Treasury would normally be at an informational disadvantage to management in these interactions.

Today, the Morrisonian model's value is as a lesson showing the need to separate management from politics, and an understanding (drawn from the nationalisation experience) of the inability to achieve this without formal structures geared to that end. The Thatcher privatisation program was enacted partly in response to this failure to achieve managerial autonomy. The Thatcher reforms represented a mandate that a public enterprise achieve financial success while also attaining social objectives as inherently contradictory. The lack of clear objectives would produce inefficient and ineffective organisations. Entrenched political and bureaucratic interference added to this lack of clarity. This contributed to a loss of accountability (due to competing objectives and continued political interference). Thus, the agency costs of governance were singularly high.

The fact that *some* of these entities were natural monopolies (a fact that had been used to justify their public ownership) sheltered *all* of them from competition, and so waste and inefficiency thrived. The costs associated with these businesses can be seen to be made up of both the social costs of monopoly and the agency costs of management.

Other factors, besides these inefficiencies associated with GC governance, also played a role. Ideologically, the Cold War politics of the day also influenced the Thatcher agenda, so that purging British society of socialism was an end in itself. Relatedly, the privatisation of these GCs was intended to harm trade unions (and indirectly the Labour Party), much as their creation was attended by the opposite purpose (see generally Longstreth 1989). The relation between these GCs and the budget was also problematic. The nationalised industries were capital-hungry, but at the same time, were, by design, not meant to produce surpluses. Thus, the financing burden fell to Treasury. At this time, the budget bore the scars of the 'stagflation' of the 1970s, so that financing these industries propelled public debt to unsustainable levels. Accordingly, privatisation had the merit of furnishing a one-off credit bonanza which would enable public debt to be reduced.

Even though Thatcherism has fallen from favour in the United Kingdom, the clean sweep of British SOEs has left a much smaller SOE sector (some of which is only partly government-owned). This includes such entities as the Post Office and the BBC. There is no general statute governing corporate governance in GCs.

The World Bank's World Development Indicators (2000) show that Investment by State Owned Enterprises in the UK for 1990–1997 was 4.6% of Gross Domestic Investment, a figure on par with the United States (4.0%), but much smaller than that for Australia (12%).

New Zealand

In New Zealand, the economy in the early 1980s was a mirror of that in the UK. Public debt was approaching endemic levels, and the inefficiencies of entities under government control were draining the public coffers, reducing funds available for social welfare programmes. The initial corporatisation reform program quickly became a privatisation program. This readied government bodies for private ownership, while softening the blow to the public when the sales eventually began. The provenance of this corporatisation model as an interim process before divestment has cast doubt on its governance value for those entities not thereafter privatised.

Again, it was the problems of endemic loss-making in SOEs, a perceived loss of accountability through conflicting objectives and the breakdown of channels of responsibility that drove the reforms (Duncan and Bollard 1992, p. 15). While the UK reforms sought to produce accountability and profitability through wholesale privatisations combined with structural reform of monopolistic markets, the NZ model was somewhat different. At least initially, it sought to create a model whereby government ownership was retained, and SOEs were restructured to reflect as closely as possible the system of incentives faced by private firms. However, the retention of public ownership came to be seen as limiting the ability to replicate such incentives, leading many commentators to advocate a fully-fledged privatisation programme. Property rights economics (Alchian 1965; Demsetz 1967; De Alessi 1969) gave a theoretical pedigree for a process that seemed to have a more pragmatic basis in reducing the amount of public debt (Mascarenhas 1998, pp. 30-1, 43-4). While this was also true of the United Kingdom, the New Zealand experience was not the ideological anti-socialist crusade we saw in Britain.

Privatisations were not so prevalent in New Zealand as in the United Kingdom, with the result that the *State Owned Enterprises Act* 1986 retains

28   *Corporate Governance in Government Corporations*

importance as legislation regulating GC governance. Currently, SOEs include the Airways Corporation of New Zealand, the Electricity and Forestry Corporations, the Land Corporation, New Zealand Post, New Zealand Railways, Radio NZ and TVNZ, and TransPower New Zealand. The governance arrangements of the Act are examined below. In addition, there are other important Crown companies that form the remainder of the SOE sector. These fall into two main groups — research institutes, and other limited liability companies incorporated under New Zealand companies legislation in which the Crown has an ownership interest.

Australia

History Although in the last two decades, Australia has followed a similar path to England and, more particularly, New Zealand, in the corporatisation, and subsequent privatisation, of many important GBEs, there has been an important and idiosyncratic difference in the historical reliance on state-owned enterprises in Australia.[1] From the outset, British governance of the Australia colonies involved an interventionist approach to economic development. In this process, one important objective was to minimise the risk of nuclei of private economic power developing, that might be capable of fuelling secessionist tendencies (as with the American colonies). The role of the state in the economy provided a solution, as in the development of railways. Public enterprise also addressed a 'lack of private entrepreneurial activity and private access to capital' (Butlin *et al.* 1982, pp. 259, 262). Far from 'driving out' private capital, this market intervention was 'not regarded by those who benefited from it (the major capital owners) as odd or threatening ... [because] its major redistributive consequences have, on the whole, advantaged private capital' (Patience and Head 1979, pp. 283–284).

> Primitive Benthamism ... has triumphed in Australia in a manner that would be inconceivable in Bentham's native land. ... [T]he image ... is of a body which, to paraphrase one of the most famous of all definitions, acts as the administrative agency of the masses. ... The concept is one of a state which is committed rather than neutral. To mitigate the effects of the commitment, state intervention, whether of a regulatory or operating character, tends to be detached as much as possible from the traditional state machine and dealt with in either a quasi-judicial or 'non-political' manner, or to be diffused among a number of organs with claims to sovereignty in their own sphere (Encel 1968, pp. 44–45).

Hancock (1930, p. 65) refers to the 'Australian tendency' of employing 'collective power to foster interests which are primarily individual'. This,

Historical and Comparative Issues 29

he said, was not socialism, as that term was understood, but 'more primitive', and perhaps more pragmatic (see also Encel 1968). Brown (2003, p. 17) refers to the role of state-owned enterprise as one that did not '*change*, mitigate or displace market activity, but ... *enable*[*d*] it to occur' [emphasis in original].

Butlin *et al.* (1982) refer to substantial change to this approach in the role of the state at the onset of the Great Depression. Initially, the government made a marked withdrawal from public enterprise as part of a commitment to reducing budgetary expenditures. Subsequently, the demands of world war required this conservative approach to be abandoned, as was also true of the United Kingdom government. However, government policy on public enterprise sharply diverged from the United Kingdom's after the war. In contrast to the far-reaching nationalisation policies of British Labour, Australian Labor's nationalisation platforms were substantially thwarted by High Court rulings that they were unconstitutional (McMinn 1979, pp. 182–185). When Labor was displaced in 1949 by a conservative government, Australia returned to a policy not dissimilar to the historical business-state partnership that preceded the Depression (Brown 2003). This led to substantial divestitures (*i.e.*, privatisations) and the encouragement of competition (Wettenhall 1987, p. 3), at odds with the progressive 'big government' then observable in the United States and Britain.

Australia and neo-liberalism Despite the marked difference between the historical role, efficiency, and extent of SOEs in Australia, compared to the United Kingdom and New Zealand, the Commonwealth and State governments were not immune from the siren song of SOE reform and divestment. Government was perceived to have become too large and too unaccountable (Curnow and Saunders 1983), and the statutory corporations managing business enterprises were implicated in the problem (Wettenhall 1987). It fell to a Labor government to undertake the bulk of the reform. Despite its social-democratic ideology, it was unable to eschew the burden of reform when its sister party in New Zealand, and state governments within Australia embraced privatisation. As in New Zealand, privatisation and SOE reform were driven in the Australian states by a combination of budgetary deficits and accountability breakdowns in the relation between SOEs and government ministers (the worst of which occurred in Labor administrations). In Queensland, like New South Wales, privatisation was employed more sparingly than elsewhere. This reflected, first, Queensland's stronger budgetary position (De Lacy 1993), and the weaker sympathy for privatisation in the dominant partner in Queensland conservative politics, the National Party, which has a rural support base

30   *Corporate Governance in Government Corporations*

concerned by changes to SOE service levels. However, Queensland did commit emphatically to SOE reform and to increasing efficiency in the delivery of government functions (Davis 1993; Ahern *et al*. 1989).

Federally, the reform process entered its final phase with the conservative Howard government, elected in 1996, to which the political aspirations of the Thatcher regime had revenant appeal, such as empowering household shareholding and breaking up public sector unions. This curiously protracted cycle of reform, spanning three decades, has the effect that the corporatisation process is often tainted by the suspicion that its reforms are temporary and incomplete. A GC is represented as a privatised entity that failed, either commercially or through lack of political will. In part, this reform process offered less than it seemed as a governance framework for these corporatised entities, primarily because it failed to take the GC seriously as a form in its own right (Brown 2003).

By comparison, the important role of GCs prior to the Great Depression saw a clear recognition of governance problems and solutions quite as innovative as most of those articulated in the neo-liberal reforms of the 1980s. Had the former regime been less brusquely dismissed, more attention could have been directed to the experience of the governance processes of former regimes. After all, those foreshadowed the corporatisation philosophies of the 1980s quite closely. A brief account of some of these follows, which are then compared to the dominant principles of the extant Australian corporatisation model.

The fundamental problem with agency costs of governance has long been recognised in Australia. It has been translated into a policy imperative of giving GC management substantial independence from traditional ministerial or 'political' lines of control. One of the principal loci for working this principle out was in the governance of public railways.

Butlin *et al*. (1982, pp. 259–278) argue that, from earliest times, the use of independent technical managers in the railways provided some measure of independence. However, in the event, bad management occurred, and where it did occur, it usually coincided with political pressure and influence. The railways were restructured with a board of independent commissioners. This occurred first in Victoria and then in New South Wales. The Victorian framework specifically regulates the operation of Ministerial control by formally confining ministerial powers of direction via declaration or 'writ' to 'general matters of policy, in an attempt to reconcile democratic control with a degree of real autonomy for public corporations' (Butlin *et al*. 1982, p. 263). The New South Wales Premier, Henry Parkes, a key figure in the federation movement, declared that:

Historical and Comparative Issues   31

These great national properties must be at once withdrawn from all political influence, and worked on principles of economy and efficiency, and of commercial benefit to the State as well as of general convenience to all classes of the people (Parkes 1892, pp. 453, 469–473).

Closely related to the separation of Ministers from management control was the need for a device that explicitly recognised and funded any non-commercial objectives of the GC. In this way, democratic goals may be served without obscuring the commercial motivations of the GC. In more recent times, this has been developed as the 'community service obligation' (CSO). In Australia, this mechanism can be traced back to the 1890s and the railway commissions. These used a 'recoup' mechanism which required governments to bear the costs associated with diverting railways from maximising business performance (Wettenhall 1966).

Implicit in the CSO mechanism is the proposition that GCs should, in general, be managed to maximise the firm's financial performance. Recognising such an objective, and enforcing it, is an important part of economising on the agency costs of management. Brown (2003) points out that at least by the 1950s, at which time a conservative government made significant divestitures, it explicitly recognised that those GCs that remained were to be managed in a way that as closely as possible replicated a private firm, and that the role of the state was that of 'sole shareholder' (see also Wettenhall 1987, p. 4). This is a significant difference to the Morrisonian GCs of the United Kingdom which adopted the commercial objective of breaking even.

The final general objective for a system of governance for GCs is minimising the social costs of monopoly. In part, the recoup/CSO mechanism serves this objective since it permits government to serve social justice concerns while mitigating the effects of a monopoly. In addition, the Australian approach to GCs detached not only commercial activities, but also regulatory functions, into semi-autonomous quasi-judicial or 'non-political' forms. This enabled 'competitive neutrality' in state involvement to be maintained long before that term was coined in the 1980s and 1990s. Such a separation reduces the risk of the use of these regulatory and policy functions being pressed into the service of maximising GCs profits while generating negative externalities for social welfare.

Having examined something of Australia's important history of GCs and the principles attending their governance, we may now complete the Australian history by comparing aspects of the extant system in more detail. This has expository value for the analysis in Chapters 3–5 since it provides a detailed exposition of the regime in which the analysed GCs were examined.

32   *Corporate Governance in Government Corporations*

Following the historic Hilmer report (Hilmer *et al.* 1992), a committee of inquiry examining competition policy and related microeconomic issues, the Commonwealth and all state governments agreed to implement legislation that fundamentally reviewed anti-competitive legislation and the operations of government business enterprises. The so-called National Competition Policy required a wide range of activities previously undertaken by governments or statutory authorities to be fundamentally overhauled. A range of measures were involved in the reform — they included subjecting provision to competitive tendering, full-cost pricing by, and within, government, and commercialisation (that is, a neologism referring to the imposition of market objectives and disciplines on SOEs). A case was also made for extensive corporatisation, and in some cases, privatisation of these SOEs (see generally Forsyth 1992; Quiggin 2003).

As noted above, the balance between corporatisation and privatisation varied between the federal and state governments. Influences on this variation included the exigency of the budget situation, the ideological predisposition towards privatisation of the government, and the extent to which a jurisdiction was 'reform-fatigued' (generally, reform fatigue has increased with time). Thus, the strength and significance of the GC sector in each of the Australian jurisdictions varies sharply — strongest in Queensland and New South Wales, much weaker in Victoria and South Australia, with the Commonwealth somewhere in the middle.

As part of the corporatisation process, four values emerged as guiding principles for the restructuring of SOEs. These were first articulated in the Hilmer Report (1992, p. 300). These were clarity of objectives, fostering managerial responsibility and accountability, managerial authority and autonomy, and competitive neutrality. Reynolds and Von Nessen (1999) state that these principles emerged from the problems that the reforms were aimed at addressing — a lack of responsibility, the obfuscation of the lines of accountability and authority, and an insulation of SOEs against market forces.

The most important governance features of the new generation of GCs follow from the first three, in particular, of the four corporatisation principles. In outline, they define the functions of a board of directors of the GC, and of the Ministerial shareholders, and the principal processes by means of which the two interact. Establishing a board and endowing it with independence furthers the management autonomy and authority principle. By requiring the processes for interaction between the Ministers and the board, the legislation can allow clear objectives to be set, and accountability for achieving these can be enforced. We expand on these points below.

The Australian corporatisation framework[2] is generally a two-tier system, although some jurisdictions only have a single tier.[3] The tiers correspond to the extent to which a commercial orientation has penetrated the GC. Entities in the first tier take the *company GC* form, in which a corporation is registered under the *Corporations Act* 2001, Australia's general incorporation legislation. Ministers, on behalf of the State, hold all shares in the corporation. These GCs are fully commercialised, and are expected to operate in competitive markets. Less commercialised bodies, which may be unable to compete successfully in a competitive marketplace, are incorporated as *statutory GCs* until sufficient skills, procedures and systems are developed to complete the move to the company GC form. The key difference is that company GCs are exposed from the outset to the provisions and constraints in the *Corporations Act*, such as those governing directors' duties, like any other business corporations. The statutory GCs are subject only to the provisions in the corporatisation legislation of the jurisdiction in which they are formed. However, at the governance level, core features are common to both, and we discuss these below.

At the pinnacle of the corporatisation governance system, corporatisation legislation establishes processes by which Ministers negotiate with the board the formal goals the GC is, from time to time, to pursue. This formal planning process reinforces the principle that Ministers must set clear objectives and the board and the GC are accountable for achieving them. Most jurisdictions adopt some form of performance contract between the board of directors and the shareholding Minister(s). This is called, in Queensland, the *Statement of Corporate Intent* ('SCI').[4] This is the primary mechanism by which incentives are imposed in imitation of those operating in the private sector.[5] It is the principal means of governmental input into the objectives, and governmental monitoring of the performance, of public enterprise. Originating in New Zealand legislation passed in 1986, a SCI-like mechanism can be found throughout the Australasian legislation, with a notable exception at the Commonwealth level. As a general summary, the SCI contains the GC's financial and non-financial performance targets for the relevant financial year,[6] an outline of the GC's objectives, the nature and scope of proposed activities for that financial year, capital structure and dividend policies, and policies and plans relating to major asset acquisition or divestiture.[7] The content of these matters is negotiated between the Board and the relevant shareholding Minister(s) to form a formal performance contract that creates the primary accountability mechanism in the GC framework.[8] The result is supposed to ensure a substitution of bureaucratic and political involvement in the day-to-day decision-making of the GC for medium- to long-term goal-setting

34   *Corporate Governance in Government Corporations*

and monitoring of an independent and commercially focused board of directors.

Operating at a much less specific level than the SCI are the general purpose statements of GC objectives in corporatisation legislation. Legislation indicates that a GC's board of directors is appointed primarily for its ability to realise the objectives of the GC.[9] The principal objective is couched in general terms, such as 'to operate as a successful business',[10] or to 'perform its functions for the public benefit'.[11] More specific requirements are to 'act as profitably and efficiently as comparable private businesses',[12] combined with injunctions that the GC pursue some public good. New Zealand SOEs, for example, are specifically obliged to be a good employer and exhibit a sense of social responsibility.[13] Other Acts specify that an objective of a GC is to 'maximise [their] contribution to the economy and well-being of the State',[14] to pursue their non-commercial activities 'efficiently and effectively',[15] or to maximise their sustainable return, while having regard to the 'economic and social objectives of the State'.[16] Thus, in summary, legislation typically refers to a requirement for commercial success and efficient pursuit of recognised public interest goals. The ambiguity leaves scope for management discretion, and thus for potential influences on that discretion (of which government pressure is the most obvious). However, the SCI and like mechanisms, have the potential to eliminate much of this ambiguity and provide for more specific goals.

In general, corporatisation legislation does not provide specifically for director qualifications or for the mix of backgrounds and experience to be present on the board. It simply provides for a process by which the governor in council (that is, the executive government, via cabinet) may appoint persons to GC boards.[17] We saw above that the legislation indicates that the board is responsible for management, and obliges the board to achieve goals in the SCI and to ensure the GC otherwise performs in a proper, effective and efficient way.[18]

More onerous obligations (for individual directors) are found, in the case of the more commercially oriented company GCs, in the *Corporations Act*, and, in the case of statutory GCs, in the corporatisation legislation. Many of the provisions applying to statutory GCs are modelled on those in general companies legislation. Sch. 10 of the New South Wales *State Owned Corporations Act* 1989 sets out certain duties governing directors of statutory GCs. These are largely modelled on the provisions of the legislation preceding the *Corporations Act* (prior to amendments made in 2000).

There are, however, some instances where corporations legislation is modified substantively, not just for statutory GCs, but for company GCs as well. An example is found which accommodates the special characteristics

Historical and Comparative Issues   35

of company GCs to the application of directors duties. Section 3(8) of the Schedule provides that:

> in determining ... the degree of care and diligence that a reasonable person in a like position in a company [GC] would exercise ... regard must be had to
>
> (a)   the fact that the person is an officer of a company [GC], and
> (b)   the application of this Act to the [GC], and
> (c)   relevant matters required or permitted to be done under this Act ...
>
> including, for example, any relevant directions, notifications or approvals given to the [GC] by the [GC]'s voting shareholders or portfolio Minister.[19]

Corporatisation legislation provides specifically for the shares in GCs to be held by Ministers. The configuration of the shareholding Ministers changes at the level of detail from jurisdiction to jurisdiction and as between statutory and company GCs. Generally, provision is made for two shareholding Ministers, one being the portfolio Minister (*i.e.*, the Minister responsible for implementing the GC's Corporate Charter), the other being (typically) the Treasurer or Finance Minister. There may be provision for *more* shareholders but, in general, only these two Ministers have formal governance entitlements.[20]

The portfolio Minister is generally responsible to parliament for the administration of the government department most concerned with the GC in question. This department may well have been responsible for the business enterprise conducted by the GC prior to its corporatisation. Typically, the department has extensive interactions with the GC above and beyond its governance functions. It may be a budget competitor, it may be a customer, it may often be a regulator, it may have an advisory role.[21] These complex interactions potentially confer power on the portfolio Minister above and beyond the formal governance entitlements under corporatisation legislation. The risks associated with this model are apparently reduced by the New Zealand model, which creates a Minister for SOEs, who is responsible for portfolio management, rather than the Minister of the portfolio department. In practice, however, the differences may not be great.

Shareholding (or 'voting') Ministers retain substantial powers over GC governance. This reflects the state's position as the 'owner' of the entity and allows for democratic control to be exercised in the public interest. The main powers of shareholding Ministers include control over the content of the SCI, and reserve powers of direction where these are thought to be justified in the public interest, which directors are obliged to obey.[22] The SCI is negotiated between the board of directors and the shareholding

36 *Corporate Governance in Government Corporations*

Ministers. The legislation provides for a process by which the SCI is to be negotiated, although the Minister is able to mandate content,[23] if the board's agreement cannot be obtained.[24]

Closely related to the SCI mechanism is the system of mandated Community Service Obligations ('CSOs'). CSOs are designed to resolve the cost inefficiencies and goal conflicts inherent in the practice of cross-subsidising loss-generating 'social' activities with the profits drawn from commercial activities. Five out of the eight Australasian jurisdictions provide for this, or a similar, mechanism. Of these, the Queensland framework is typical.[25] A GC's board must satisfy the shareholding Ministers that certain activities, which the GC is obliged to perform under Ministerial directions, are not in the commercial interests of the GC to perform. If the Ministers are satisfied, the obligation is specified in the SCI, along with the explicit costings and government funding of the obligation. Similarly, in New Zealand, when the Crown wishes an SOE to perform non-commercial functions, an agreement is entered into, by which the SOE provides the function in return for 'the payment by the Crown of the whole or part of the price thereof'.[26]

The power to mandate CSOs, where it is not a separate subject of legislation, is founded on the general 'reserve powers' of the shareholding Minister. These powers ensure that, as a matter of last resort, Government policy can prevail over the wishes of GC directors and management. There is a public interest qualification that must be satisfied before notifying a GC board of Government policy; further, written directions must only be given in exceptional circumstances where justified by the public interest.[27] In Tasmania, the Treasurer alone is given power to issue directions on a specified range of matters.[28] In most jurisdictions those directions must then be gazetted,[29] tabled in Parliament,[30] or at least made explicit in the annual general report. Only South Australia and New Zealand do not provide for a reserve power of direction to shareholding Ministers. There, the Ministers' powers are limited to directing the board to modify the SCI,[31] or altering unilaterally the corporation's Charter.[32]

Finally, corporatisation has been accompanied by microeconomic (specifically market structure) reforms following from the 1992 Hilmer Report into competition. Policymakers in Australia, and to a lesser degree,[33] New Zealand, were cognisant of the need to introduce competitive market structures to avoid the creation of monopolies — a result that would negate the efficiency gains of corporatisation. All Australian jurisdictions are bound to implement the outcomes of the 1992 Hilmer inquiry into competition, which include the establishment of a competitively neutral environment for the operation of SOEs. The Queensland legislation, for example, mandates that GCs cannot enjoy nor suffer from any special

Historical and Comparative Issues 37

advantage or disadvantage stemming from either their public ownership or market power.[34] This translates into a requirement that all SOEs pay federal income tax equivalents to their respective owners.[35] This principle also authorises a range of exceptions to administrative law mechanisms, such as Freedom of Information legislation and other public sector accountability processes.[36] In cases where a GC does enjoy a degree of market power deemed excessive, structural reform will be undertaken, or, where this is not feasible, special monitoring processes will be installed to prevent the abuse of that power. The application of this principle has been most keenly felt in the electricity generation and distribution markets, where GCs have undergone substantial restructuring since 1993, and compete directly with both GCs and BCs based in other jurisdictions. While initial gains in profit and productivity among the electricity GCs were both substantial and significant, the increased competition with interstate GCs is having an impact on profit margins.[37]

As Brown (2003) suggests, this reform process is perhaps most significant in its recognition of the importance of market structure and the use of a formalised performance contract (the SCI) as a basis for incentives. In other respects, the regime reinvents many of the parameters of GCs in the early twentieth century.

United States and Canada

Although the United States has been dominated historically by privately-owned, heavily-regulated business entities in markets characterised by natural monopoly, the government played an important historical role in a range of aspects of the economy (Goodrich 1967). The post office has always been publicly run, for example, and government played important roles, sometimes as 'entrepreneur', on other occasions by providing subsidies, in the development of infrastructure, such as canals, harbours, roads and railways, as well as other core government services such as policing, defence and revenue collection. Nonetheless, in the individualistic American climate, privately owned providers of utilities developed at the same time, to a much greater extent than elsewhere.

Swann (1988) examines the history of regulation in the United States and United Kingdom. He cites as a foundational influence the 1905 National Civic Federation study of the relative merits of public versus private ownership of utilities. While this study primarily relied on the British experience, it heavily influenced the structure of American governmental economic involvement. That study concluded that early attempts to regulate gas, water and transport utilities had been unsatisfactory. Private utilities had exploited consumers as to price and had provided poor levels of service. Regulation, or at least that form which had been sanctioned by Parliament, had not worked. A second reason which led to municipal operation was concerned with the profits enjoyed by private companies. Municipalities, lacking funds for their own development, saw utilities as a useful source of income (Swann 1988, p. 77).

This second factor, combined with restrictions on municipal borrowings, explains the predominance of American SOEs at the local governance level. Municipalities would create public enterprises to move debt off public balance sheets, thereby evading the debt restrictions.

The key to the unique American SOE experience lies in the history of government-business relations in the US. The period between 1870 and 1930 has been described as the pinnacle of *laissez-faire* capitalism. This bias towards *laissez-faire* was reinforced by the historic conservatism of the Supreme Court's interpretations of the Constitution, and its enforcement of the Madisonian federal system and state rights. The Federal government of 1871 employed 51,020 civilians, of whom nearly 37,000 were postal employees (McCraw 1981, p. 5). Thus, the US federal government was not in a position to play a role in the economy as either the provider of public infrastructure (as in Australia), or as a regulator (as in Europe). This was to prove determinative of future US government-business relations.

> Following the Civil War, industry became increasingly complex, and mass production techniques enabled producers to expand their output ... The economic pendulum, which before the Civil War had favored competition among a large number of sellers, swung over to the large-scale enterprise with an ever-increasing need for capital. Various business abuses followed that contributed to a decline in competition (Schnitzer 1987, p. 23).

The creation of industrial and railroad monopolies soon followed. So, given the historical 'watchman' role of the US government, private enterprise had become the overwhelmingly dominant engine of economic growth. Following the Civil War, technology facilitated the formation of giant firms that greatly reduced the level of market competition. While the Sherman Act was passed in 1890, to prohibit anticompetitive practices,

> the laws directed against industrial concentration and the accumulation of wealth did not have much effect, and by 1920 industrial concentration was more pronounced than it had been in 1880 (Schnitzer 1987, p. 21).

Historical and Comparative Issues   39

In certain industries, notably petroleum and steel (dominated by Rockefeller's Standard Oil Trust and the Carnegie Company (later US Steel) respectively), the government was content to focus on specific acts of anti-competitive behaviour through antitrust laws; in other industries where political lobbying from aggrieved parties was intense (*i.e.*, railways), regulatory structures were established to oversee market behaviour. This provided a precedent for the eventual expansion of the regulated private enterprise model to other areas of the US economy, including telecommunications and broadcasting, air and trucking transport, and of course, public utilities.

Thus, the role of government in the economy is an important difference between Australian and American approaches to market failure. While the Australian government was expected to provide a helping hand in setting up public infrastructure requirements, in the US private enterprise took responsibility for establishing railroads, granaries, and utilities. When the outcome of competition in those markets led to monopolistic dominance, the government imposed regulation to decrease the social costs of monopoly. Given the size of the US federal government at the time, and in light of the historical role of government, public ownership was never seriously considered.

Perhaps as a consequence, the structure of the SOE sector in the US is characterised by a lack of uniformity, and a lack of clear governance structures. This has wide-reaching constitutional implications. Federal Government Corporations (FGCs) straddle the unclear line between public and private. Despite their relative obscurity, FGCs 'manage communication satellites, museums, railroads, and power generation. They provide specialized credit and insurance for housing and agriculture' (Froomkin 1995, p. 547). What differentiates US FGCs from, say, Australian GCs is the lack of uniformity in their ownership structure. While some are wholly government-owned, others are partially or even wholly owned by private persons. Privately held FGCs gain their apparently contradictory status through the provision of public funds to private actors. Froomkin (1995, p. 548) states that this practice 'poses a serious and largely unexplored challenge to accountable, efficient, democratic national government'. What follows in this section focuses on FGCs in which the government owns shares or appoints directors.

The nearest equivalent to a corporatisation statute is the *Government Corporation Control Act*.[38] However, that statute does not necessarily regulate the FGCs currently in existence, as exceptions to it are given to certain FGCs. This adds to the lack of uniformity in structure and regulatory framework. Further, that legislation only regulates FGCs in existence; it does not provide a formal, uniform structure for the creation of new FGCs. New corporations are chartered in most instances by legislation, which may provide a federal charter to incorporate the new company under the corporate law of the District of Columbia (Froomkin 1995, p. 552). The incorporating Act will also generally define the body's powers, structures, obligations, and purposes. In this sense, the incorporating statute bears some relation to the role played in Australasia by the SCI.

Power to appoint directors rests primarily with the President. He may have the power to appoint all, a majority, or a minority of directors on any particular FGC. As in Australasia, FGCs are generally exempt from public service limits on pay levels, tenure, and other administrative functions such as freedom of information legislation. Many FGCs also issue stock, leading to a loose categorisation of FGCs as either 'wholly-owned', 'mixed-ownership', or 'private'. Wholly-owned FGCs (*e.g.*, Commodity Credit Corp.) are generally subject to a greater degree of administrative law. Mixed-ownership FGCs (including Amtrak and the Tennessee Valley Authority) are generally seen to carry an implicit government guarantee from the federal government, distorting their borrowing rates. Finally, a private FGC limits government control to board member appointment. Private FGCs are not subject to the *Government Corporation Control Act*. Against this informal categorisation is the loose regulatory structure contained in the above-mentioned *Government Corporation Control Act*. Compared to the Australasian statutes, this legislation sets out only a very limited regulatory framework for FGCs. Broad requirements include the preparation and submission to the President of annual budgets and other financial information, including the expected return to Treasury, and capital requirements from Treasury. Treasury approval must also be gained prior to the issuing of any securities to the public. The Comptroller General audits wholly-and partially-owned FGCs. These audits and the material submitted to the President are then submitted to Congress for approval.

The Act is therefore designed to provide for information flows from FGCs to the President and Congress. There is no equivalent of the CSO mechanism or the SCI, apart from targets implicit in budgets. FGCs are subject to a regulatory patchwork that needs to be consolidated and updated.

Despite its geographical proximity to the United States, Canada's historical experience of GCs is more similar to its peers in the Commonwealth. Its environment resembles Australia's — a vast country, sparsely settled, in which a severe climate challenges the exploitation of prodigious natural resources. We find that public enterprise has been extensively used for public policy objectives, not just in infrastructure and natural monopoly areas (Chorney 1998) but in more contestable markets, such as air travel, natural resources, the production of staples, and so on

Historical and Comparative Issues

(Tupper 1998). The ideology of the government seems to be an important influence on the creation of GCs, although conservative governments have created GCs as well (Chandler 1983).

Canada is a federal system. Its experience with GCs (called Crown Corporations) has depended on the relevant jurisdiction in question; unlike Australia, there has not been an analogous process of microeconomic reform that has standardised governance procedures. As such, the many 'Crowns' tend to be subject either to generic companies legislation or *sui generis* enabling legislation. Canadian GCs feature similar accountability principles to those elsewhere, which are based on Ministerial and parliamentary oversight.

The federal government's GCs, which manage total assets of more than $C68 million (Treasury Board of Canada Secretariat 2001), are subject to an accountability framework set out in the *Financial Administration Act*. This framework allocates power to a board of directors to approve strategic plans for the GCs, to manage risk, and to supervise management. The board is accountable to a (single) responsible Minister, who is in turn accountable to the government. The Executive approves an annual corporate plan for each GC. The board is also responsible for ongoing examination of the GC's public policy objectives and its statutory mandate, and for appreciation of how these objectives should trade-off with commercial objectives (Minister of Finance and the President of the Treasury Board 1996). Although corporate governance guidelines indicate the importance of board independence (ibid), public servants can and do serve on GC boards. By contrast, Australian jurisdictions generally prohibit this.[39]

There are, however, divergent governance arrangements as between the various provinces and the federal government. Stevens (1993) demonstrates this in his incisive comparison between GCs in Alberta, Manitoba, and Saskatchewan. The most important differences relates to the balance between the autonomy of management and the level of institutional control in the relevant government. The Albertan approach has been one that has favoured a much greater level of managerial autonomy; the other two provinces have opted for a much higher level of institutional control over, and political involvement in, the management of the GC, albeit by very different means. The Manitoban approach has relied on a powerful bureaucratic monitoring model through a Department of Crown Investments, which provides government considerable information advantages. By contrast, the Saskatchewan approach relies instead on a model in which GCs are subject to the control of a holding company which itself is under Ministerial management, a structure which runs in parallel with the location of Ministers in strategic positions on the 'subsidiary' GC boards. Saskatchewan and Manitoba have more experience of left-leaning governments than Alberta.

Canada, too, has experienced substantial privatisation reforms. Brian Mulroney's administration, between 1984 and 1993, sought to privatise to reduce budgetary deficits and national debt. One of its major projects was the privatisation of Air Canada (1988) and Petro-Canada (1991). The Liberal Chrétien government took this process further, privatising Canadian National Railways (1995) and Nav Canada (1996). Nonetheless, the pace of privatization reforms has been more moderate than in the United Kingdom (Levac and Wooldridge 1997). The provinces also undertook their own divestments for fiscal reasons, such as the telecommunications bodies in Alberta (1990) and Manitoba (1996).

To conclude this section on SOEs in English speaking countries, each of the jurisdictions considered above has addressed the regulatory issues associated with market failure or natural monopoly in ways that raise different governance issues. While the United Kingdom has gone down the American path of regulated private monopolies in recent times, it has only done so after an extreme experiment with nationalisation and a consequent set of privatisations which raised complex governance issues that the Americans have never had to seriously consider (see, *e.g.*, Jones *et al.* 1999). These include the issues of the pricing of the assets privatised (see, *e.g.*, Perotti and Guney 1993), the choices between more concentrated and dispersed ownership, the impact on those choices on agency costs of management, the distribution of the proceeds of privatisation amongst interest groups, and the issues related to the retention of residual powers over the privatised entity for national interest considerations (such as via a golden share). The Australian experience can, as was noted above, be described as unique in evidencing a clear preference for situating publicly-owned enterprise in a context that acknowledges the need for appropriate governance parameters. It was therefore predictable that Australia would follow the example of New Zealand, by adopting reforms aimed at capturing the benefits of private enterprise while avoiding the costs and difficulties of regulating private actors. Nonetheless, privatisation of utilities in many Australian states, and the gradual privatisation of the national telecommunications utility, Telstra, raise similar issues of price regulation. Some Australian economists have a dim view of the enhancements of the efficiency of the part-privatised Telstra (*e.g.*, Quiggin 2003). At the same time, in areas such as electricity, states, such as Queensland, that retain publicly-owned energy companies have achieved

Historical and Comparative Issues

efficiency gains through increased interstate competition with private companies under the guidance of the competitive neutrality principle. While the UK also has a significant history of GCs from the Morrisonian period, it demonstrates clearly how the combination of ideology and inefficient governance create the conditions for reactive cycling between aggressive nationalisation and privatisation.

This review shows how the three governance problems identified in Chapter 1 pervade the regulatory landscape. Agency costs of management and governance rose to crippling levels in the United Kingdom GCs of the pre-Thatcher era because of their confused objectives, loose budget constraints, and Ministerial micro-management. The ideologically neutral Australian model of the early twentieth century was far preferable in its recognition of the need for limiting government intervention in management, for the separate funding of non-commercial activities, and private sector benchmarks. The revisitation of these principles in the 1980s and 1990s, coupled with enhanced knowledge of the important role of markets, property rights and incentives is a testament to the enduring insights of the older model, and the sufficiently unbiased approach of Australasian governments not to throw out the public enterprise baby with the less efficient governance practice bathwater.

We now turn to examine the role of SOEs in emerging economies and the response to the inheritance of central economic planning.

Eastern European and Chinese Privatisations

The fall of the Berlin Wall heralded the collapse of the command economies of the ex-Soviet Union and its network of Eastern bloc satellite states. Post-Cold War policy makers in Eastern Europe and post-Soviet Russia looked to the economic success of the West for future direction, and sought to construct Western economic and political institutions on the ruins of fallen socialist institutions. Attendant with this institution building was a desire to shed the state of its role as the decision-maker regarding economic activity and to develop a thriving private sector. In fact, aside from programmes of price liberalisation (which have engendered pervasive social hardship), the main issue in these reforms was not whether privatisation should occur, it was how quickly the programme should proceed. In light of the political turmoil that existed (and continues to exist) in many former Eastern bloc states, it was thought that a lengthy reform programme would stagnate, provoking popular resentment that would cause the privatisation agenda to be thwarted. It was therefore seen to be preferable to embark on a programme of rapid privatisation, in a manner that has been called 'shock

44   *Corporate Governance in Government Corporations*

therapy' (Weisskopf 1998, p. 106), in order to credibly demonstrate a government's commitment to economic reform. While this was expected to involve massive social dislocation (which it has, to the resentment of large sections of the populace), by concentrating the pain of reform in a short timeframe, reformers hoped that once the benefits began to accumulate, popular support would emerge, adding weight to the liberalisation of the economy. That view was also taken by bodies such as the International Monetary Fund, who tied financial assistance to reforms of this sort (see generally Stiglitz 2002). After a decade, social dislocation remains, with benefits only slowly emerging. In their literature review, Megginson and Netter (2001) note that the case for privatisation has often been weakest in Eastern Europe where the pace of reform has been greatest.

Juxtaposed against the shock therapy approach adopted in Eastern Europe is the 'crossing the river by feeling for stones' (Deng Xiao Ping, quoted in Chen *et al.* [2000, p. 4]) approach of the remaining communist superpower, China. The strength of the Chinese government has made possible the gradual liberalisation of the Chinese economy. Popular resentment has been suppressed by both the totalitarianism of the Communist regime, as well as the high levels of economic growth that have occurred as a result of official endorsement of the private sector. While hardly endorsing totalitarianism as a means of attaining political stability, the avoidance of massive social dislocation via a programme of gradual reform represents an alternative to the shock therapy of Eastern European reforms. To view matters from the governmental perspective, a more gradual approach may be regarded as desirable for an established regime clinging to power. Minimising social dislocation decreases the need to enforce its reforms by totalitarian means. By way of contrast, the newer political orders of Eastern Europe had less time to work out reforms, and depended on the support of organised interest groups, specifically executives and workers in privatised enterprises (Kapstein and Milanovic 1999).

Russia

Under the influence of Marxist-Leninism, the private sector was suppressed in Eastern bloc economies, surviving only in black market transactions. Heavy industry was in the hands of the state, along with distributional chains and retail outlets. Lacking the incentive structures of private market actors, command economies quickly descended into massive waste and inefficiency, typified in sprawling industrial conglomerates, integrated both vertically and horizontally (Kornai 1992). Investment and production was geared primarily towards the massive industrial-military sector. Consumer goods were much more limited in these economies. When the Eastern bloc collapsed, in part as a result of these economic inefficiencies (Olson 2001), reformers were faced with the task of privatising tens of thousands of small shops and retail outlets, along with the medium-to-large size industrial firms that constituted the driving force in the Russian economy. These industrial behemoths, some of them employing tens of thousands of workers and producing a peculiarly wide range of goods, proved to be one the most significant stumbling blocks to the completion of a rapid and comprehensive reform programme in Russia.

Privatisation in Russia, as in the rest of Eastern Europe, proceeded primarily through the issue of vouchers to citizens. Theoretically, this reflects the people as the ultimate 'owners' of the state-owned enterprises, while engendering popular participation in the reform programme. Individuals interested in participating could then purchase further vouchers from those reluctant to take part in the sales, while others could place their vouchers in mutual funds, who would then purchase shares in privatised firms. The majority of the 170,000 small shops and retail stores were then auctioned off. This worked quite well for these small enterprises, and the foundation of a private market sector was laid.

Much more problematic was the privatisation of medium-to-large enterprises, particularly the massive industrial conglomerates — the 'crown jewels' of the old Soviet regime. The primary concern was with the eventual ownership mix of the privatised firms. While some advocated a diffuse and widespread body of shareholders, others drew attention to the problems of lack of control over managerial power that would result if a substantial bloc of shares was not in the hands of an individual (*e.g.*, Frydman and Rapaczynski 1994). In light of these concerns, and due to the politicking of managers and employees:

> Workers and managers wanted these enterprises to be given or sold cheaply to them and to no one else. Workers opposed any significant role for domestic or foreign investors because they feared that outsiders would drastically cut employees, and managers feared outside owners would fire them or curtail their power. Both were also concerned that outsiders who had criminal connections might get control of their enterprise (Blasi *et al.* 1997, p. 36).

The reform team in Moscow was also concerned that the managerial elite would become entrenched, and support for dominant employee ownership was hesitant due to fears that the workers would run the enterprise into the ground for their own short-term advantage.

The final programme was passed into law on June 11, 1992. During an initial stage of corporatisation, the SOE acquired a legal personality separate from the state, was assigned an economic (assets-based) value, acquired stock (enumerated by dividing the asset value by 1000 (roubles)), and established its senior management, and a board of directors. Employees were then given three options to choose from at a general meeting.

The options involved varying levels of employee ownership, ranging from minority employee ownership, being 40/60 split between employee ownership and shares sold to the public, majority employee ownership, being 51/49 split between the same groups, or a management buyout. Majority employee ownership was the preferred model in almost three out of four cases. Importantly,

> Managers and employees did not have to compete with anyone to buy this initial package of shares. They simply decided what they wanted and bought the shares in their company on the basis of the low value assigned to it. No outsiders, no Mafia, no foreigners, no former Soviet bureaucrats had any formal role in the process at this stage (Blasi *et al.* 1997, p. 42).

There are three discernible stages in the privatisation process (Broadman 2001). The first stage, in 1993–1995, focused somewhat more on smaller firms than the larger firms, and employed the voucher approach described above, in which employees gained majority ownership. The second stage, in 1995–1996, raised more problems. Important financial industrial groups secured securities in the largest and most attractive firms in exchange for loans to the budget under the 'loans for shares' scheme in 1995. At the same time the managers of other corporations obtained control of their organisations, sometimes legally, sometimes through coercive and unscrupulous means, such as stripping employee shares of voting rights. Managers blocked outsiders from acquiring seats on the board of directors. Corporate governance in many of these organisations was deplorable during this period. The third stage, beginning in 1997, was far better managed. It focused on the sale of controlling shares in large SOEs through more transparent means such as competitive tenders. Independent financial consultants were involved both to improve the SOE's governance and to conduct the sale.

Broadman (2001) notes that the state continues to hold major equity stakes in about 2500 companies and about 14,000 uncorporatised SOEs. With a few exceptions, government officials have primary managerial involvement. This management, he observes, continues to be seen as inefficient, unaccountable, and often corrupt. There are some signs of reform, such as the use of holding company structures for the companies, and an increased tendency to try to professionalise management through management contracts. However, there is continued internal resistance within these firms to increased exposure to markets.

Historical and Comparative Issues 47

One may conclude that, while the legal structures of corporate governance are in place, there is little understanding of how the norms and practices associated with corporate governance are supposed to function. It will clearly take some time before a functioning corporate governance culture is established. This will prolong the social dislocation already caused by wider economic reforms (most especially the freeing of prices from state control). We therefore find that with relatively weak governance, the agency costs of management are high in these privatised entities.

Poland

Privatisation experiences have varied from jurisdiction to jurisdiction, even though it is fair to say that the principles behind the Russian reforms are common throughout Eastern Europe (Hlaváček and Mejstřick 1997). Despite this commonality, differences in the pace of reforms and in political stability quickly appeared. Kapstein and Milanovic (1999) note that political interest groups differed markedly as between Poland and Russia — the strength of unions and farmers in Polish politics prior to the demise of communism enabled them to contest the power of insiders in privatised firms. Unions and farmers were weaker in Russia (see generally Hellman 1998; Shleifer and Treisman 1997).

Poland has been especially plagued by political instability, with more fierce resistance to privatisation from both left and right parties than any other European transition economy (Winiecki 1997). The initial reform programme, commenced in June 1990, incorporated both voucher style coupons, distributed to Polish citizens free-of-charge, and the liquidation of unprofitable companies and their sale or lease to third parties. Polish SOEs were divided into 500 large firms and a body of 5500 small-to-medium size firms. Large firms might then be liquidated and transferred to the small-to-medium category. As in Russia, the initial ownership mix post-privatisation was mandated by the state, and is set out in Table 2.1.

48   *Corporate Governance in Government Corporations*

Table 2.1   Initial Equity Shares in Privatisations in Poland

Proportion of equity	Identity of recipients
30%	Special purpose investment funds for distribution to public
20%	Pension funds
10%	Employees (entitled to buy at a 50% discount from the purchase price)
10%	Banking sector.
30%	State, for subsequent sale to outside investors (including foreigners).

Source: Blaszczyk and Dabrowski 1993, p. 17.

Political instability halted this first attempt at reform. A weak economy, industrial disputes with increasingly nervous workers, and shifting political coalitions (there were 29 political parties in the Sejn in 1993) necessitated changes to the reform agenda (Klich 1998). The Mass Privatization Plan (MPP) was proposed in 1992, and envisaged each Polish citizen over 18 years of age one certificate of ownership in each of the special purpose investment funds. The programme was rejected in March 1993 and subsequently separated into two stages. First, fifteen National Investment Funds assumed control of 200 firms that had previously undergone preparations for privatisation. Shares in these firms were to go to pensioners and public servants. Second, 400 of the largest state enterprises would be privatised by providing shares to all Polish citizens at massively discounted prices. This was accompanied by a separate issue of vouchers (15%) to SOE employees to purchase shares in the privatised firms. These reforms were passed into law on 30 April 1993 and, 'after long and often heated debates' (Klich 1998, p. 90), initiated in November 1995.

A problem that has affected Poland and other post-communist economies, is the conflict between encouraging support and participation of the reforms (which requires a widely dispersed shareholder base) and overcoming disincentives to the taking of collective action by shareholders in corporate governance (which requires larger shareholders). This latter requirement is the impetus behind the mutual and investment funds set up in Poland, Russia and elsewhere.

Overall, the absence of stable government and lack of a unified vision has hampered ongoing reform in Poland. It has also hampered foreign investment, while general economic weakness has limited support and participation in the privatisation process. The initial programme led some to comment that extensive 'shock' had been produced for very little 'therapy' (Poznanski 1993, p. 15). Polish governments have since proceeded more gradually, however, this has lead to the accumulation of substantial losses in firms waiting for privatisation (Klich 1998, p. 94). This may lend

Historical and Comparative Issues

credence to the Russian reformers' 'shock therapy'. However, some measure of political stability is necessary to push fast-tracked reforms through, while proposed shock therapies may arouse sufficient popular opposition that political stability quickly disintegrates, slowing reform and allowing SOE sector losses to accumulate. It should be noted that while the rapid reforms were forecast to produce rapid (and positive) outcomes, 10 years later, many benefits have been slow to appear.

The Czech Republic and Slovakia

The separation of the former Czechoslovakia into the Czech Republic and the Republic of Slovakia has denied observers what may have been a model emphasising transitional reform from a centrally planned economy to a market economy. The former Czechoslovakia had an unusual degree of political stability and internal cohesion. This has enabled it to remain the only post-communist state that has provided no preferences to SOE sector employees (Mládek 1997, p. 50). Market institutions such as a functioning banking sector, stock exchanges and a stable property rights regime were established, and overall the government enjoyed relatively high levels of popular support for its privatisation programme.[40]

The initial reform of the federated Czechoslovakia provided for the public auctioning of over 10,000 small shops and enterprises that weren't contested by descendants of pre-war property owners, who could file claims to regain ownership under the Restitution Law. This was successful. Political momentum was maintained throughout the process and the measurable improvement in retail and wholesale trades and services became symbolic of future benefits to the Czech people (Mládek 1997). Further, popular grievances against the communist regime were addressed through the restitution process, which 'actually resulted in the privatisation of a vastly larger portion of state-controlled assets than did the [small privatisation process]' (Hopkins 1998, p. 63).

A 'large privatisation' law covering some 4000 firms was then instigated in 1991 using a voucher system. While these firms were given some say in the planning of privatisation for their own enterprises, the final decision rested with the federal Privatisation Minister. The voucher system aimed at providing the 'widest possible dispersion of assets' with 'approximately 8.5 million of the country's 15 million eligible citizens participating' (Balfour and Crise 1993, p. 94). Ownership soon concentrated, however, as private investment funds began bidding up the value of the vouchers. This raised concerns about anti-competitive behaviour, and a single fund was limited to owning a maximum of 20% of any one company's stock. As of 1992, almost 1500 firms had been

50   *Corporate Governance in Government Corporations*

privatised, involving property worth $US10 billion (Balfour and Crise, 1993, p. 95).

However, on 1 January 1993, the former Czechoslovakia was divided into the Czech Republic and Slovakia. This partition was a substantial set back to reforms in both countries. Slovakia, due to its weaker economy and greater political instability, predictably bore large costs. Czech reforms continued, and by early 1995 the capitalisation of the Prague stock exchange was estimated at US$25 billion (Hopkins 1998, p. 66). At the end of 2001, the Czech Republic still held interests of more than 30% in over 20 large companies in industries including steel, oil and energy (Muzikar and Drevinek 2002). Slovakia has been beset by difficulties. Popular support for the reforms was sliding, necessitating a slower agenda of privatisation.

Harper (2001) finds that, by way of contrast to the normal finding that privatisation improves firm performance (*e.g.*, Boubakri and Cosset 1998; Megginson *et al.* 1994; Megginson and Netter 2001), efficiency and profitability actually *decreased* in privatised firms in the Czech Republic (although firms did take steps to decrease employment). That evidence is perhaps consistent with the finding of Pinto *et al.* (1993) that efficiency improved considerably in Czech firms in a period after incentives were increased and competition introduced, but before privatisation. A cross-sectional study of SOEs and privatised firms in the Czech Republic, however, finds that the privatised firms perform better in generating revenue (although not in reducing costs) (Frydman *et al.* 1999).

Both countries face difficulties stemming from the state's previous monopolisation of real property, and the bifurcation of state and private property. Contract law is a new body of knowledge in both jurisdictions, and uncertainty will prevail for some time in the interpretation and application of the new laws. Similarly, bankruptcy and competition laws are not only novel, but contain concepts wholly alien to a society accustomed to a half century of socialist thinking. The application of these laws is, for a time, likely to bring frustration and social dislocation.

The experience of the former Eastern bloc countries makes a fascinating contrast to economic restructuring in Commonwealth countries. Undoubtedly, most of the former state owned assets needed privatisation, because the state had little comparative advantage in managing these, especially shops and other enterprises without elements of natural monopoly. In the same way, the political volatility of these countries places heavy compromises on the capacity of a government to administer a viable SOE sector and build a governance culture. At the same time, the market institutions needed to support the ownership transition inherent in privatisation have been on the weak side. We now turn to examine the success of SOE reform in China where the totalitarian regime has enjoyed

Historical and Comparative Issues 51

the stability needed to choose between shock therapy and transitory approaches.

China

The Chinese experience in transitory reform stands in marked contrast to the 'shock therapy' approach adopted throughout the former Eastern bloc economies. While economic liberalisation in Eastern Europe has been accompanied by democratisation, in China:

> political repression coexist[s] with an economy currently experiencing one of the most rapid growth rates in the world. Nominally socialist but steadfastly market-oriented, China is embarking on a strategy of slow but steady economic transformation (Cao 1995, p. 98).

Thus, the Chinese State has been able to keep a tight grip on the reigns of economic reform; in the words of Deng Xiao Ping, 'China wants modernization, not democratisation' (Shen 2000, pp. 42). There is little immediate problem of political instability derailing or postponing reforms. To this end, reform can proceed at a slower, more gradual pace. By comparison, the sudden collapse of the Eastern bloc negated the existence of a strong government guiding an economy slowly towards market liberalisation. Local government, in particular, has encouraged the development of private firms in China, whereas in Russia local government has retarded the growth of new firms. Blanchard and Schleifer (2000) attribute this to the strength of the party-controlled *central* government in China, which has encouraged local policies conducive to growth. This has not been present in Russia. Overall, 'unlike economic liberalization in Eastern European nations, the process of opening up in China was gradual and calculated' (Shen 2000, p. 45).

We can see the incidents of the slow Chinese transition to private markets in the changing share of National Gross Output Value of Chinese Industrial Enterprises. From 1993 to 1999, SOEs' share of output has fallen from 47% to 28%. Collectives have stayed constant in the vicinity of 35%. The share of enterprises owned by individuals have more than doubled from 8% to 18% (although the *number* has fallen by 20%), as have all 'other' entities (including local corporations and foreign firms), increasing from 11% to 26%. Yet a problem remains with the productivity of these SOEs. Although they account for less than a third of total output, they own two thirds of total assets and account for approximately three-quarters of investment (Broadman 2001).

52   *Corporate Governance in Government Corporations*

Fundamentally, the Chinese reforms maintain a strong distinction between privatising state owned businesses and creating a private sector. Summarily, 'Chinese privatisation has evolved over time into three manageable sequences: the creation of a new, non-state sector, the reformation of the existing state sector, and the privatisation of the state sector' (Cao 1995, p. 102). Rather than concentrating on the transfer of assets to private ownership, China has concentrated on independently fostering a nonstate sector to create market institutions to support the eventual transition of state owned enterprises to private hands. In 1997, less than 5% of the 118,000 industrial SOEs had been transferred to private ownership (World Bank, 1997, p. 1), but the number had risen to 61,000 in 1999 (Broadman 2001). Shen (2000, p. 145) draws the conclusion that a primary purpose of private enterprise in China is to supplement the state sector's function in the economy.

This approach is centred on the premise that working institutions of a market-based economy must be securely established before wholesale privatisations can occur. '[G]overnment policy placed increasing emphasis on building a market economy and shifted towards a rules-based framework, [paving] the way for rapid growth of private enterprises' (International Finance Corporation 2000, p. vii) but always in the shadow of the still dominant SOE sector. Instead of privatisation, '[p]roduction planning [did] not vanish, but its span of control [has] gradually [shrunk]' (Rawski 1996, p. 190). Cao (1995) even doubts whether wholesale privatisations should occur at all. Cao represents the Chinese approach to market liberalisation as containing an entirely new approach to economic prosperity, based less on individual property and more on communal enterprise. In this sense, the need for an effective governance framework for enterprises remaining in State ownership is heightened far more than is true of the former Eastern bloc countries.

The fostering of a non-state sector has been, by all accounts, a remarkable success. By 1996, this sector was responsible for three-quarters of industrial output (Shen 2000, p. 148). Economic growth rates, particularly in the special economic zones (mainly on the south-east coast) have been spectacular. Cao (1995) sees the provision of an up- and down-stream market for the goods of the non-state sector as one of the most important functions the state sector plays. Without this initial demand from state-owned firms, the private sector may have had a much shakier start. Nonetheless, China's economy is still heavily dependent on its state sector, as the figures quoted above in Broadman (2001) indicate.

What are the characteristics of governance in the state sector? In the late 1980s, Chinese reformers turned their attention to the reform of the country's state-owned enterprises. From the Communist takeover until

Historical and Comparative Issues 53

1984, SOEs were not even regarded as having separate legal personality from the state — much less economic independence (Schipani and Liu 2002). The state funded the SOE, which in turn produced goods distributed by the State and provided economic security to SOE employees. In 1988, an SOEs Law, was enacted which was a turning point in the reform process (*ibid*). It articulated a separation of ownership and management by recognising the managerial authority of the chief executive of an enterprise. The enterprise was subject to the supervision of the local organisation of the Communist Party. The creation of the non-state sector has been seen to aid the reformation of the state-owned sector. State enterprises have been under pressure to adopt characteristics of their private counterparts to compete effectively. Further, performance-based compensation and initiatives have also encouraged reform of work practices. Responsibility was given back to managers in an attempt to foster accountability. Rewards include profit-sharing plans, and the freeing of prices (to an extent) from central control. Further, by way of contrast to the SCI mechanism in Australasia, SOE management has, since 1983, been able to take advantage of a contract responsibility system whereby:

> An SOE would sign an individually-negotiated contract with its supervising agency specifying the annual amount of revenue (tax-cum-profit) to be turned over to the state, thereby ... giving the firm the incentive to maximise its financial surplus (Sachs and Wing 1996, p. 281).

Subsequently, 'new forms of contracting gradually supplanted annual plan targets even for the largest firms' (Jefferson and Rawski 2001, p.247). As Cao points out, this involves the creation of property rights, moving the locus of such rights down the chain of command from 'the central plan towards more enterprise autonomy' (1995, p. 148). Similarly, a two-tiered pricing structure was introduced. Production quotas are mandated and the goods manufactured are sold at the price set by central authorities. Any production over that quota can then be sold at the market price, reflecting the distribution of supply and demand. This has the effect of slowly introducing state-firms to price competition, with less social dislocation than the shock associated with freeing prices from state control in Eastern Europe. The evidence on the productivity gains from these incentives is somewhat mixed: Li (1997) finds productivity gains, but Shirley and Xu (1998), in a study using a small sample of 12 monopoly SOEs, do not.

In summary, productivity picked up significantly in the 1980s (Jefferson *et al.* 1996; Zhuang and Xu 1996). However, by the 1990s it became clear that those successes were limited and structural problems remained (Lardy 1998). The system depended on the capacity to define an

54   *Corporate Governance in Government Corporations*

appropriate amount of profit to be paid to the State, and agency costs associated with misuse of assets remained high. As central control is divested to regional and local government authorities, the SOE sector is experiencing a loss of control (a 'governance vacuum' according to Broadman [2001, p. 15]) that is becoming manifest in widespread asset stripping. Essentially, assets become privatised while liabilities become socialised. This has wide-ranging ramifications for macroeconomic stability (World Bank 1997, ch. 1). Further, despite the productivity and efficiency gains (including those for the private sector), the state-owned sector constitutes a massive financial burden on the government. This increased the pressure for a privatisation programme for smaller entities and for corporatisation reforms for larger entities, culminating in the Communist Party's plan to privatise all but the largest 300 or so SOEs in China (Lin 2000).

Since 1993, the reform process in SOEs has been tied to developments in corporate governance. A general corporations statute was introduced in 1993, and a securities regulation statute in 1998. This enabled increased corporatisation of SOEs. Nonetheless, the potential for improved corporate governance has had equivocal effects. Schipani and Liu (2002) refer to a 1999 survey by the China Confederation of Enterprises which indicated that only a seventh of corporatised SOEs reported better economic performance although more than a half reported better corporate governance. They refer to infrequent board and shareholders' meetings, blurred lines between executive and director roles, and ubiquitous government intervention in management. Referring to survey evidence undertaken in China suggesting similar conclusions to our own, they report that managers 'are so busy dealing with unlimited and repeated inspections and examinations organized by government agencies that their business suffers' (p. 29).

The dilemma facing China is how to pursue the needed reforms (mainly through allowing outside equity interests in SOEs) in a manner consistent with socialist ideology. The model adopted 'reflects the quandaries of its genetically mixed origins but also the hiccups of political deadlock and compromise' (Cao, 1995, p. 152). The model shows a preference for debt over equity financing, consistent with the state's second goal to maintain majority ownership. Cao comments:

> the Chinese model of privatisation has produced a distinctively Chinese reality — state sector privatisation motivated by the surplus, not the dearth of domestic capital. This fact makes the free distribution schemes adopted in Eastern Europe economically unnecessary (1995, p. 152).

To maintain some level of ideological consistency, initial issues of bonds were made primarily to workers. Cao suggests that:

> Bonds represented a noncontroversial financing tool, providing the Chinese government with an ideologically compatible vehicle for raising need capital. Debt instruments wholly void of equity interests allowed the government to raise money without implicating socialist ownership of the means of production and without undermining government control of state enterprises (p. 157).

The success of this reform led the Chinese to experiment with a shareholding system. However, the experimentation has been limited and distorted by the need to maintain ideological consistency with socialist theory. The primary limitation has been the state's insistence on retaining majority ownership. The Chinese government rejects the need for the separation of ownership from control that typifies private corporations in the West. The outcome is that Chinese corporate law classifies shares by ownership status rather than the rights attached to different classes of shares. Governmental departments retain majority shareholdings. Although since 1984 (Otsuka *et al.* 1998, p. 33), management in principle holds responsibility and decision-making authority, we have seen that the evidence on government interference suggests otherwise. Majority state-ownership has inevitably hampered the proper functioning of Chinese stock markets, serving more as a financing tool for the government than a corporate governance mechanism. This can occur, as above, because of the surplus availability of domestic capital. Consequently, Chinese SOEs continue to enjoy soft budget constraints. In an attempt to harden the budget constraint, the Chinese government has moved to using bankruptcy laws to force the grossest offenders into liquidation.

Even though China prefers debt financing over equity, securitisation of selected SOEs has occurred, and some enterprises are now traded on the stock exchange. The surplus of domestic capital that the government has been able to tap into, a surplus previously denied to it, has curtailed the need for direct foreign credits or foreign investment, a factor of obvious appeal to the Chinese authorities. This pool of investment funds has been of special importance, given the rate at which the SOE sector bleeds red ink. In Cao's words, 'private capital [has been utilized] to finance public debt' (1995, p. 154). This point makes an interesting comparison with SOEs in South East Asia, where public money is often used to finance the private debt of politically-connected 'crony' or 'client capitalists' (Alatas 1997, pp. 123-4; Milne and Mauzy 1999; Rodan *et al.* 1997).

Although taking SOEs public seems to offer a solution to the incentive problems associated with SOEs, empirical evidence is less supportive. Wang *et al.* (2001) find that taking SOEs public has actually had *negative*

56 *Corporate Governance in Government Corporations*

effects on efficiency — performance in the years following a listing are sharply lower than their levels in both the pre-listing years and the initial public offering years, and that capital expenditure appears to fall. Moreover, they find that the effects of listing on performance are substantially unaffected by the percentage of equity held by the state or the concentration of shareholdings. This result is at odds with the normal trend in privatised SOEs (Megginson and Netter 2001), although it is similar to the result discussed above for the Czech Republic (Harper 2001) and the evidence of Ehrlich *et al.* (1994) that partial privatisations achieve little. Harper also found ownership concentration to be irrelevant.

On a philosophical note, one might question how this manner of financing highly leveraged SOEs accords with the socialist notion that 'the people' ultimately own SOEs, through the agency of the government. Should the Chinese people have to pay for direct property rights in Chinese SOEs? On the Eastern European model of rapid privatisation, underpinned by the rationale that free distribution is mandated morally and theoretically (and, no doubt, politically), they should not. There is an irony here — the region of reform moving most quickly towards market liberalisation bases its reform model on a socialist theory of property rights, while the state most concerned with fitting market liberalisation into a socialist government appears, in this respect, to be more willing to deny communal ownership through the state.

Cao (1995, p. 120), speaking of the importance of the Chinese experience, states that 'whether it is a model or accident, it cannot be denied that the Chinese experience challenges economic dogma and presents legitimate alternatives for other transitional economies'. Ultimately, China faces the same dilemma as other transitional economies — reforms may destabilise the economy and society, the long-term costs of avoiding it may be far greater. But, despite the progress made:

> in practice, from the perspective of institutional reform, the government-enterprise relationship has not materially changed much, with effectively little separation between the affairs of business and those of administration. Substantial progress is thus needed on mechanisms for the implementation of the economic legal framework and clear assignment of property rights (World Bank 1997, p. 28).

Synthesis

In this chapter, we have reviewed different responses in a wide range of jurisdictions over the last hundred years to the problems associated with the governance and reform of SOEs. Corporatisation and privatisation have both featured in these responses. Our analysis has suggested that the choice of reform strategies depends on a wide range of factors.

On the one hand, they should be influenced by the three considerations advanced in Chapter 1. As between privatisation and corporatisation, privatisation has the edge in its capacity to eliminate the agency costs of governance. However, in this situation, the 'governance' focus then shifts to the appropriate means of regulating privately owned, natural monopolies. To put that another way, it depends on the efficacy of regulation as a means of decreasing the social costs of monopoly, compared to more direct forms of intervention. At the same time, the agency costs of management may be lowered by privatisation, through stronger market disciplines, such as takeovers, bankruptcy, and so on. However, corporatisation continues to reserve a range of direct governance interventions by government to respond to inefficiency, so the proposition that privatisation necessarily decreases agency costs of management more than corporatisation must be considered as an empirical proposition. Moreover, the choice between corporatisation and privatisation is not by any means a simple binary choice. To choose corporatisation requires choices on a range of governance mechanisms. It is certainly asserted in various parts of this book that the extant corporatisation models in Australasia are anything but perfect, and could in some respects be gainfully altered. Likewise, to opt for privatisation similarly requires a range of choices. One is the degree of privatisation, or the extent to which a government sells down its interest.

The British experience suggests that the combined agency costs of management and governance behave as they do in Figure 2.1 — strictly increasing in the proportion of government ownership (O) and therefore minimised by a full privatisation ($O=0$). Both components of total agency cost (C), agency costs of management (M) and agency costs of governance (G), are strictly increasing in O, so $\partial C/\partial O > 0$ for all values of O.

Yet, it is far from clear why these functions could not behave differently. In particular, there may be situations at which $\partial C/\partial O = 0$, $\partial^2 C/\partial O^2 > 0$, for some value of O where $O>0$. For example, creating a minority class of shareholders ($O>0.5$) whose equity is publicly traded may be optimal. There are in such a situation opportunities to examine the impact of the government's governance of the GC on the value of the firm and a class of shareholders with standing to impeach activities that decrease the value of the firm. These factors may greatly decrease G. Likewise, market values may enable more efficient compensation contracts to be written for managers that also decrease M. However, as O falls further, so that as $O \rightarrow 0$, M may rise in a proportion greater than the fall (if any) in G, perhaps because the government is an efficient monitor of management and the cost of collective action amongst other shareholders is relatively high. In these circumstances, a partial privatisation may dominate a full privatisation (see also Schmitz 2000; *cf.* Ehrlich *et al.* 1994). Even where full privatisations are more efficient, fundamental questions remain regarding the optimal concentration of the buyers of equity.

Figure 2.1   Total Agency Costs in Government Corporations as a Function of Ministerial Discretion

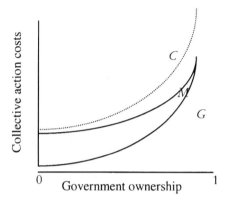

On the other hand, we have seen that other extraneous issues may often dominate these factors. Ideology may be a factor, as it was in the Thatcher era in the United Kingdom, and, similarly, the extirpation of communism in Eastern Europe. Ideology itself often is inherently part of a second, larger factor — politics. The anti-communist ideals of the Conservatives in the United Kingdom were always intended to translate into interest group support, for example by debilitating public sector unions and the opposition party, British Labour, allied with them. In addition to specifically partisan issues, we have seen from Eastern Europe that political climates influence the timing and dynamics of SOE reform. Abrupt shock therapy may be the only viable solution where a political environment is unstable; gradual transitions may be impossible. The fiscal position of a state is also a crucial influence on the reform strategy chosen. The appeal of privatisation is much greater — even irresistible — in circumstances where there is a substantial budgetary deficit or government debt reaches dangerous levels, especially in situations where the SOEs do not return to dividends to the state or require continued investment or debt service. It is no great surprise that the modern era of privatisations occurred in the wake of major economic slowdowns in the early 1980s.

When these extraneous factors influence the decision on SOE governance, it is impossible to say for certain how the overall level of agency costs and the social costs of monopoly will be influenced. Incompetently designed privatisations may easily generate high agency costs of management, while being impossible to reverse. The opportunity costs of these decisions are rarely easy to observe.

Can we say anything about convergence in the corporate governance of SOEs? First, the influence of extraneous factors makes convergence less likely. Political and fiscal considerations will be jurisdiction-specific, although world economic conditions inevitably cause corporations to move together to a certain degree. Extraneous factors are likely to influence governments in idiosyncratic ways, and because the costs associated with the response to these factors are unlikely to be fully internalised by politicians, the response that maximises social welfare is only intermittently likely to be chosen. This is also true of the agency costs of management and governance, and the social costs of monopoly — there is no market mechanism that encourages governments to select an optimal form, even if one could be demonstrated to exist. Most of the costs of inefficient governance choices are borne by the residents of the state, usually in the form of higher taxes and higher prices. The scope for arbitrage and other market-correcting devices is minimal. Product markets exert little influence on natural monopolies, bankruptcy is unlikely where there are soft budget constraints, and takeovers and capital market discipline are impossible when equity is not traded.

Some degree of convergence, however, may come from the dissemination of governance practices through the conscious emulation of those in leading BCs (Hansmann and Kraakman 2000). A bottom-up form of convergence may come from the influence of persons who have sat on BC boards, and want to bring their practices with them. It may also occur by the emulation of a demonstrable innovator in an area in which there are few clearcut optimal responses. Hence, the British experience of privatisation, and, to a lesser extent, the New Zealand approach to corporatisation, have been influential.

Conclusion

In this chapter we studied some of the reform processes used in relation to SOEs and their governance. We can see evidence that economising on the agency costs of management and governance, and the social costs of monopoly have an influence on reforms as do other local and more tendentious factors. However, the absence of market incentives for optimal

60 *Corporate Governance in Government Corporations*

SOE governance and the tendency for copycat emulation amongst jurisdictions, situated within larger political cycles, leave one agnostic whether we should accept the merits of the range of governance mechanisms we observe across the world today. There is, therefore, scope for a detailed examination of how these governance processes operate in practice, especially in corporatised entities.

Notes

1. The following analysis is much indebted to the analysis in Brown (2003).
2. In Australasia, the legislation providing for corporatisation frameworks are *State-Owned Corporations Act* 1989 (NSW); *Government Owned Corporations Act* 1993 (Qld); *Government Business Enterprises Act* 1995 (Tas); *Commonwealth Authorities and Company Act* 1997 (Cth); *State Owned Enterprises Act* 1992 (Vic); *Public Corporations Act* 1993 (SA), *Territory Owned Corporations Act* 1990 (ACT), *State-Owned Enterprises Act* 1986 (NZ). References to legislation below are by the state enacting it.
3. Tasmania, and South Australia are slightly different, in that those jurisdictions only provide for the formation of statutory GCs: Tas: s. 3; SA: s. 5. Therefore, the provisions set out in the corporatisation legislation of those states are exhaustive as to the duties of directors in those GCs. The Australian Capital Territory and New Zealand statutes, on the other hand, provide only for the establishment of company GCs: ACT: ss. 3, 6(1); NZ: s. 2.
4. There are similar documents that go under different names in other states, such as the Corporate Plan (Cth) or Performance Statement (SA). These jurisdictions do not utilise a separate SCI-like statement, and consequently, the CP incorporates specific performance targets over the life of the plan: SA, ss. 12, 13; Cth, s. 42.
5. The governance requirements differ slightly in form, but perform similar functions in substance. New Zealand, the first Australasian jurisdiction to enact a corporatisation framework, does not require a Corporate Plan, with performance criteria being set out on a three year basis in the SCI, reviewed annually. Similarly, NSW and the ACT, following closely behind NZ, also forego CPs, relying on the SCI as the sole governance document. Victoria, Qld, and Tasmania utilise the SCI, but also provide for a CP. In Qld, the CP is agreed between the shareholding Minister(s) and the board. The legislation is silent as to content, but the requirement that the SCI be consistent with the CP suggests that the later functions as a broad guide to SCI content. The Tasmanian model is more opaque. The CP sets out projected financial results and the principal assets and undertakings of the GC. It also contains details of the SCI, unusual in that the SCI functions as 'a summary of the corporate plan' (s. 41). The Victorian CP similarly requires the inclusion of the SCI, in addition

Historical and Comparative Issues

to a business plan, and financial statements as required by the Treasurer (s. 41). The SCI in turn sets out the objectives, main undertakings, nature and scope of activities, accounting policies, performance targets and any further information required by the Treasurer and relevant Minister (s. 42). The Commonwealth, on the other hand, only requires a CP, containing the GC's objectives, assumptions about the business environment, business strategies, investment and financial programs, dividends policy, non-financial performance measures, CSOs, and performance reviews. SA utilises a Corporate Charter, similar in operation to the CP, and separate 'performance statements'. Overall, the SCI or equivalent generally functions as a detailed performance review, while the CP or Charter deals with the broader strategic aspects of an SOE's operations.

6. Qld: s. 114. In New Zealand and Victoria, the SCI for the current financial year, in addition to the two following years, are required: NZ: s. 14(2); Vic.: s. 42. This is also the case for Tasmania's 'corporate plan', of which the SCI is a summary: Tas. ss. 39–41.

7. Qld: s. 115(1)(a)–(j); NSW: s. 22(a)–(g); NZ: s. 14(2)–(3); Tas.: ss. 39–41; SA: s. 13(1); Vic.: s. 42.

8. Qld: ss. 116–120; NSW: s. 21(1)–(3); NZ: s. 14(4); Tas. s. 13(2),(3).

9. NZ: s. 5(1); NSW: s. 10(1); Tas.: s. 11(3); Vic.: s. 25(1). The South Australian and Queensland legislation contain different provisions, requiring that directors achieve a more specific range of objectives, all of which are consistent with the commercial focus of the principle GC objective: SA: s. 14, Qld: ss. 92, 96(2).

10. NZ: s. 4; Tas.: s. 7(1)(a); ACT: s. 7; NSW: ss. 8(1)(a), 20E(1)(a). The Queensland legislation (s. 20(1)) requires GCs to be 'commercially successful in the conduct of its activities and efficient in the delivery of its community service obligations'.

11. Vic: s. 18.

12. NZ: s. 4(a); NSW: s 8(1)(a)(i). Victorian legislation (s. 18(a)) imposes the standard, 'as efficiently as possible consistent with prudent commercial practice'. To similar effect, see Tas: s. 1(a)(i), SA: s 11(1).

13. NZ: s. 4(b), (c).

14. Vic.: s 18(b).

15. SA: s. 11(2); Qld: s. 20(1); Tas.: s. 1(b).

16. Tas.: s 1(a)(i)–(ii).

17. Qld: s. 96(1); NSW: ss. 20J, Pt 2, Sch 2 s. 1(6); Vic. s. 25(1); Tas.: s. 11(2). The Commonwealth, South Australian and New Zealand Acts are silent on the issue.

18. Qld: ss. 95(a)–(d).

19. See also Qld: s. 145(1).

20. Queensland GCs, for example, are obliged to have five shareholding ministers in the case of company GCs: Qld: s. 76. Why five? The number reflects a former requirement of the then *Corporations Law* that a public company that is not a wholly owned subsidiary have five shareholders. That requirement has

62   *Corporate Governance in Government Corporations*

since been repealed: *Corporations Act* 2001 (Cth) s. 114. The historical excrescence persists, nonetheless, in the GC legislation.

21. See below, chapter 4, p. 114 below.
22. See, *e.g.*, NSW: s. 33AA(1).
23. NZ: s. 14(1); ACT: s. 19; NSW: s. 21(1); Vic.: s. 41(1); Cth: s. 42 (Cth); Tas.: s. 39; Qld: ss. 106, 116.
24. Qld: ss. 105, 107, 110(2), 117, 120(2); NSW: s. 21(7); NZ: s. 13(1); Vic.: s 41(9); Tas.: ss. 39, 40; SA: s. 13; cf. Cth: s 42; ACT: ss. 19, 21, where no power of mandatory modification is provided.
25. Qld: ss. 121(1), 122; Tas.: Pt 9, ss. 59–65; NSW: ss. 11, 20N.
26. NZ: s 7.
27. Qld: ss. 123, 124; NSW: ss. 20O, 20P (statutory SOEs only); Cth: ss. 28, 43.
28. Tas.: ss. 114, 115.
29. Qld: ss. 110(3), 120(4); NSW: ss. 200, 20P; SA: s .6(5)(a)(i).Tas: s 7(2).
30. NSW: s. 26(1)(j); SA: s. 6(5)(a)(ii); NZ: ss. 13(3), 17(3).
31. NZ: s. 13(1).
32. SA: s. 12(6).
33. New Zealand competition law is rather different from the regime of the *Trade Practices Act* 1974 (Cth), being heavily influenced by the efficiency-based Chicago school of antitrust theory (Patterson 1996). NZ is experiencing problems of regulating private actors who hold excessive market power, as in the UK.
34. Qld: s. 19(d).
35. See Pt 14 (Qld); ss. 15, 20T (NSW); s. 29 (SA); ss. 67-76 (Tas); and ss. 30B, 30C (ACT). New Zealand, the Commonwealth, and Victoria do not mandate tax equivalents. Victoria does provide that an SOC is not exempt from taxes or duties by virtue of public ownership: s. 70(b).
36. To take a few examples, in NSW: s. 26(4) gives the Treasurer power to delete commercially sensitive information from documents laid before Parliament, while s. 7(1)(a)(i) *Freedom of Information Act* 1989 excludes incorporated companies. At Commonwealth level, the *Freedom of Information Act* 1982 Sch. 2 sets out entities exempt from providing commercially sensitive information, while s 43 excludes documents relating to business affairs. NZ: ss. 9(1)(b)(i), (ii) and 9(1)(c) protects commercially sensitive documents that might inhibit the Crown's capacity to perform commercial functions.
37. Johnstone (2002). The Opposition sought to dubiously attribute the slump to a failure to privatise electricity entities.
38. 31 USC § 9101.
39. Qld: s. 96A.
40. The discussion of Poland, the Czech Republic and Slovakia is indebted to Balfour and Crise (1993).

Chapter 3

The Management of the Government Corporation

Since Berle and Means (1932) documented the prevalence in the United States of corporations that are incapable of effective control by their shareholders, the study of corporate regulation has focused on controlling the abuse of power and resources by those who manage the corporation. Management, thereafter, came to be regarded as the central constituency of the firm, and scholarship divided along pro- and anti-managerial lines, according to the perception of how responsibly management might act (Bratton 1989). Since the late 1970s, considerable attention has been paid to the means by which contracts and markets are capable of motivating managers to act consistently with the interests of shareholders. These include the use of incentive compensation, including stock options, and the effects of takeovers and capital raising.

To what extent, then, are the things that we think we know about the governance of the relation between management and shareholders capable of application to GCs? The governance of the relation in the GC is both harder and easier. Harder, because the benchmarks for the successful discharge of the relation are fewer, and because there are fewer markets to correct overreaching. Easier, because members of the executive government are able to take timely action to address governance problems, unhindered by the collective action problems experienced by BC shareholders (Hirshhorn, 1984). Market discipline is weaker, but potentially less necessary.

As we saw in Chapter 1, minimising the agency costs associated with management must be approached in conjunction with the counterpart process of minimising the agency costs of governance. It follows that any system of governance for GCs must simultaneously attempt to minimise the sum of both categories of agency costs. Therefore, this chapter overlaps with the material in Chapter 4. Initially, the chapter will introduce some of the material discussing the governance of the management–investor relation in BCs. We then examine the limitations on the application of the conclusions from this literature to GCs. In this context, we discuss relevant

64 *Corporate Governance in Government Corporations*

evidence from the Queensland sample, and form some tentative conclusions in relation to the governance of the management relation in GCs.

Corporate Governance of Management: Comparing Government and Business Corporations

Governance Problems and Contracts

The development of the theory of the firm in economics permitted a conceptual understanding of the accountability problems arising from the appointment of a manager. One of the most familiar treatments of the problem is by Jensen and Meckling (1976), which modelled the delegation of management power to an agent as a moral hazard problem. After the contract is struck between principal and agent, the agent's incentives to maximise the value of the principal's interests are altered. Jensen and Meckling examined one form of behaviour by the agent that reduced the principal's welfare, namely, the consumption of perquisites. In that analysis, the agent overconsumes perquisites because he does not bear the cost of the perquisites and his consumption of them is imperfectly observable. According to Jensen and Meckling, however, that incentive is anticipated by the principal who will alter the terms of trade with the agent, diminishing the agent's compensation consistently with the loss that the principal anticipates. Jensen and Meckling argued that agents may be willing to bond themselves credibly not to overconsume perquisites and allow their promise not to do so to be monitored, in return for greater compensation. In equilibrium, not all perquisite overconsumption is eliminated. A residual loss remains as bonding and monitoring are costly; thus, a dollar spent on bonding and monitoring will be equated at the margin with a dollar saved from reduced overconsumption.

This analysis applies without substantial change to other moral hazard-like behaviours. These include on-the-job shirking, expropriation of assets, conflicts of interest, excessive retention of cash instead of payment of dividends, and so on. In each case, the parties seeks a contract to align the agent's incentives with the principal's own.

Much of the economic literature now recognises that a central problem requiring governance arises from transaction-specific investment (Hart 1995; Klein *et al.* 1978; Williamson 1985). That is, problems arise from investments which generate returns that are contingent on the use of the investment in a specific exchange context. These investments are usually used in conjunction with other physical or human assets. The capacity of a party to walk away from the exchange would dissipate the returns (*quasi-*

rents) associated with the transaction-specific investment. That enables that party to demand the redistribution of the gains from trade. The governance problem therefore involves determining how to protect transaction-specific investments from opportunism ex post, so that parties have incentives to make them ex ante. Williamson (1985, 1996) has argued that the use of a 'hierarchical' governance process may be useful in responding to this problem, by giving flexibility in response that is not possible in autonomous spot-exchange market contracting. Hart (1995) has argued in favour of the discriminating allocation of property rights over the assets with which transaction-specific investments are 'matched'. This problem applies with particular force to managers themselves, because a firm's competitive advantage will often depend on investments by managers of their human capital, matched to its assets, rather than investments of generic appeal (Rajan and Zingales 2000). However, the risk of an agent being terminated will deter these investments. The nature and incidence of termination depends on the type of organisation. Shareholders have little or no power to terminate managers in a publicly traded BC; that power resides in the board of directors, which is often thought to be closely aligned to top management. However, a takeover represents a very important means by which an entire management team can be changed. The basic allocation of entitlements and property rights by corporate law, and the powers and responsibilities defined by the corporate governance system, represent a means of responding to the hold up problems that effect BCs (Armour and Whincop 2003).

We may now examine the translation of these problems and their solutions from the BC to the GC. As we know, compensating the BC manager by giving him a source of income tied to the value of the firm encourages the manager to maximise his welfare by equating the marginal cost of his effort with the marginal impact on that proportion of the value of the firm that he or she internalises. Increasing the proportion of the manager's remuneration that is tied to firm value ought to be efficient.[1] We also know that CEOs internalise only small percentages of changes in the value of the firm in large, listed BCs (Jensen and Murphy 1990; Perry and Zenner 2000), but that in entrepreneurial firms financed by venture capitalists capable of more active involvement in corporate governance, those percentages are much higher (Baker and Gompers 1999).

As King (2003) shows, there are unavoidable problems in the adaptation of the contractual bonding devices used in BCs. The problem that is experienced is twofold. First, it is not entirely clear that one actually *wants* the CEO of such an organisation to maximise the value of the firm, in light of social justice and equity objectives, and the possible concern associated with maximising monopoly rents. Unless there are other

66 *Corporate Governance in Government Corporations*

regulatory devices that sufficiently address these matters, an unfettered maximisation objective may not be desirable.

Second, even if the ultimate 'principals' of the GC managers, the citizens, wanted the managers to maximise value, it is less than clear that those members of the executive government who represent citizens are willing to enforce that incentive. One particular problem in this regard occurs where there is a divided accountability to more than one member of the executive government. The GCs in the Queensland sample, for example, are in this situation, because they have two shareholders with governance power. Where these governance agents have different objectives, the capacity for either one of them to enforce their objectives is substantially weakened, reflecting the interplay between these parties (Dixit 1996, 2000).

Third, it is not easy, if it is possible at all, to write a contract creating an incentive to maximise the value of the GC even assuming the appropriateness of that as an objective. Most GCs lacks a verifiable market value, unlike a listed BC. As such, no contract can predicate on that value. The GC can, at best, use some form of proxy measure of firm value, such as reported net assets. As King (2003) demonstrates, a contract encouraging the GC manager to maximise that measure may be dysfunctional. The manager has incentives to undertake activities that increase the measure of value that do not increase true value. These may crowd out activities that increase true value, or these activities may in some situations actually decrease value in the long term. An example may be cribbing on research expenditure in order to increase current profits.

These problems with contracts affect the alternative forms of dysfunctional management in different ways. Behaviour such as expropriation of assets or diversion of corporate opportunities doesn't change between the BC and the GC. Both are unequivocally contrary to the standards that should be expected of managers. It is not hard to prohibit them contractually or by way of fiduciary duties. By contrast, the problem of encouraging directors to exert appropriate effort and to make appropriate investments is much harder. It is caught most directly by this contracting problem.

Some of the other characteristic problems in BCs translate ambiguously into GCs. One important example is the dividend retention problem. In BCs, one of the key agency problems lies in the incentive of managers to retain cash in the firm, rather than paying it out as dividends. Retaining it enables managers to finance pet projects, irrespective of their profitability, and to develop a cushion of slack should there be a change in market conditions (Jensen 1986). In the BC, the case for paying the amount out is patent where the rate of return from reinvestment within the firm is lower than the shareholders' market return. In GCs, however, dividends are not

The Management of the Government Corporation 67

paid to citizens — they are usually paid back into consolidated revenue. It is much less clear how to compare the marginal return on the best reinvestment project foregone within the firm, and on the use of the dividend within government (lowering other taxes would be ideal, porkbarrelling would be the opposite). That comparison may be impossible if the government uses the dividend to achieve social justice outcomes.

Finally, to what extent is hold-up behaviour, connected with investments in match, a problem in the GC? The problem changes somewhat in its relevance. It seems likely that, as in a BC, citizens and properly motivated governance agents would like GC managers to invest their human capital in match with the productive assets of the GC in order to create new sources of value that are not easily replicated in the market. What are the incentives of a GC manager to do that?

Compared to a BC, there is one advantage. The incidence of quasi-rent-seeking by hold-up behaviour is likely to be less severe, because those members of the executive government with governance power in the GC, usually will not internalise the result of any renegotiations. For example, a ministerial shareholder will have no incentive to renegotiate a contract with a GC manager who has invested his human capital in match with the GC assets, since he will not benefit personally by attempting to hold up the manager.

On the other hand, other factors more specific to the governmental context of the GC may cut strongly in the opposite direction. The key consideration relates to the tenure of the GC manager. One marked difference between the US and the UK government bureaucracies is that the tenure of senior public servants in the former is tied to the term of government of the party in power (Davies 1998). By contrast, the public service is markedly more independent in the UK. The Australian public service is moving from a UK model of independence, to a US model. As we shall see later in this chapter, turnover in directors in GCs in the Queensland sample is high. These environments change the incentives to invest in match.[2]

The UK model arguably provides an environment in which hold-up is relatively unlikely, although of course it may not provide adequate incentives for the manager to invest unless the remuneration package allows the manager to capture at least some of the quasi-rents associated with it.

The US model is very different, because the expected tenure of the manager is much shorter. This makes investments in match with the assets of the GC rather less likely. The manager will prefer to substitute generalised human capital skills for firm-specific ones, and we should consequently expect a relatively greater mobility of managers between sectors of the government. This situation can be contrasted with the effect

68   *Corporate Governance in Government Corporations*

of takeovers on investments in human capital in BCs. As with parties going in and out of office, the threat of a loss of tenure can discourage investments with low opportunity costs. However, the incidence of takeover will often be endogenous to the making of these investments. A CEO who can make profitable firm-specific investments that increase the value of the firm diminishes the likelihood of a hostile takeover designed to displace him. Also, a hostile takeover that is successful may often depend on the ability of the successful bidder to create value through firm-specific investment. By contrast, because elections are rarely influenced by GC performance, a GC manager may *lose* office in circumstances where he has *made* successful investments in match — or may *keep* office despite having *failed* to do so. The cyclicality of politics, and the fact that it is not necessary for the party winning an election to 'pay' for the right to govern a GC, or all GCs, reinforce these outcomes.

That is not to say that the GC manager in a party-oriented system will have *no* incentive to invest in match. However, the match assets are likely to be those of a particular political party, rather than the productive assets of a government firm. In other words, a manager will attempt to cultivate his skills in dealing with the formal organisation of a particular party, the interest groups associated with it, and so on. There may be corresponding investments by the political party in the manager's human capital, designed to enable the manager to be considered favourably for particular government jobs as they arise.

Governance Problems and the Board of Directors

So far, we have examined what might be described as generalised governance processes (mostly contracts) that are capable of being instituted ex ante. Governance processes also include hierarchical processes which are capable of ongoing operation and ex post adaptation. In BCs, the board of directors is of pivotal importance, because of its capacity to monitor, hire, and fire senior managers, and to ratify their most important decisions. Much analysis has focused on whether the directors appointed to the BC are likely to act in the interests of their appointors, the shareholders, in holding managers to account for their performance (for a novel examination of this question with references to the earlier literature, see Blair and Stout [1999]).

In recent times, there have been moves by shareholder constituencies, especially institutional investors, to ensure that those appointed to the board are independent non-executives (and therefore less amenable to the CEO).[3] Closely related are the moves to allow independent non-executives to dominate decision-making in areas that are fraught with intense conflicts of interest. The key examples here are the use of a non-executive chairman, rather than permitting the CEO to hold that position, and the devolution of key responsibilities to committees staffed by independent non-executives. These include the audit and executive compensation committees; the former is crucial to reporting on the discharge of management's stewardship, and the latter is crucial to ensuring that executives do not write their own pay cheques.

In general, the weight of opinion in English-speaking countries has been that the board of directors should be a one-constituency organ — that is, it should act in the shareholders' interests, and only in the shareholders' interests. The logic for this identity has been much defended by economists. Shareholders must invest for the life of the firm, and are least well-placed to write a contract enabling them to define events enabling them to withdraw their capital, as lenders may demand the repayment of their debts on default or employees may resign (see, *e.g.*, Williamson 1984; Macey 1991). The other reason for focusing the board exclusively on shareholders' interests is that unlike other constituencies, selecting their interests as the ones to be maximised by the directors allows for a clear and unconflicting imperative to be given to managers and directors — maximise the value of the corporation. Compared to other constituencies, shareholders are likely to agree unanimously to that goal (De Angelo 1981). Other constituencies will favour other goals, likely to conflict with maximisation, creating a greater zone of discretion for management.

Instances of participation by non-shareholder constituencies, such as employees and affected local communities, are rare and company-specific, in the BCs of the English-speaking economies of the world, unlike the situation in Japan or Germany where the norm of shareholder primacy has been historically less significant.

GCs are also established with a board of directors, typically appointed by the executive government. The question that arises is how its duties, constitution and accountabilities should be conceived. Obviously, unlike the BC stereotype of days gone by, the board is most unlikely to be a self-perpetuating constituency, since management will have little or no power over appointment apparatus compared to the government shareholder. On the contrary, the board is likely to resemble a revolving door, with boards going in and out of power as parties go in and out of government. We should expect potentially high turnover in the board, just as we saw above in relation to management.

The more complex question relates to the criteria for choosing board members. The complexities of the GC pulls these criteria in two opposite directions. On the one hand, a GC is an organisational arrangement that is designed to improve efficiency in delivery of particular forms of

70 *Corporate Governance in Government Corporations*

government services. As we saw in Chapter 2, that purpose has explicit imprimatur in the Anglo-Australian corporatisation legislation. As such, one might expect that appointments to the GC board would be similar persons to those appointed to BC boards. One would therefore expect to see most of those sitting on GC boards to have corporate governance experience. On the other hand, the ultimate residual claimants of the GC are the citizens, so that the appointor might attempt, at least in part, to try to make the board representative of a wide range of constituencies and interest groups. There would, accordingly, be employees, consumer representatives, and other community appointments. Public interest objectives also have a place in the corporatisation legislation. This distinction tracks Kelly-Escobar's (1982) typology of managers in state-owned enterprises, which distinguishes 'engineers' from 'commissars'.

> [T]he engineer is assumed to choose strategies prompted by the same motivations as his colleague in private business, although he does confront a different political environment, which he may have to manipulate for his own good or that of the firm ... The commissar's principal interest lays outside the firm. ... For the commissar, days spent in a state-owned company make up a season in a political career (1982, pp. 105–108; emphasis in original removed).

It is difficult to resolve the impasse between these efficiency and communitarian perspectives, in part because they both represent a part of the objective function that citizens would like to see maximised, but the way in which they combine with each other, if at all, is unclear (see generally Chang 1997). Different citizens will want different things. For example, in respect of a utility corporation supplying electricity to a rural region, the citizens of that region may want low tariffs, and that goal may be appropriate for equity and social justice reasons. By contrast, the other citizens of the state outside that region may want those tariffs to be set equal to marginal cost for efficiency reasons. Such conflicts demonstrate the difficulty of knowing whether or not to prefer an efficiency or communitarian perspective on board membership.

It may also be the case that effective GCs do in fact need both types of appointments if the GC is to survive (Stevens 1993). The greater the political sensitivity of a GC, the less practical it is to think the board can limit itself to an exclusively commercial orientation.[4] Some ability as a 'commissar' may be necessary in responding to complex environment, and in providing scope for management to function effectively.

Tied to the question of what sorts of people should sit on the board is a more complex question of the constitution of a director's term. More representative or communitarian perspectives on the board may incline one to the belief that terms should be shorter in order to decrease the 'distance'

The Management of the Government Corporation

between community and representatives. By contrast, an efficiency perspective may suggest a greater domain of autonomy may be required for better management. This question is linked to the degree of independence that a board (and management) should possess vis-à-vis the government. For example, how long should a director be appointed for? Should a director's position be terminable at will, or should it only be terminable for cause? In the BC, the notion that directors should have independence from shareholders is heretical — such an insulation from the shareholders would violate accountability, and increase agency costs. However, the GC is different because of the agency costs of governance, arising from self-serving behaviour by the executive government. Thus, there may be a certain appeal in some of the practices that protect the tenure of directors that might be considered as featherbedding in BCs. This issue is closely related to the membership of the board. It is arguable that professional directors would be expected to act more independently than representative directors. That is because the former are less vulnerable to a threat of termination by the government. The effectiveness of the threat is weakest where the opportunity cost of the director's time spent on the board is relatively low. Highly 'professional' directors, for example, will not find this a threat, since they are likely to find replacement directorships easy to procure, and they may find a reputation for standing up to the shareholder as something of value to them. Less highly valued directors and persons appointed to the board from outside traditional directorial ranks seem more likely to take the intimation as a threat, because there are far fewer positions for such persons as directors of private firms. Although some of these persons will place a high value on their reputations for serving their constituencies, in many cases the constituency's interests and those of the party holding government would be expected to be consonant in order for that group to be favoured by winning a position on the board.

Governance Problems and Legal Rules

The notion that legal rules may assist in corporate governance is a relatively old insight that English judges of the nineteenth century seemed to understand quite well (Whincop 2001). Law and economics scholarship harnessed the idea in the theorisation of BCs as complex contracts, and asserted that legal rules allowed the parties to save on the transaction costs that would be generated in drafting many commonly used terms (Easterbrook and Fischel 1991). They took that idea further by asserting the desirability that these legal rules be contractible — that they yield to the parties' decision to exclude or modify their operation contractually. That enabled parties to substitute terms they valued more, where the transaction

72   *Corporate Governance in Government Corporations*

costs of writing such a contract were justified by the advantages of the term.

Of great importance amongst the range of legal rules relevant to corporate governance are the fiduciary duties imposed on top managers and directors. These impose prohibitions on any dealings or transactions that would create interests or obligations that conflict with the duty of the officer to act in the best interests of the corporation. Such a transaction can be addressed in two ways. One, conforming with the economic scholarship on contractibility, recognises that the fiduciary duty can be modified contractually to allow transactions to proceed if there is adequate disclosure of the details to the board of directors. The constitutional documents of an overwhelming majority of corporations allow transactions to proceed in these circumstances (Whincop 2002b). The other is for the shareholders to give majority consent to the specifics of a transaction that conflicts with the fiduciary duty (Whincop 1999). Both methods make good economic sense in the BC, since they allow a more tractable version of prudential obligations to apply, while requiring more aberrant transactions to respond to a more demanding procedure.

How does the fiduciary duty operate when it is exported to the GC? Certainly, some forms of transactions don't change in their undesirability, such as misappropriation of assets. However, other transactions can become more complicated. This is particularly true in situations where the board is constituted by representative directors, since conflicts of interest are intended to pervade the decision-making of the board. For example, employee representatives may be required to vote on collective bargains or responses to industrial action. Community representatives may be required to vote on service levels for particular regions.

Similarly, there is a fundamental question regarding the construction of the best interests of the 'corporation' in which fiduciaries are thought to be obliged to act. There is no clear answer to this question. In BCs, it is customary to treat the corporation as being substantially identical to its shareholders. However, in the GC, this identity fragments. If the corporation is conceived to be its shareholders, the duty becomes a duty to the executive government, or one of its members. That compounds the agency costs of governance since it is that person's interests who become paramount, and that person who has the final say in any situation raising a conflict of interest. If the corporation is conceived to be the citizens as a whole, the above described problem of incommensurable and conflicting interests makes the application of the standard extremely difficult. If the corporation is conceived of as its population of affected stakeholders, the notion of a conflict of interest becomes almost otiose, since most interests become internal to the corporation's interests. Finally, if the interests of the

The Management of the Government Corporation 73

corporation are defined to remain substantially the same as maximising value, as in a BC, the perplexing question that then arises is how to identify any constituency in whose interests the furtherance of this objective necessarily lies.

The consequences that flow from a breach of fiduciary duty are also particularly uncomfortable in GCs, when one looks at conflicts of interest that are not of the strict pecuniary kind but are more political in nature. The usual remedy associated with breach of fiduciary duty is to rescind a transaction and restore the status quo ante. However, for courts to do that would often require them to be actively involved in the management of the GC. Consider two examples. First, how could a court require a pricing policy, for example, to be rescinded without determining prices for the future? Second, a court faces even more intense problems, should it be obliged to rescind something like capital works, after costs are sunk. The conventional permission that shareholders should be entitled to ratify a conflict of interest is less desirable in the GC because it concentrates power in the hands of the executive government. The government is then able to be the final arbiter of how particular political tradeoffs are to be resolved, and limiting the independence of the board to make commercial decisions.

The foregoing concentrates on the characteristic Anglo-Commonwealth conception of the fiduciary duty. The somewhat more flexible US approach emphasises the judicial review of the 'entire fairness' of an interested transaction. Although avoiding the undesirable politicisation of giving a Minister the right to proceed, or the impossibility of giving the choice to citizens, it nonetheless focuses the court itself on these highly difficulty questions. In a majority of situations, where the interest is indirect or not held by a majority of directors, American courts would fall back on the low-order scrutiny of the business judgment rule and focus instead on the clearer terrain of public law remedies (see, *e.g.*, Stearns 2003).

Corporate Governance and Executives: Empirical Evidence

In this section, I review evidence which illuminates aspects of the governance of management in GCs; in the next section we turn to corporate governance at the level of the board of directors. Most of the evidence, although not all of it, is taken from the sample, described in Chapter 1.

Level of Executive Compensation

As noted above, the means by which to remunerate GC managers is a complex subject. On the one hand, increasing the amount of incentive

74   *Corporate Governance in Government Corporations*

compensation may motivate managers to achieve greater efficiencies and add more value. On the other hand, greater incentives may be dysfunctional in two senses. In the absence of a strict measure of firm performance, the incentive may encourage the manager to maximise some measure that does not increase welfare at the expense of other activities that do, or to maximise monopoly rents. In addition, increasing the stake wagered on performance as between the senior managers and the executive government can lead to collusion between these two levels of 'agents', at the expense of the ultimate principal, the citizens (Dixit 1996, 2000; Skeel 2003). For example, the CEO has a very strong incentive to encourage the executive government to relax certain constraints on the GC collecting monopoly rents. As Skeel (2003, p. 107) puts it, incentive compensation 'put[s] more money on the table'. The likelihood of this happening is instantiated by the Enron scandal. There, the siren-song of profits from stock options encouraged Enron to use fraudulent means to bid up the energy prices over their competitive value in the new deregulated Californian energy environment (Alonso-Zaldivar *et al.* 2002).

The empirical evidence on management compensation in GCs is limited in its public availability. Korn/Ferry International (2001), in a survey of companies in Australia, report that the mean remuneration of a CEO of a government enterprise is $295,460, and that the value of the 75th percentile is $367,300. The mean is slightly higher than private companies ($270,000), and much lower than either public unlisted ($586,660) or public listed ($656,490) companies. We can also make this comparison in respect of the industries which are closest to those of corporatised enterprises. In the case of the GCs included in the Queensland sample, the industries are principally energy and transportation. The mean salary for utility companies and transportation companies are $722,330 and $270,000 respectively. The comparison seems to be quite favourable compared to transportation companies but much lower when compared to other utilities. These figures, however, do not control for the effects of company size, which influences the magnitude of salary substantially. The more general comparison suggests that compensation in GCs is low. On balance, the evidence does not indicate that problems associated with high executive compensation are of much concern here.

A matter examined in the survey is to what extent GC directors thought the CEO was undercompensated. We asked directors to answer the question, 'In your opinion, was the CEO adequately compensated for the job?' Directors could answer 'over-compensated', 'under-compensated', or 'neither over nor under'. The results are tabulated by portfolio in Table 3.1. They indicate that a majority of responses favour the view that the CEO

The Management of the Government Corporation

was adequately compensated. However, a large minority, a little under 40%, consider remuneration is too low.

Table 3.1 Overcompensation of the CEO (by Portfolio)

	Portfolio A GCs	Portfolio B GCs	Portfolio C GCs	Total
Overcompensated	4	5		9
Neither over not under	33	28	5	66
Undercompensated	17	18	9	44
Total	54	51	14	119

If the responses are coded so that overcompensation equals 1, undercompensation equals -1, and neither over nor under equals 0, an analysis of variance (ANOVA) indicates that the directors of the Portfolio C GCs are more likely to regard the CEO as undercompensated than the directors of the other GOCs, at the $p<0.1$ level ($F=2.753$). What is surprising is that the Portfolio A directors' responses are not significantly different from the Portfolio B directors, despite the major compensation differential, which was referred to above, between transportation and utilities. When the sample is partitioned for the director's experience of corporate governance in a listed public company,[5] the differences in mean are not statistically significant. This suggests that these directors are *not* biased to thinking compensation is inadequate.

Effects of Undercompensation

Some of the consequences of undercompensating managers were examined above. We probed this issue in the survey by asking directors which of eight possible effects they would expect undercompensation to cause. Table 3.2 sets out the different effects, with the responses segmented by portfolio.

Slightly more than a quarter of the sample thought the CEO would be unaffected. This may be consistent with King's conjecture that 'public spiritedness' can influence management behaviour (King 2003). This is the most optimistic assessment. At the opposite extreme, very few directors thought the CEO would shirk on his obligations. This is unsurprising. Shirking is a different concept to failing to add value, and it would be surprising if the work ethics of CEOs were so lax as to permit this (Eisenberg 1989).

76   *Corporate Governance in Government Corporations*

Table 3.2   Effects of Undercompensating the CEO (by Portfolio)

	Portfolio A GCs	Portfolio B GCs	Portfolio C GCs
The CEO will shirk on his obligations	6%	8%	7%
The CEO will be more willing to resign	61%	57%	60%
The CEO will be less inclined to favour risky projects, investments or decisions	26%	18%	0%
The CEO will be less inclined to acquire specialisation or expertise relating to the firm	20%	12%	0%
The CEO will be less inclined to compete in the market	24%	10%	7%
The CEO will be more inclined to favour decisions that improve his political reputation	20%	16%	27%
The CEO will be more inclined to favour decisions that correspond with his private preferences	6%	4%	20%
The CEO will be unaffected by under-compensation	26%	27%	20%

By contrast to shirking, directors thought undercompensation made CEOs more willing to resign. Just under 60% of directors thought this was the case. This suggests that the opportunity cost of employment as a CEO in a GC may often be relatively high. However, that scenario would seem to depend on their capacity to compete for jobs in private firms. The responses are not significantly different between portfolios. This may be surprising in light of the market remuneration differential referred to above. It is important to note that directors with corporate governance experience in listed public companies were more likely to think that the director would resign than those lacking that experience.[6] Their greater experience suggests that the probability of resignation may be higher than the statistics reported.

Even if undercompensation does not cause directors to shirk on their obligations, it may discourage them from taking risks. Risk aversion is a common problem cited in the corporate governance literature, which is attributable to the fact that managers are less capable of reducing the company-specific risk they bear than the shareholders are (Kraakman 1984). A manager, working for one company at a time, is inherently undiversified. Risk aversion takes on particular resonance in GCs, where worthwhile risks may be avoided because of the high level of political costs and similar fallout associated with publicly visible failure. Nineteen per cent of the sample thought the CEO was 'less inclined to favour risky projects, investments or decisions'. There is also a marked portfolio effect — not a single respondent in Portfolio C thought it was true, whereas 26% of the respondents from Portfolio A thought so. The chi-square statistic indicates that this difference is statistically significant.[7] Closely related to risk aversion is the effect of undercompensation on competitive incentives. The lower compensation is and the less sensitive it is to performance, the less incentive a director has to disturb the market equilibrium and provoke more aggressive competitive behaviour (Baird et al. 1994, pp. 165–178). Nineteen respondents thought this was an effect of undercompensation, mostly from Portfolios A and B. The portfolio differences may reflect differences in the competition in the different industries. Another way of interpreting these results is that 'undercompensation' may be used to decrease the likelihood that CEOs will use the market power associated with a monopoly to harm private competitors (King 2003; Skeel 2003).

Above, we considered the incentive of the manager of a GC to invest human capital in match with the other assets of the GC. Various factors will affect the incentives of CEOs to make firm-specific investments of their human capital. Compensation may be one of them. The lower the level of compensation, the less justification the CEO has to sink investments in the firm. She is being paid a market wage, rather than one reflecting the higher returns to the GC from a firm-specific investment. Thus, she has no incentive to invest her human capital in skills and expertise not highly valued by other firms. There is a marked portfolio effect. Fourteen per cent of respondents agreed with this as an effect; the responses in Portfolios A, B, and C were 20%, 12%, and 0%. The likelihood ratio indicates the difference is statistically significant between portfolios at $p<0.05$. One marked difference in the response to these questions came from current and former directors. Fifteen of the 66 former directors thought the CEO would underinvest in firm-specific capital, compared to two of the current 54 directors. The chi-square statistic is statistically significant at $p<0.005$. It should be pointed out that other factors may also influence the decision of managers to invest in match, and this association may simply reflect the likely coincidence of undercompensation with these other factors.

The final two matters we asked directors to consider was the extent to which undercompensated CEOs would be more inclined to favour decisions that improve their political reputation, or to favour decisions that correspond with his private preferences. Twenty-three respondents thought that CEOs were more likely to favour decisions that improve their political reputation. A quarter of the 66 former directors thought so, although only slightly more than a tenth of the 54 current directors did. This difference is statistically significant at $p<0.05$. This is consistent with the earlier analysis that although GC managers may be unwilling to invest in match with firm

78   *Corporate Governance in Government Corporations*

assets, they may well invest in match with a political party. Only eight directors thought directors would make decisions to maximise their private preferences.

To conclude, there is some evidence that managers are undercompensated in GCs. The effects of that are unclear, but there is some perceptual evidence that it leads to increased risk aversion, increased sensitivity to political considerations, decreased competition, and decreased investment in match. Against that must be set the problems associated with stronger incentives, including the risk of manipulating activities that increase compensation but not the value of the firm, and of socially costly behaviour such as maximising monopoly rents. In the next section, we examine the related issues associated with the board of directors.

Corporate Governance and the Board of Directors: Empirical Evidence

Aspects of Appointment

Empirical analysis of the relation between the constitution of a board of directors and the corporation's performance does not reveal any clear value added by appointing non-executive directors to the board (Romano 1996). Even if we accept this evidence, that is not to say that the matter is an issue of minor inportance for GCs.

First, BCs listed on the stock exchange have continuing incentives to create strong, effective boards. This begins at the time they go public, when the offeror will try to attract a reputable, effective board in order to maximise the value of the offering. Thus the absence of clear evidence on boards may reflect the fact that all listed BCs are subject to similar incentives (Romano 1996). By comparison, the GC is not subject to similar market forces, since it has no traded stock.

Second, governments have political incentives to make board appointments with a view to constituting a tractable board (not unlike CEOs, but with even fewer market disciplines). The more tractable a board, the more easily it can be influenced in ways that maximise political support. By contrast, maximising the value of a GC may require a board willing to oppose some of the shareholders' wishes.

Third, the connection of GCs to the public sector and their continuing interface with government departments may leave an organisational culture wanting in private sector business and governance practices. An appropriately constituted board can redress this deficiency by importing superior norms into the organisation.

The Management of the Government Corporation 79

It follows that the processes for appointing directors, their qualifications and experience, the means by which they are acquainted with their responsibilities, and so on, are all of critical importance to GC boards. Before analysing the evidence on these propositions, it is important to note, for this and subsequent sections, that the applicable corporatisation legislation in Queensland provides that a GC's board is responsible for commercial policy and management, to achieve its formal performance and operating targets established in its statement of corporate intent, and ensuring that the GC performs its functions in a proper, effective and efficient way.[8] So the legislation is consistent with the proposition that the board should further similar objectives to those of a board of a normal, commercially-motivated BC.

In the survey, we asked various questions regarding the experience and backgrounds of GC directors. Of the 118 respondents answering the relevant question, 35% indicated they had professional qualifications (for example, legal qualifications). Arguably of more importance than professional qualifications are the directors' experiences in corporate governance. Corporate governance experience, however, may be immensely varied — it could range from being a non-executive director of a family company, to a chairman of a listed company. We therefore sought evidence on a wide range of experience types and company types. We asked directors to indicate whether they had experience as: (a) a chief executive; (b) a senior manager; (c) a board chairman; (d) a non-executive director; and (e) a substantial shareholder holding more than 20% of the voting equity. These questions were asked with respect to seven different types of company: (a) a family company; (b) other private or proprietary company; (c) a start-up venture or entrepreneurial company; (d) a listed public company; (e) other Queensland GCs; and (f) or other GCs (*e.g.*, a GC in another state). Where possible, we verified, from public records, involvement as a chief executive, board chairman or non-executive director in listed companies and GCs. Table 3.3 records the results.

Table 3.3 Experience in Corporate Governance

	Chief Executive	Senior Manager	Chairman	Non-executive	Share-holder	No involvement
Family	22%	6%	13%	7%	12%	40%
Other private	17%	8%	13%	19%	6%	36%
Entrepreneurial	5%	2%	3%	7%	3%	81%
Listed	6%	7%	4%	9%	—	74%
Qld GC	1%	1%	7%	17%	—	74%
Other GC	3%	1%	3%	11%	—	83%
Charitable	4%	2%	12%	13%	—	70%

Ten directors have no experience in *any* of these companies; four in Portfolio A, and five in Portfolio B. What is notable is that only 26% of directors have experience in the corporate governance of listed companies. Thus, there is relatively limited familiarity with corporate governance procedures in those corporations where they are most important. Agency costs, although still significant should be lower in family, private and entrepreneurial companies, than in listed companies, because of the relative concentration of shareholdings. We use listed company corporate governance experience as an explanatory variable at various points in this work. We may note that a *third* of the 29 GCs had no respondents with public company experience amongst either their current *or* former directors.

In order to determine the opinions of GC directors regarding the desirability of increasing the number of directors with experience of corporate governance in listed public companies, we asked directors, 'How should the composition and functioning of the GC board be improved?' We asked them to indicate the extent of their agreement with various statements on a scale of 1–5, where 1 was strong disagreement and 5 was strong agreement. Two statements were, 'There should be more professional directors with experience in listed companies' and 'GC boards need more experienced and professional chairmen'. The mean for these two items was 3.54 and 3.47. The responses were slightly higher in Portfolio C, but the difference is not statistically significant. There is, however, a significant difference in the means for the responses of former and current directors. For the question on directors, the responses were 3.71 (for former directors) and 3.34 (for current directors); for the question on chairmen, the responses were 3.72 and 3.17. The former result is significant at $p<0.1$ and the latter result at $p<0.05$.

In view of the low level of formal corporate governance experience on some boards, other skills and experience may also be considered relevant — which would shed light on the role that executive governments want boards to serve. Directors were asked, in respect of each of a series of skills

The Management of the Government Corporation

and experience, to select a response on a scale of one to three, where one was highly relevant and three was not relevant. We asked directors the following question, 'What skills and experience do you feel qualified you to act as a GC director?' Directors were asked to limit their answers to skills and experience at the time of appointment. Table 3.4 sets out the list of skills and experience, and the means for each, segmented by portfolio. It reports whether a one-way Analysis of Variance (ANOVA) indicates a statistically significant difference between the grouped means, and where one exists, the probability level.

The results indicate that managerial skills are highly relevant, and that professional or financial qualifications are also important. Of the least importance were community service, political party membership and political experience. The results also seem to indicate that governance skills are most likely to be relatively generic, since the results for experience in the industry area or with the GC are relatively low.

Table 3.4   Experience and Qualifications (by Portfolio)

	Portfolio A GCs	Portfolio B GCs	Portfolio C GCs	ANOVA
Formal educational qualifications	2.20	1.88	2.57	$p<0.01$
Private sector experience in this GC's industry area	1.56	1.75	2.08	NS
Experience with this GC	1.50	1.59	1.83	NS
Experience with other GCs or public enterprises	2.02	1.83	1.95	NS
Policy experience in this area	1.77	1.65	2.00	NS
Professional or trade qualifications	2.23	2.00	2.36	NS
Managerial skills	2.44	2.40	2.54	NS
Financial or investment experience	1.98	2.00	2.36	NS
Industrial relations experience	1.77	1.75	1.42	NS
Ability to represent a specific constituency	1.55	1.77	1.00	$p<0.05$
Community or social service	1.90	1.89	1.25	$p<0.05$
Political party membership	1.22	1.16	1.00	NS
Political experience	1.17	1.26	1.17	NS

Note: 'NS' indicates the ANOVA does not reveal a significant difference between means.

The comparisons between the portfolios suggest further propositions. The most significant differences are between the miscellaneous corporations, many of which operate financial businesses, and the other two portfolios. The miscellaneous companies in Portfolio C rated formal educational qualifications, private sector experience, trade qualifications,

82   *Corporate Governance in Government Corporations*

and financial experience higher, and industrial relations, community service and constituency representation lower than the other two portfolios. This is consistent with their characteristics as corporations with important financial responsibilities, a workforce professionalised to a higher degree, and less in the way of political interest group effects compared to the other portfolios.

In the question, referred to above, where we asked directors how the composition and functioning of the board could be improved, we also asked, besides the propositions regarding more professional chairmen and directors, a number of other propositions regarding the board. Table 3.5 sets out these propositions, and the means for the three portfolios:

None of these propositions was supported in a single portfolio (3 being the undecided mean). When the means are compared for current and former directors, former directors tended to agree more than current directors with the proposition that there should be more customer and community appointments. The means are 3.11 and 2.29, significant at $p<0.001$. Directors who had corporate governance experience in public companies differed from other directors in agreeing somewhat more with the proposition that boards need to be smaller (2.81 versus 2.31, significant at $p<0.05$). There are some predictable correlations between the scores on these propositions (results not reported). Those favouring more community appointments favour more labour representatives, and those favouring professional directors favour fewer of both. On the other hand, those preferring more communitarian boards comprised of a wider range of stakeholders coincidentally support the appointment of more executives. This may reflect a stronger advocacy of non-executive directors by professional directors. The other surprising result is that those supporting professional chairmen support smaller boards.[9]

Table 3.5 Agreement with Propositions to Improve Board Composition and Functioning (by Portfolio)

	Portfolio A GCs	Portfolio B GCs	Portfolio C GCs	ANOVA
There should be more appointments to the board from the community and customers	2.83	2.90	1.93	$p<0.01$
There should be more representatives of labour on the board	2.34	2.22	1.80	NS
There should be more executive appointments to the board (*i.e.* more managers appointed)	2.17	2.26	1.80	NS
Boards need to be smaller than currently	2.28	2.69	2.20	$p<0.05$

Supply Side Influences on Directorship

The decision by a person to accept appointment as a director depends on a number of factors. These include, first, the marginal benefit from accepting appointment, measured by directors' fees. There may be other indirect benefits as well, such as an anticipation of future business, based on improved contacts or superior information about the firm or the industry. Second, there is the opportunity cost of accepting appointment, which may include foregone remuneration from appointments in other companies, both BCs and GCs. Third, there may be other, indirect costs to the director. These include the risk of reputational damage should some crisis befall the corporation, the expected value of personal legal liability, the utility gained (or disutility borne) from working with the other directors and the management of the GC and working with the Minister, the utility gained (or disutility borne) from any political intervention by the government, and so on. We address these issues in this section, other than those concerning the impact on the Minister's governance, which is a focus in Chapter 4.

To probe these issues, we surveyed the nature of expectations and beliefs about directors. When appointed, directors will have expectations about what will happen while they are directors. These are likely to be the basis of their estimate of the costs associated with directorship, and will therefore influence the persons who become and who do not become directors. The evidence below is biased as there is no 'control' sample of persons who choose not to become GC directors, a population of imprecise extent.

84   *Corporate Governance in Government Corporations*

Remuneration   GCs will find it hard to attract the most experienced directors, to the extent that they cannot or will not pay comparable fees to those received by directors in other companies. We examined this issue in two ways. First, we asked directors to indicate the extent to which they were influenced by specified factors. One of these was remuneration. The general instruction for this question was, 'Which factors encouraged or discouraged you from becoming a GC director? Please limit your answer to factors influencing you at the time of appointment.' Directors were asked to select a response from 1–5, where 5 was strong encouragement, 1 was strong discouragement and 3 was no influence. For remuneration, the specific statement was 'The amount of remuneration, relative to the time commitment I needed to make to do the job.' Second, we asked directors to respond to the following statement: 'I thought the remuneration paid to GCs directors was: (a) generous; (b) about right; (c) inadequate.' We asked the two questions, because the two may in combination give some indication of the elasticity of supply of GC directorship. In other words, directors may vary in the extent to which they are influenced by perceived inadequacies in remuneration.

In relation to the issue of encouragement, one director was strongly encouraged, six were slightly encouraged, 79 were neither encouraged nor discouraged, 21 were slightly discouraged, and 9 were strongly discouraged. If each response is coded by the number circled, the mean is 2.61, which is significantly different from the mean of 3 (representing no influence), based on a one-sample t-test (t=7.515, df=115, p<0.001). In relation to the generosity (or otherwise) of GC remuneration, the figures are quite stark: four directors thought remuneration generous, 37 thought them about right, and 75 thought them inadequate. Clearly, there is a strong perception that directors' remuneration is too low. Taking these results together, it appears to be the case that the supply of GC directors' services is somewhat inelastic, since although a majority thought remuneration inadequate, only a minority are discouraged by it. This could suggest that there are other sources of benefits from being on the board; alternatively, it could reflect a sampling bias that the persons most discouraged by the level of remuneration did not accept appointment.

These results are influenced by whether or not the director has had experience in a listed public company. Directors are more likely to regard remuneration as inadequate where they have listed company experience. Table 3.6 sets out the cross-tabulation of listed company experience and the influence of remuneration levels. A t-test calculating means on a scale of 1–5 (for encouragement) and a scale of 1–3 (for adequacy) rejects the hypothesis of equality of means at p<0.05.

Table 3.6 Cross-tabulation of Remuneration Perceptions and Listed Company Experience

	Listed company experience	No listed company experience	Total
Panel I: *Effect of Remuneration Level*			
Strongly encouraged	1	—	1
Slightly encouraged	2	4	6
No influence	14	65	79
Slightly discouraged	7	14	21
Strongly discouraged	6	3	9
Panel II: *Adequacy of Remuneration*			
Generous	—	4	4
About right	5	32	37
Inadequate	25	50	75
Total	30	86	116

Directors' liability Another source of disincentives to directors is the possibility of legal liabilities to the company or to stakeholders interested in it. This has become increasingly contentious since the early 1990s, when both legislatures and courts imposed more onerous standards on directors (Whincop 1996). It is common to cite increased liability as deterring a decision to accept appointment as a director. That officially justified the introduction in Australia in 2000 of a statutory business judgment rule in the *Corporations Law*.[10] The question of directors' duties, from a prescriptive perspective of what those duties should be and how they operate, is considered in the next section of this chapter. This section considers the impact of perceived liability on accepting appointment. Again, we approached this question from an angle permitting examination of both the relative magnitude of the problem and its effect on accepting directorship. The relative magnitude question asked directors to respond to the following statement: 'I thought the potential legal liabilities I could incur as a GC director were: (a) substantial; (b) trivial; (c) I never considered them.' The question gauging their influence on accepting appointment was 'Expectations as to the legal liabilities I might incur in serving as a GC director', with the same 1–5 response scale.

In relation to the effect of the relative magnitude of legal liability, 99 directors thought liabilities were substantial, nine thought them trivial, and eleven did not consider them. The fact that five-sixths of the sample thought them substantial should be a matter of concern, since there is a widely held perception amongst respondents that directors' fees are also too low. An obvious question is what other benefits of board membership a director envisages to compensate him for both inadequate remuneration and substantial liabilities. These results are borne out when we examine the

86 *Corporate Governance in Government Corporations*

issue of encouragement. We find that two directors were slightly encouraged, 54 were not influenced, 51 were slightly discouraged, and 6 were strongly discouraged. If each response is coded on a 1–5 basis in which 5 is strong discouragement, the mean is 2.46, which is statistically significantly different from the mean of 3 (representing no influence), based on a one-sample t-test ($p<0.001$). Thus, the interaction of lower fees and substantial liabilities will inevitably deter directors at the margin from accepting GC appointments. We can see this by examining Table 3.7, which cross-tabulates the perceptions of the relative magnitude of remuneration and of legal liabilities.[11]

Table 3.7   Cross-tabulation of Perception of Adequacy of Remuneration and Effects of Legal Liability

	Remuneration:			
	Generous	About right	Inadequate	Total
Substantial liabilities	3	31	63	97
Trivial liabilities		1	7	8
Liabilities unconsidered	1	4	5	10
Total	4	36	75	115

Thus, over half of the sample fall into the cell of Table 3.7 that has been shaded in grey, where they appeared to have a double disincentive of accepting appointment, since they regard remuneration as being inadequate and liabilities as substantial. The overall population of potential directors from the respondents self-select by becoming directors would be expected to share this double disincentive, since compensation or liabilities is a likely reason not to accept the offer of a position.

Perceived Quality of Directors and Management A possible concern with the interaction of high liability and low remuneration is that directors will be discouraged from accepting appointment, and in continuing to remain a director. If that is so, other appointees may be discouraged from accepting appointment based on an expectation that the best directors will be unrepresented. This may be a discouragement because of the utility foregone when one is unable to work with the best directors and the disutility and higher risks of working with less competent colleagues. We therefore examined this issue by analysing perceived quality and effect on appointment.

Directors were asked, 'I thought the other members of the GC board were, on the whole: (a) competent and professional; (b) incompetent and

The Management of the Government Corporation

unprofessional; (c) I didn't know.' They were also asked in the question examining the effect that different factors had on their decision to accept appointment, to analyse the proposition, 'Expectations as to the competence, professionalism or ethics of other directors', on the same 1–5 scale. In general, directors had a high perception of each other. As regards the first question, 97 respondents thought the other directors competent and professional, one respondent thought the other directors incompetent and unprofessional, and 22 did not know. As regards the second question, one respondent was strongly discouraged, three were slightly discouraged, 36 were slightly encouraged, 29 were strongly encouraged, and 43 said they were not influenced. The mean response is 3.79, which is significantly higher than the mean of 3 ($p<0.001$). Portfolio C had the highest incidence of encouragement; thirteen out of fifteen directors were encouraged slightly or strongly, and the other two were not influenced. This proportion, 87%, was much higher than that Portfolio A (49%) or B (58%).

A related question, which might be thought to be linked indirectly to the magnitude of directors' liability, is the perception of management quality.[12] A lack of confidence in management would be a disincentive to act as a director, both because of the association with poor performance and the greater likelihood of directors' liability being imposed. To the question, 'I thought GOC management was, on the whole: (a) competent and professional; (b) incompetent and unprofessional; (c) I didn't know', 96 selected (a), six selected (b), and seventeen selected (c). They were also asked in the section on the effect of factors on appointment to analyse the proposition, 'Expectations as to the competence, professionalism or ethics of GOC management' on their decision to accept appointment. The results are similar to the effects regarding other directors. One respondent was strongly discouraged, one was slightly discouraged, 46 were slightly encouraged, 43 were strongly encouraged, and 22 said they were not influenced. The mean response is 3.79, which is statistically significantly higher than the mean of 3 ($p<0.001$). There are no significant differences between portfolios.

These results seem to indicate that the perception of other directors and management is favourable, and has some attractions to other directors, although a self-selecting bias precludes too much being made of this.

Reputational Effects The extent to which directors perceive service on the board of a GC to effect their reputation will influence their decision as to whether or not to serve on the board. To gauge relative magnitude of reputational effects, directors were asked:

I thought that serving on the board of this GC would:

88   *Corporate Governance in Government Corporations*

(a)   Improve my reputation as a potential director on other companies' boards;
(b)   Damage my reputation as a potential director on other companies' boards;
(c)   I didn't expect any effect on my reputation.

Directors were also asked in the section on the effect of factors on appointment to analyse the proposition, 'Expectations as to the effect of GC service on my reputation as a candidate for other boards', on the same 1–5 scale. Both questions sought to confine respondents' answers to reputations relevant to corporate governance, and to exclude other reputational issues such as those involving political persuasion.

The relative magnitude question indicates that no respondents anticipated a damaged reputation, 56 thought their reputations would be improved, and 64 anticipated no effect. The reputational effects on their decision to accept appointment are similar. Three were slightly discouraged, 47 were slightly encouraged, twelve were strongly encouraged, and 52 were not influenced. We also find that those persons who have corporate governance experience in a public company (either as a director, a CEO, or a senior manager) are much less likely to anticipate an improved reputation. This is indicated in Table 3.8.

Table 3.8   Relation between Effect on Reputation and Public Company Experience

	No public company experience	Public company experience	Total
Expect improved reputation	48	8	56
No expected effect	41	23	64
Total	89	31	120

The chi-square statistic is significant at $p<0.01$. This result suggests that the return to reputation at the margin is lower for those with public company experience. There is also a portfolio effect (unreported), albeit only weakly significant at $p<0.1$. namely that the reputational effect is strongest in Portfolio C, and is weakest in Portfolio B. This may reflect the relative levels of professionalisation in the different portfolios.

The Management of the Government Corporation   89

Fiduciary Duties

Both directors and a corporation's most senior managers are subject to fiduciary duties. We observed above that the application of these duties to the governance environment of a GC is fraught with many complexities, attributable to the absence of a clear standard such as value maximisation. This is especially noticeable in the areas of 'political conflicts'. In order to examine this issue, we sought evidence of various kinds. We first examined how GC directors perceived the nature of their fiduciary duty.

We asked directors to select the best response to the following question, the answers to which are summarised in Table 3.9:

I anticipated that my duty as a director would be to:
(a)   Maximise the value of the corporation;
(b)   Act according to the interests and wishes of the Minister;
(c)   Serve the interests of the constituency I was to represent;
(d)   Serve the interests of the people of Queensland as a whole;
(e)   Reconcile the conflicting demands and interests as to how the GOC should be managed.

Table 3.9   Perceptions of Directors' Duties

	%
Maximise the value of the corporation	51.3
Act according to the interests and wishes of the Minister	2.5
Serve the interests of the constituency I was to represent	8.4
Serve the interests of the people of Queensland as a whole	28.6
Reconcile conflicting demands	9.2
Total	100.0

This reinforces the idea that accountability relations in GCs are somewhat imprecise, since there is support for different ways of constructing these relations. It is interesting that support was predominantly expressed for two formulations that are *most* imprecise in the specification of the beneficiaries in whose interest the GC should be run. The 'maximise value' standard is premised on the assumption that maximising value is in the best interests of all constituencies, while the 'people ... as a whole' standard presupposes that there are valid means by which to resolve conflicts between different constituencies.

The problems that such imprecision causes can be seen when we examine how directors thought they ought to respond to a range of hypothetical conflicts of interest, in light of their fiduciary duties. The

90   *Corporate Governance in Government Corporations*

question raised two different types of conflict — the conventional interested contract, and forms of conflicts of interest with more political overtones.

In order to gauge how fiduciary standards might apply to some of these more government-specific transactions, our survey asked directors to specify how examples of these transactions *would* have been handled in their GC, and how they *should* have been handled. For each case, we offered directors four generalised responses as to what the director with the conflict should do:

(a)   The director declares her interest and absents herself from deliberations and the vote;

(b)   The director declares her interest and abstains from voting, but is present for deliberation;

(c)   The director declares her interest but deliberates and votes;

(d)   The director discusses and votes on the issue without reference to any interest.

These were the three hypotheticals:

1.   The GC is deciding whether to provide new services to country regions. The board has an appointee who resides in such an area and often advocates rural interests.

2.   The board is considering how it will approach the next enterprise bargain with labour. The board includes a director who has been appointed to represent the interests of workers in this and allied industries.

3.   A director has a substantial pecuniary interest in a company which has tendered for a contract being considered by the board.

The results are summarised in Table 3.10. What is immediately noticeable about these results is that the respondents believe, on the whole, that the conflicts are handled in the manner as they should be — the would/should differential is minor. But even though respondents appear to think that the conflicts are handled as they should be, in the first two cases there is evidently no consensus as to how the transactions should be handled.

The Management of the Government Corporation

Table 3.10 Means by which a Conflict Would and Should be Handled

Transaction	Declare, absent (%)	Declare, deliberate, abstain (%)	Declare, deliberate (%)	No reference to interest (%)
Services to country (n=116)	28.4%/28.7%	35.3%/40.0%	23.3%/20.9%	12.9%/10.4%
Enterprise bargain (n=110)	30.0%/33.0%	32.7%/36.5%	30.0%/27.0%	7.3%/3.5%
Interested contract (n=117)	95.8%/97.4%	4.2%/2.6%	—/—	—/—

Note: The percentage appearing in each cell before the solidus is the percentage of respondents who thought that the transaction would be handled in this way; the percentage after the solidus is the percentage of respondents who thought that the transaction should be handled in this way.

Although I have not reported it, this variation cannot be attributed to practices varying by company, as there is substantial variation within the responses for individual GCs. There is not a single GC, for which responses were received from two or more directors, in which all respondents were unanimous on a method for handling the first two transactions. Only the third transaction, the paradigm conflict, elicited unanimous responses, indicating that the perceptions of the handling of political conflicts are highly imprecise, and confirms the point that I have made in the theoretical analysis above.

When the 'would' and 'should' results are cross-tabulated, the results are more complicated than Table 3.10 suggests. The proximity of the results for the 'would' and 'should' percentages for each of the options for the first two hypotheticals suggests that most respondents gave the same answer for both questions. That is not, in fact, the case. The divergence is greater for the Enterprise Bargain hypothetical, which is set out in Table 3.11:

92   *Corporate Governance in Government Corporations*

Table 3.11 Crosstabulation of Responses to how the Conflict in the Enterprise Bargain Transaction Would and Should be Handled

	Should be handled:				
Would be handled:	Declare, absent	Declare, deliberate, abstain	Declare, deliberate	No reference to interest	Total
Declare, absent	27	3	3		33
Declare, deliberate, abstain	5	30			35
Declare, deliberate	1	7	25		33
No reference to interest	1	1	1	4	7
Total	34	41	29	4	108

Note: The cell records the count of the number of directors who offered the particular combination of responses paired for each cell. There are 13 missing values.

The shaded cells are those where the transaction would be handled as the respondent thinks it should be. The cells to the south-west of the shaded diagonal (containing fifteen responses) are those where the respondent thinks that the transaction is handled *less* onerously than it should be. The cells to the north-east of the shaded diagonal (containing six responses) are those where the respondent thinks that the transaction is handled *more* onerously than it should be. The equivalent numbers for the country services hypothetical are nine and three. It is a particular concern when the actual handling of a transaction is less onerous than it should be. It reflects perceptions of weak governance or doubtful procedures.

The ambiguity associated with the treatment of these transactions is also reflected when we cross-tabulate separately the 'would' responses for both the Enterprise Bargain and the Country Services hypothetical, and then the 'should' responses. The similar percentage of respondents for each category reported in Table 3.10 implies substantial convergence, but Table 3.12 gives the lie to this perception:

The Management of the Government Corporation

Table 3.12 Crosstabulation of Responses to how the Conflict in the Enterprise Bargain Transaction and the Country Services Transaction Would be Handled

| | *Enterprise Bargain:* | | | | |
Country Services:	Declare, absent	Declare, deliberate, abstain	Declare, deliberate	No reference to interest	Total
Declare, absent	15	9	5	1	30
Declare, deliberate, abstain	10	26	6	1	43
Declare, deliberate	5	4	17		26
No reference to interest	3	2	5	4	14
Total	33	41	33	6	113

Note: The cell records the count of the number of directors who offered the particular combination of responses paired for each cell. There are 13 missing values.

In this table, the shaded cells are those where the respondents thought that both transactions should be handled in the same way. The cells to the south-west of the shaded diagonal (containing twenty-nine responses) are those where the respondent thinks that the conflict in the case of the Enterprise Bargain would be handled more onerously than the conflict in the case of Country Services. The cells to the north-east of the shaded diagonal (containing twenty-two responses) are those where the respondent thinks that the conflict in the Enterprise Bargain would be handled less onerously than the conflict in the Country Services case. There is clearly much disagreement, reflecting the imprecision of the legal principle's application.[13]

How does the handling of the conflict vary between the respondents for their perception of their generic director's duty, as reported in Table 3.9? Surprisingly, it has little or no effect at all. For the country services transaction, it is unsurprising that those who see themselves as implementing the Minister's wishes or serving constituency interests all chose to be absent or to abstain. By contrast, the lowest percentage of respondents who would choose to absent themselves were those regarding their duty as being to maximise value. The effect is not, however, significant, and disappears in the Enterprise Bargain transaction. Directors with experience of corporate governance in listed companies do not respond significantly differently to other directors.

Portfolio has some weak effects on the perception of directors duties. In the country services transaction, 87% of respondents in Portfolio C would have absented themselves or abstained, compared to an average of 60% for

94   *Corporate Governance in Government Corporations*

the other portfolios. The response is much the same for how those respondents thought that transaction should have been handled. Neither effect is, however, significant. These results are stronger in relation to the Enterprise Bargain transaction, as Table 3.13 demonstrates. The result is significant at $p<0.05$. The result for the same test on how the transaction should have been handled is significant at $p<0.01$.

Table 3.13 How the Conflict in the Enterprise Bargain Transaction Would be Handled (by Portfolio)

	Portfolio A GCs	Portfolio B GCs	Portfolio C GCs	Total
Declare, absent	13	14	6	33
Declare, deliberate, abstain	15	14	7	36
Declare, deliberate	21	11	1	33
No reference to interest	1	7	—	8
Total	50	46	14	110

Director Tenure and Termination

The official tenure of directors in GCs and listed BCs is not radically different — both serve for a limited period, usually three years, at which point they must be reelected in order to continue. Both are also in principle subject to more direct displacement. Anglo-Australian law gives shareholders the right to pass a resolution to remove a director at any time. That right is inalienable in a public company, but is contractible in other companies.[14] Similarly, directors of GCs can usually be displaced at the will of the executive government.[15] However, there are very different dynamics in corporate control vis-à-vis political power. Governments go in and out of power cyclically, whereas the boards of BCs have often been regarded as a self-perpetuating constituency, in view of the power the board can exert over the proxy voting process. Therefore, the *de facto* tenure may differ radically between the two, despite the similarities of *de jure* tenure. In order to examine this, we gathered empirical evidence in relation to termination of director appointments. Initially, we examine some quantitative evidence in relation to director tenure. We then review the survey evidence on that subject.

Quantitative Evidence In this section, we use a concept of a 'term' to measure aspects of the appointment and reappointment of a director. Thus, a reappointed director will have more than one term. Table 3.14 describes the number of GCs, the number of director appointments, and the number

The Management of the Government Corporation 95

of terms, divided across total appointments, continuing appointments, completed appointments, and those appointments related to defunct GCs.[16] For the analysis that follows, we work with the data in relation to completed terms in continuing GCs — the continuing appointments are not relevant because they do not raise turnover issues until the end of the term, and defunct GCs are a special case of termination. Our attention is directed to two topics — whether or not the director was reappointed and whether or not a director's term was terminated early. We examine these in simple univariate terms, and then provide econometric evidence.

Table 3.14 Summary Statistics of Director Terms

	GCs	Directors	Terms
Total	29	311	392
Continuing	22	133	133
Completed	29	203	259
Defunct GCs	7	44	44
Completed in continuing GCs	22	159	215

Note: The number of directors serving completed terms is not the difference between Total and Continuing Directors because some Continuing Directors have also Completed Terms.

Evidence on whether directors were reappointed at the end of their terms may point to two different phenomena. It may, on one hand, reflect the preferences of the government — the government may wish to see either more competent or more 'simpatico' appointments. It may also reflect the preferences of the director. His outside opportunities may have changed so that the opportunity cost of his time spent as a director is substantially higher, his information about the benefits to him about being a director may have changed, or the political environment may have changed (either by a change of Minister within the government or a change of the party forming government). To summarise, these differences may either be 'political' (either reflecting the preferences of the government, or the preferences of the director arising from political change), or 'non-political'. Political change should be greatest where there is a change in the party forming government. If political change does have an effect on continuance, we should expect to see lower levels of continuance around the time of a change in party forming government than at other times. Table 3.15 provides summary statistics on how many of the terms were associated with either change in government (but not change in party), or change in party.

96   *Corporate Governance in Government Corporations*

Table 3.15 Completed Director Terms in Continuing GCs Associated with Change of Government and Party

	Change in government	No change in government	Total
Change in party	152	n/a	152
No change in party	42	21	63
Total	194	21	215

Note: The top right cell is not applicable, because there cannot normally be a change in the party forming government without a change in the government.

It follows that we can explore the question of how change in government, and change in party can impact on continuation by directors, and the effect of other potentially relevant variables. To examine portfolio first, Table 3.16 sets out the difference in continuation statistics between portfolios. We can see clear differences between portfolios (significant at $p<0.005$) — reappointment occurs most often in Portfolio C (where reappointments are the rule, not the exception), and least often in Portfolio A (where the reverse is true).

Table 3.16 Directors Reappointed at the End of their Terms (by Portfolio)

	Portfolio A GCs	Portfolio B GCs	Portfolio C GCs	Total
Reappointed	9	55	19	83
Not reappointed	33	87	12	132
Total	42	142	31	215

The reappointment of directors with listed company experience is an important issue to study. On the one hand, these directors, having more extensive corporate governance experience, are arguably the most important to retain. On the other hand, these directors are likely to have the highest opportunity costs of serving on GCs, because they have the most alternatives to choose from. Table 3.17 demonstrates that directors with listed company experience are more likely to be reappointed — just under 60% are reappointed, compared to just over a third of other directors ($p<0.005$).

The Management of the Government Corporation

Table 3.17 Relation of Experience in Listed Companies to Reappointment

	Experience with listed companies	No experience with listed companies	Total
Reappointed	21	62	83
Not reappointed	15	117	132
Total	36	179	215

Table 3.18 Relation of Experience in Listed Companies to Reappointment (by Portfolio)

Portfolio		Experience with listed companies	No experience with listed companies	Total
A	Reappointed	3	6	9
	Not reappointed	6	27	33
B	Reappointed	5	50	55
	Not reappointed	7	80	87
C	Reappointed	13	6	19
	Not reappointed	2	10	12
	Total	36	179	215

It should, however, be pointed out that this result is driven by the Portfolio C GCs, as Table 3.18 demonstrates. When a chi-square statistic is computed for each of the three two-by-two tables, only the chi-square for the miscellaneous GCs is significant ($p<0.005$).

We turn now to political factors. Table 3.19 sets out the relation between reappointment and change in government. It indicates that although about 60% of directors are not reappointed where there is a change in government, change in government does not, itself, have a statistically significant effect on reappointment. However, the story is very different when we study the effect of a change in the party forming government. Table 3.20 sets out this relation. It indicates unequivocally that change of party is associated with a significantly lower level of reappointment ($p<0.001$).

98 *Corporate Governance in Government Corporations*

Table 3.19 Relation of Change of Government to Reappointment

	Change of government	No change of government	Total
Reappointed	77	6	83
Not reappointed	117	15	132
Total	194	21	215

Table 3.20 Relation of Change of Party Forming Government to Reappointment

	Change of party forming govt	No change of party	Total
Reappointed	47	36	83
Not reappointed	105	27	132
Total	152	63	215

Examining these statistics at portfolio level in Table 3.21, reveals some interesting trends. It shows that Portfolio B is the department where the trend in the aggregate data is most clearly apparent (the chi-square statistic is significant). However, the trend is less well-defined in the other portfolios. In the case of Portfolio A, reappointment levels are lower where there is a change in party but the effect is not significant — it seems dominated by the incredibly high levels of turnover. The effect is also not significant in the miscellaneous GCs, where turnover is lowest.

Table 3.21 Relation of Change of Party Forming Government to Reappointment (by Portfolio)

Portfolio		Change of party forming govt	No change of party	Total
A	Reappointed	5	4	9
	Not reappointed	23	10	33
B	Reappointed	32	23	55
	Not reappointed	74	13	87
C	Reappointed	10	9	19
	Not reappointed	8	4	12
	Total	152	63	215

In order to provide econometric evidence on turnover, director reappointment was modelled by way of a logit regression, using the above factors as the independent variables. This enables the effect of all of these

The Management of the Government Corporation

variables to be examined simultaneously. A logit regression is the appropriate econometric technique when the dependent variable — here, director reappointment (*Reappointment*) — takes binary (0/1) form (0 when not reappointed, 1 otherwise). Two dummy variables are used to model portfolio — *Portfolio A*, which takes the value of 1 for a GC in Portfolio A, and *Portfolio B*, which takes the value of 1 for a GC in Portfolio B (GCs in Portfolio C are therefore identified by both values being equal to zero). *Change in Government* takes the value of 1 when there has been a change in government between the time of appointment and the end of the time, and 0 otherwise. *Change in Party* takes the value of 1 when there has been a change in the party forming government between the time of appointment and the end of the term, and 0 otherwise. We also add one further variable, *Days to Next Election*, measuring the number of days between the termination of the director's term and the next general election, in order to gauge whether reappointment decisions are affected by the proximity to an election. The general form of the regression is:

$$Reappointment = a + b_1.Portfolio\ A + b_2.Portfolio\ B + b_3.Listed\ Experience +$$
$$b_4.Change\ in\ Government + b_5.Change\ in\ Party + b_6.Days\ to$$
$$Next\ Election$$

The results, set out in Table 3.22, confirm most of the univariate results. Experience in a listed company increases the odds of reappointment, and change in the party forming government decreases the odds of reappointment. Directors of GCs in Portfolio A are less likely to be reappointed (although the significance of this effect is relatively weak).

The only unexpected result is the fact that change in government is strongly significant — but the sign of the coefficient is positive, which is precisely the opposite direction to change in party. This result underlines the effects of the party system on GCs. The statistics for the model indicate that it is well supported. Political change is evidently a major influence on board reappointment. The econometric evidence's suggestion that change of government leads to reappointment is consistent with the idea that governments become more, not less, conservative with time, a result suggested by Chandler (1983), regarding the creation of GCs in Canada.

100　*Corporate Governance in Government Corporations*

Table 3.22 Econometric Model of Reappointment (Logit Regression)

Variable	Coefficient	Wald-stat	Significance (p)
Constant	−0.592	0.709	0.400
Portfolio A	−1.139	3.585	0.058
Portfolio B	−0.224	0.213	0.645
Listed Experience	1.242	7.343	0.007
Change in Government	2.440	12.885	0.000
Change in Party	−2.183	23.855	0.000
Days to Next Election	−0.001	0.883	0.347

Final model: -2 log likelihood: 236.796; χ^2-stat: 46.041 ($p<0.001$); R^2 (Cox & Snell): 0.196.

The office of a director may terminate before its formal end. There may be several reasons for this. It may be that the director has formally been terminated or has become disqualified (for instance, because of insolvency). Alternatively, the director may simply resign. Again, there may be both political and non-political reasons for the change. It may reflect changes in outside opportunities, disappointment with the nature of directorship in a GC vis-à-vis initial expectations, or it may be attributable to changes in the political environment. These factors may be tested in much the same way as they were tested for reappointment. Univariate tests and econometric evidence are offered below. Before doing so, it is useful to examine the relation between early termination and reappointment — of those directors who have served their full terms, how many are reappointed? There were 83 directors who served a full term and were reappointed, 85 who did not serve a full term, and 47 were not reappointed after serving a full term. The breakdown by portfolio is set out in Table 3.23.

Table 3.23 Early Termination of Directorships (by Portfolio)

Portfolio		Reappointed	Not reappointed	Total
A	Early termination		26	26
	Full term	9	7	16
B	Early termination		49	49
	Full term	55	38	93
C	Early termination		10	10
	Full term	19	2	21
	Total	83	132	215

To examine portfolio first, Table 3.24 sets out the difference in early terminations between portfolios. We can see very clear differences between

The Management of the Government Corporation 101

portfolios, very similar to those on reappointment — early termination occurs least often in Portfolio C, and most often in Portfolio A. The chi-square statistic is statistically significant at $p<0.005$.

Table 3.24 Early Termination of Directorships (by Portfolio)

	Portfolio A GCs	Portfolio B GCs	Portfolio C GCs	Total
Early termination	26	49	10	85
Full term	16	93	21	130
Total	42	142	31	215

The finding in relation to early termination where directors have experience of listed public companies is particularly important. Directors of listed public companies are likely to have the greatest range of outside opportunities — their opportunity costs of serving on GC boards should be higher, and their willingness to terminate their position may be greater. On the other hand, they may be more professional in outlook and willing to work with either side of politics.

Table 3.25 sets out the difference in early terminations between directors with listed experience. It is clear that directors with listed experience are more likely to serve a full term than other directors. The chi-square statistic is statistically significant at $p<0.05$. This result is common to Portfolios A and C, but not Portfolio B (where the difference is not statistically significant, although it is in the same direction), as Table 3.26 demonstrates. The chi-squares for each of the three two-by-two tables are significant for Portfolios A and C at $p<0.05$. The results suggest that by serving full terms and being reappointed more often, the expected directors form a more enduring core of governance processes.

102　　*Corporate Governance in Government Corporations*

Table 3.25 Relation of Experience in Listed Companies to Early Termination

	Experience with listed companies	No experience with listed companies	Total
Early termination	8	77	85
Full term	28	102	130
Total	36	179	215

Table 3.26 Relation of Experience in Listed Companies to Early Termination (by Portfolio)

Portfolio		Experience with listed companies	No experience with listed companies	Total
A	Early termination	3	23	26
	Full term	6	10	16
B	Early termination	3	46	49
	Full term	9	84	93
C	Early termination	2	8	10
	Full term	13	8	21
	Total	36	179	215

We turn now to political factors. Table 3.27 sets out the relation between reappointment and change in government. It suggests a result that is consistent with the econometric evidence on reappointment — namely that a change of government is not, per se, associated with more earlier terminations, but, on the contrary, is associated with more full terms. The result is highly significant ($p<0.005$).

Table 3.27 Relation of Change of Government to Early Termination

	Change of government	No change of government	Total
Early termination	70	15	85
Full term	124	6	130
Total	194	21	215

The Management of the Government Corporation   103

Table 3.28 Relation of Change of Government to Early Termination (by Portfolio)

Portfolio		Change of government	No change of government	Total
A	Early termination	21	5	26
	Full term	16	—	16
B	Early termination	42	7	49
	Full term	87	6	93
C	Early termination	7	3	10
	Full term	21	—	21
	Total	194	21	215

Table 3.28 indicates that this trend exists in all three portfolios — most strongly in the GCs in Portfolio C (significant at $p<0.01$), followed by Portfolio A (weakly significant at $p<0.1$), with the result in Portfolio B not far off the level of weak significance ($p<0.1$). These individual results are occluded somewhat by small numbers of terminations in each portfolio.

Change of party forming government affects early termination in exactly the opposite direction, as it did for reappointment. Table 3.29 sets out this relation. It indicates that change of party is associated with early termination ($p<0.05$), although the effect is not so strong as with reappointment. Examining these statistics at portfolio level, as in Table 3.30, reveals that these trends are apparent in each of the portfolios, but that none of them is more than weakly significant in its own right (Portfolio A is the only portfolio significant at $p<0.1$).

Table 3.29 Relation of Change of Party Forming Government to Early Termination

	Change of party forming govt	No change of party	Total
Early termination	67	18	85
Full term	85	45	130
Total	152	63	215

Table 3.30 Relation of Change of Party Forming Government to Early Termination (by Portfolio)

Portfolio		Change of party forming govt	No change of party	Total
A	Early termination	20	6	26
	Full term	8	8	16
B	Early termination	40	9	49
	Full term	66	27	93
C	Early termination	7	3	10
	Full term	11	10	21
	Total	152	63	215

In order to provide econometric evidence, early termination was modelled by way of a logit regression, using a similar model to the one used for reappointment. This enables the effect of all of these variables to be examined simultaneously. The dependent variable is early termination, *Early Termination*, which takes the value of 0 when the full term was served, and 1 otherwise. The other variables are the same as the ones used previously. The general form of the regression is:

Early Termination = a + b_1.Portfolio A + b_2.Portfolio B + b_3.Listed Experience + b_4.Change in Government + b_5.Change in Party + b_6.Days to Next Election

The results, studied in Table 3.31, confirm the univariate evidence and are substantially similar to the results for the logit model of reappointment. The reader will observe that, with one (insignificant) exception, coefficients for the variables and the constant all take the opposite sign to those for the reappointment model (as is to be expected).

Table 3.31 Econometric Model of Reappointment (Logit Regression)

Variable	Coefficient	Wald-stat	Significance (p)
Constant	1.310	2.917	0.088
Portfolio A	0.933	2.202	0.138
Portfolio B	−0.830	2.268	0.132
Listed Experience	−1.452	7.333	0.007
Change in Government	−4.185	21.405	0.000
Change in Party	2.739	15.920	0.000
Days to Next Election	0.001	2.917	0.201

Final model: -2 log likelihood: 226.496; χ^2-stat: 57.994 ($p<0.001$); R^2 (Cox & Snell): 0.240.

The Management of the Government Corporation   105

To summarise, experience in a listed company and change of government decrease the odds of early termination, while change in the party forming government increases the odds of early termination. Companies in Portfolio A are more likely to terminate early, and companies in the Portfolio B are less likely to do so, but neither effect is significant.[17] The statistics for the model indicate that it is well supported. Again, political change is a major influence on early terminations.

The econometric evidence indicates that the level of turnover on boards is high. The Korn/Ferry International (2000) survey shows that only a relatively low percentage of directors of BCs retire from office. Twelve percent retired in 1999, of which a quarter are by choice. Other significant reasons are reaching the maximum age set either by legislation or specific to the company, or reaching the end of a maximum length of service set for the company. Given these rates, and the average board size of between six and eight directors, less than one person per year retires on the board.[18] By contrast, our evidence of GCs indicates that turnover is unlikely to be principally caused by changes in the value of outside opportunities — those most likely to have the best outside opportunities are the least likely to resign, and most likely to be reappointed. Additionally, the evidence indicates that the principal influence on board turnover is the change in the party that is the driving cause. Losing substantial numbers of directors is, in any event, substantially problematic because of the loss of corporate memory, and, when politics is influential, the GC may well be adversely affected by 'cycling' tendencies in the makeup of the board.

Qualitative Evidence In the survey, we sought evidence from directors in relation to aspects of termination of director appointments on the board of directors. The principal subjects were examining the principal factors likely to lead to termination or non-reappointment, the views of those not reappointed to the board, and the circumstances in which their appointment ended.

We asked directors, 'What factors are likely to result in a decision to terminate or not reappoint a director?' Directors were asked to respond as to how likely they thought each of twelve stated factors were in relation to termination and reappointment, on a scale of 1–3, where 3 was very likely, and 1 was not likely. Table 3.32 sets out these factors, the mean for each of the three portfolios, and the results of an ANOVA comparing these means.

Table 3.32 Factors Likely to Result in Termination or Non-reappointment (Means by Portfolio)

	Portfolio A GCs	Portfolio B GCs	Portfolio C GCs	ANOVA
Corporate failure to meet goals in the SCI or Corporate Plan	2.04	1.86	2.00	NS
General financial underperformance by the GC	2.17	2.02	1.93	NS
Corporate failure to control executive remuneration	2.09	1.93	1.93	NS
A political controversy involving the whole GC	2.49	2.51	2.29	NS
Personal misbehaviour	2.56	2.59	2.36	NS
Ineptitude or slackness in performing duties	2.21	2.07	2.21	NS
Private disagreement with the Minister or Treasurer	1.94	1.93	1.71	NS
Public criticism of the government by the director	2.48	2.36	2.21	NS
Failure to follow a Minister or Treasurer's formal directions	2.67	2.56	2.50	NS
Arousing the anger of an influential interest group	1.64	1.69	1.21	$p<0.1$
Change of Minister within the same government	1.70	1.28	1.07	$p<0.001$
Change of government	2.65	2.58	2.00	$p<0.005$

Several factors emerge from these results. First, several factors likely to cause non-reappointment (personal misbehaviour and failure to follow directions) are wholly appropriate. Second, other factors likely to cause non-reappointment (political controversy, public criticism of the government, and change of government) imply a high and undesirable level of residual politicisation of the GC. Third, there are several factors which one might have thought would have been likely to lead to non-reappointment if governance powers were exercised for efficiency reasons. These are: failure to meet goals in the SCI, financial underperformance, and ineptitude. They are more appropriate motivations for changing the board but they figure lower than political controversy, public criticism, and change of government. Fourth, the differences between the portfolios are consistent with the quantitative evidence above. The responses in Portfolio C GCs tend to be lower than the responses in the other portfolios, which is consistent with the lower levels of board turnover we saw in these GCs. We can also see that change of government is less significant in Portfolio C than elsewhere. More generally, the level of politicisation is higher in Portfolio A (and, to a lesser extent, Portfolio B) than in Portfolio C, as is

The Management of the Government Corporation 107

reflected in the differences in responses to arousing the anger of an interest group or a change in Minister.

There are also important comparisons between the responses of former directors and current directors. These comparisons are not free of biases, although directors who were not reappointed by their choice may, in this case, balance the biases of those not reappointed by government choice. Current directors may also have biases of their own. Former directors should normally be more informed about termination on average than the current directors. Table 3.33 reveals some of these — former directors regard underperformance, personal misbehaviour and ineptitude as relatively less significant, and private disagreement with the Ministers and political change as more significant. In summary, the difference is one of emphasis on performance versus politics.

Table 3.33 Factors Likely to Result in Termination or Non-reappointment (comparison between current and former directors)

	Former directors	Current directors	T-test
Corporate failure to meet goals in the SCI or Corporate Plan	1.87	2.06	NS
General financial underperformance by the GC	2.00	2.16	NS
Corporate failure to control executive remuneration	1.90	2.10	NS
A political controversy involving the whole GC	2.40	2.55	NS
Personal misbehaviour	2.36	2.74	$p<0.005$
Ineptitude or slackness in performing duties	2.08	2.24	NS
Private disagreement with the Minister or Treasurer	2.06	1.75	$p<0.05$
Public criticism of the government by the director	2.43	2.35	NS
Failure to follow a Minister or Treasurer's formal directions	2.57	2.63	NS
Arousing the anger of an influential interest group	1.62	1.59	NS
Change of Minister within the same government	1.57	1.31	$p<0.05$
Change of government	2.69	2.36	$p<0.005$

We asked the former directors responding to the survey to indicate the reason they were no longer serving on the board. Of these directors, nine served on the boards of defunct GCs, twelve resigned or declined

108   *Corporate Governance in Government Corporations*

reappointment for personal or professional reasons, nineteen indicated that their term expired and they were not offered reappointment, and 25 said that their appointment was terminated. Thus, a majority of former directors were not reappointed at the instance of the government, not by their own choice. Table 3.34 summarises the breakdown between portfolios, and also according to which directors have experience in a listed public company. It can be seen that nine out of seventeen directors with listed experience were terminated or not offered reappointment, while 35 out of 47 directors lacking that experience are in that position.

Table 3.34 Reasons for Non-reappointment (by Portfolio)

		Portfolio A GCs	Portfolio B GCs	Portfolio C GCs	Total
Director has listed experience	GC no longer exists	3	—	—	3
	Resigned or declined	2	2	1	5
	Not offered	—	4	1	5
	Terminated	3	1		4
Director lacks listed experience	GC no longer exists	6	—		6
	Resigned or declined	3	2	2	7
	Not offered	4	9	1	14
	Terminated	10	10	1	21
	Total	31	28	6	65

In order to examine the circumstances associated with those directors who might resign or decline reappointment for personal or professional reasons, we asked directors to give us their opinions on the board, the Minister, and the GC. The first question was, 'I was pleased with performance of the board at the time'. Directors were asked to express their agreement with this statement on a scale of 1–5 where 5 was strong agreement and 1 was strong disagreement. Of those resigning or declining reappointment, 10 out of 12 strongly agreed and one disagreed. The second question was, 'The GC was performing well'. Eight strongly agreed, three agreed, and one strongly disagreed. These questions suggest that those resigning or declining do not do so because they have formed adverse views about the board or the GC which suggests, for example, an increased risk of liability of reputational damage.

The next three questions addressed effects of political change. The first asked, 'I approved of the Minister's involvement in the GC'. The evidence is somewhat mixed — two disagreed (one strongly), eight agreed (two

The Management of the Government Corporation 109

strongly) and two were undecided. The next two questions asked, 'I left the GC due to a change in Minister or government', and 'I left the GC in anticipation of a change in Minister or government'. All respondents disagreed with this statement, all but one strongly. It would appear that political change is not a major reason for early termination at the director's instance, or for declining reappointment.

Directors whose appointments were terminated or not offered reappointment were asked, 'If you were not offered reappointment, or your appointment was terminated, what were the reasons for this?' The following were the responses offered:

- There was a change of government and the new government wanted new directors.
- There was a change of Ministers and the new Minister wanted new directors.
- The GC had not performed well and the government wanted to improve performance.
- There had been a political controversy relating to the GC.
- The board was thought to have failed in its control over operational issues (such as executive remuneration).
- The board had opposed or criticised the Minister's wishes or directives.
- I individually opposed or criticised the Minister's wishes or directives.
- I was thought to have underperformed or misbehaved as a director.

Table 3.35 Reason for Non-reappointment (by Portfolio)

	Portfolio A GCs	Portfolio B GCs	Portfolio C GCs	Total
Change of government	15	22	2	39
Change of Ministers	2	–	–	2
Board had opposed or criticised the Minister	=	1	=	1
Total	17	23	2	42

As Table 3.35 shows, change of government (party) dominated responses, which is consistent with the quantitative evidence above. Over 90% of directors selected it — suggesting that change is often unconnected even to political controversies or opposition.

110   *Corporate Governance in Government Corporations*

Conclusion

The GC, like the BC, shares the goal of decreasing the agency costs of management. However, the governance processes associated with that goal are substantially differentiated as between the organisational forms. Even in theory, the optimal contract to compensate the manager looks very different, which is consistent with different compensation practices as between GCs and BCs.

We also find that there are marked differences between the operation of BC and GC boards of directors. Although the above empirical evidence is limited by the biases and institutional parameters of our sample it suggests that the operation of the board as a governance device in GCs is affected, probably adversely, by a number of factors. The first is the relative lack of corporate governance experience in many of the appointees, which simultaneously decreases the dissemination of best governance practices, and the homogeneity of the board's motivations. The second is the insecure tenure of GC directors, and the domination of turnover on boards by changes in the party forming government. This diminishes the likelihood that the board will function independently in the governance of management. The third is the diffusion and complication of the standards that apply under fiduciary duties to the actions of directors. The concept of the best interests of the shareholders as a whole ceases to have the coherence and tractability it has in BCs.

Notes

1. Some factors do cut in the opposite direction, specifically the effect of the manager's risk-aversion. Increasing the proportion of the manager's remuneration tied to the value of the firm increases the risk of the manager's income. The manager is not an efficient risk bearer, compared to shareholders, because of his very limited opportunities for diversifying his human capital.
2. See pp. 98–104 *infra*.
3. This issue forced its way to the top of the policy ladder in the advocacy of independent directors in the first tentative draft of *Principles of Corporate Governance* by the American Law Institute (1982), but was diluted in later drafts.
4. Arguably, this point is not limited to GCs — every politically sensitive requires political savvy. The notion that privatisation divorces the firm is politics is an overgeneralisation.

The Management of the Government Corporation   111

5. The relevant forms of experience are acting as a chief executive officer or top-management executive, or sitting on the board of directors, of a corporation whose equity is listed for quotation on a public exchange.
6. Of the 31 directors with that experience who responded, 23 thought the CEO was more willing to resign. Of the 89 other directors, 48 thought the CEO was more willing to resign (χ^2=3.907, df=1, p<0.05).
7. The Pearson chi-square is significant at p<0.1; the likelihood ratio at p<0.05.
8. Qld: s. 92.
9. This result might be thought to flow from the fact that those favouring communitarian boards would be thought to prefer larger, more representative boards, but this is not in fact supported by the correlation coefficients.
10. Cth: s. 180.
11. The totals in the Table differ from those reported in the text because of missing values.
12. That is, directors are more likely to be sued for negligence where the management they supervise are incompetent or fraudulent.
13. This also carries over when the comparison is made between how the two transactions should be handled. The results tell a similar story to Table 3.6 and are not reported.
14. *Corporations Act* 2001 (Cth) sections 203D, 203C respectively.
15. See, *e.g.*, Qld: Sch. 1, reg. 15.
16. A number of GCs in the energy portfolio were established in Queensland during the early days of the corporatisation reform process. These were later wound up and reconstituted when the electricity industry was subject to more advanced microeconomic reform. See also Chapter 2, p. 37 *infra*.
17. The coefficient for Portfolio B is the exception to the rule that the variables behave the same in both regressions, since it takes the opposite sign to Portfolio A in this regression but took the same sign in the reappointment regression.
18. The conventional assumption is that public enterprise managers have more secure tenure that private enterprise managers (*e.g.*, Hendricks 1977).

Chapter 4

The Government as Shareholder

As Chapter 1 comments, the corporate governance literature addresses the question of how to strengthen the motivations of managers to act in the best interests of shareholders. By contrast, the normative thrust of most administrative and constitutional law has been to recognise the importance of constraining the exercise of government power, based on its possible misuse in ways that are not 'public-regarding'. It follows that the relocation of some part of the enterprise of government, of business character, into a corporation, creates a fundamental question about the balance of power between managers and governmental shareholders. It cannot satisfactorily be answered by a glib premise of assimilating the GC with the BC. This is especially true if some or all of the constitutional law and administrative safeguards constraining government power, such as the right to judicial review of administrative action, are abrogated by situating the enterprise as a GC. On the other hand, the weaker controls on managers, arising from limited market forces, may require that the executive government have more power to intervene in governance than shareholders normally exercise in BCs.

It should be acknowledged that the corporate governance literature has begun to examine the agency problems associated with the exercise of governance power by agents. The principal context for this research is in relation to 'activism' by the investment managers of financial institutions with substantial block shareholdings in BCs. In the United States, the principal institutional activists are managers of superannuation funds for public sector employees (*e.g.*, CALPERS, the California Public Employees' Retirement System). The effects of activism on the value of firms are highly equivocal (Gillan and Starks 1998; Romano 1999). One explanation is the agency costs of governance by these investors, arising from the pursuit of their private interests (Romano 1993), or the divergence in the interests of shareholders per se and employee beneficiaries of superannuation funds (Schwab and Thomas 1998). These concerns apply *a fortiori* for the involvement of government shareholders in the governance of GCs. The principals of Minister-agents are as diverse as can be imagined, and the inefficiency of political markets allows Ministers scope to maximise political payoffs.[1] This underlines a theme of this book — the assimilation of the GC's practices with those of business corporations can be inappropriate where there are differences in governance problems.

The substantial disparities between the relationship of shareholders with BC management and the relationship between the executive government and GC management lie at the root of the doubtful equation of governance power between the two. The shareholder in a BC has a relatively limited and single dimensional relation with the corporation — as a residual claimant on the income generated by the business. By contrast, the relation between the executive government and the GC is more complex and layered. A member of the executive government in a Westminster system, such as a Minister, may also interact with the GC in other capacities, such as a customer, a regulator, and a broker in the competition for rents in the political process. How these diverse motivations interact with each other affects the achievement of both the efficiency and social objectives of a corporatisation regime.

To see how this point has been resolved officially, consider the design of the more advanced corporatisation models of the neo-liberal era, much used in Australia and New Zealand. We studied these designs in Chapter 2. These have been predicated on the notion that it is possible and desirable to articulate the division of powers between the board and management of the GC, on one hand, and the Ministerial shareholder, on the other. The typical balance is one which confers managerial and operating power in relation to the business on the board of directors and the management executives. Governance powers and certain other reserve powers, which may be necessary to further the 'public interest', are allocated to the executive government. This may be an ideal, or at the least the best workable, allocation of power. The problem, however, is how to find the means by which to make this allocation 'stick'.

In addition, consider some of the evidence we examined in Chapter 3. Much of it pointed to considerable politicisation of the function of the GC. There is evidence that the constitution of the board is intimately tied to party politics, and to the cycling of government between parties. Likewise, we found a considerable lack of normative convergence in the handling of transactions of likely importance to electoral politics. That lack of normative convergence suggests that governance power may be able to be used to influence management in ways that increase the agency costs of governance.

In this chapter, we examine these issues by a theoretical examination of the role of the government as shareholder and how the exercise of its power can generate agency costs of governance. We consider the relation between the two categories of agency costs (of management and governance). That

114   *Corporate Governance in Government Corporations*

leads to a discussion of the plasticity and permeability of the governance parameters established for GCs, and, finally, an empirical examination of phenomena that bear on the magnitude of the agency costs of governance.

Agency Costs of Governance in Government Corporations

Economists traditionally argue that government enterprise is less efficient than private enterprise, because the property rights in business assets are much weaker (Alchian 1965; Demsetz 1967). In private enterprise, an owner of an asset has an almost unrestricted ability to do what he likes with the asset, and to enjoy or suffer the consequences of those dealings. In the public enterprise, the ultimate owners, the public, cannot sell their interests in a GC, except by disenfranchising themselves by moving interstate (cf. Spann 1977; Tiebout 1956). In these situations, political agents, such as Ministers, are a necessity. A concern therefore arises regarding the agency costs of governance in GCs. To examine this issue, we should recognise first that a Minister is not necessarily identical to the department he administers. The Minister's incentives may be different to the department head's. It is necessary to analyse the two separately.

A Minister's welfare has only a very weak relation to the value of the GC's net assets. Provided it doesn't go broke, the Minister would seem to have the same incentives as any politician — the maximisation of political support and the chances of re-election. Maximisation of political support may involve policies that redistribute wealth in favour of small, well-organised interest groups (Buchanan and Tullock 1965; Olson 1971; Stigler 1971; Peltzman 1976). For example, the Minister may urge the GC to provide a higher level of services into his own seat, or into marginal seats necessary for his party to form government. The Minister may also indulge in inefficient pursuits of social objectives, which are not 'wrong' per se, but are inefficiently pursued through his portfolio, compared to the welfare system. An example is the use of price regulation to redistribute wealth from the rich to the poor.

The incentives in the department are different. Senior department heads, although probably less politically motivated than their Ministers, may have incentives to engage in various strategic forms of behaviour with respect to GCs that are not in the interests of social welfare. First, departments and GCs may see themselves as budgetary competitors. Thus, the department may seek to take actions which shift costs to, or revenues away from the GC. Second, department heads may want to pursue 'empire building', with respect to the allocation of responsibilities. Exactly what form empire building would take is contested by two opposed theories of bureaucratic behaviour. William Niskanen (1971) asserts that bureaucrats are budget-maximisers. Thus, a department head will oppose spinning off departmental functions into existing (or, of course, new) GCs. By comparison, Patrick Dunleavy (1991) proposes a 'bureau-shaping' theory, in which heads do not want larger budgets or departments per se, but prefer to build a bureaucracy that involves more discretionary activities, more responsibility for the formulation of policy, and so on. Unlike Niskanen's theory, heads may be willing to get rid of cost centres to GCs, if they generate little or no discretionary income. What is more important to the head is the capacity to build a bureau that has stronger policy influence, including influence over the activities of the GC, and greater discretion in the allocation of funds. In any situation, the scope for strategic behaviour by departments depends on their place with the GC governance framework. Stevens (1993) shows how a departmental bureaucracy became central to the Manitoba regime through its involvement in the budget expenditure review process. The role of bureaucracies can also be heightened if public servants are permitted to sit on GC boards.

Given the different incentives of department heads, Ministers, and GC CEOs, there is a potential for coalitions or alliances between these players. The most likely concern is that the Minister and department collude to influence GC management to deliver services in a manner that maximises political support. This outcome obviously serves the Minister. It also serves the Department, since it increases its influence over the GC. Such a coalition might adopt strategies such as tying funds to particular programs, withholding information about market conditions from the GC, or threatening to restructure the market to diminish the share of the GC.

However, the equilibrium is not wholly stable. Either the Minister or the department might defect. A Minister may defect and seek an alliance with the GC if the Minister considers that he can maximise political support by relocating departmental functions to the GC. This might be done to shelter these functions from public law review processes to which the department but not the GC is exposed. Trebilcock and Prichard (1983) also refer to the appeal of a GC to a 'selectively responsible' Minister, that is, one bent on taking credit for successes, but putting the distance of GC 'autonomy' between herself and a disaster. Finally, the GC and the department might collude. This is an unstable alliance to the extent that the two compete for funds, but the GC may often be self-funding. The GC and the department's alliance may involve a deal in which neither calls attention to the inefficiencies of the other.

The possibilities for collusion are hindered in part if the corporatisation framework provides for a second empowered Ministerial shareholder who will have different responsibilities and priorities. More parties need to be

116   *Corporate Governance in Government Corporations*

implicated in order for the collusive activity to be sustained. This result supports the general structure of corporatisation regimes in Australia, since the governance entitlements in GCs are placed in the hands of two Ministers — usually the Minister of the portfolio department, and a second Minister responsible for GCs in the government, such as the Treasurer.[2] There are other risks, however, arising from the problem of 'dual principals', discussed in detail in Chapter 6.

In light of these risks, how do corporatisation regimes attempt to economise on the agency costs of governance? The regimes in Australia, adopting the corporatisation model that was pioneered in New Zealand, and exported elsewhere, all reserve basically the same powers for the Minister and government. They represent a useful illustrative example, and also situate the later empirical analysis.

First, the shareholding Ministers are not technically responsible for making appointments to the board of directors, and for changes to the board. Directors are appointed by the Cabinet (as the Governor in Council),[3] but the Ministers hold the whip hand by normally being able to determine the recommendations the latter are to consider.

Second, the shareholding Ministers are jointly responsible for determining the principle objectives, performance targets, other financial benchmarks, and certain other operational standards. These goals are included in various important documents — in the Corporate Plan and in the Statement of Corporate Intent (SCI).[4] The board is obliged to account for the GC's performance, in light of the aims specified in the SCI. The Ministers are also expected to monitor financial performance. However, these functions are not coextensive with setting commercial policy for, or operating or managing the GC.[5] That is intended to be the preserve of the board and the CEO.

Third, the government may impose Community Service Obligations (CSOs).[6] That is, it can require the GC to undertake a non-commercial objective, which will normally be funded from consolidated revenue on the basis of the avoidable costs associated with the activity.

Fourth, the executive government retains the power to issue directives to the GC. Apart from an obligation to gazette the directive, there are no specified limitations on the frequency or subject matter of these.[7]

Providing for a regime in which the government and Ministers do not have a formal role in operations and management is done with the expectation that substantial managerial freedoms are likely to result in greater efficiencies. That explanation is defensible in theory. To see this, let us consider each of these points in detail. If the Minister is able to set performance standards, but is not able to micro-manage the GC, what sorts of performance standards will he set? The Minister only has an incentive to set low standards if he is able to engage in some form of side-deal that trades low standards for the achievement of other goals on which he sets value.[8] However, by allowing the Minister to impose CSOs and make other directives, the incentive to engage in side-deals are substantially reduced. While the Minister's incentive to set optimal standards remains on the weak side, given his or her attenuated property rights in the GC's assets, other factors such as public spiritedness and the desire to have a strong local economy will compensate to some extent. Once the standards are set, however, the Minister must leave it to the board and the management of the GC to find the optimal ways of achieving those goals. This is optimal, as the board and the management will possess more and richer information about initiating and implementing business decisions than the Minister. It is therefore optimal that the Minister not have a managerial role.

Similar comments should apply to the selection of directors. If the Minister is incapable of personally managing the firm, he should prefer to appoint a competent board, rather than an incompetent board, and ethical rather than unethical directors. To the extent the Minister does set moderately high standards, he will prefer, other things being equal, that the GC achieve its performance targets rather than miss them entirely. Similarly, there is no question that directors are preferred if they are unlikely to be followed by scandal or the hint of impropriety. However, there are other complications with board appointments, which we shall explore below, since there are more dimensions than just competence and ethics, such as ideological predisposition and sympathy to political objectives.

Some Canadian writers, including Trebilcock and Prichard (1983) and Stevens (1993), take issue with this conclusion in certain regards. They argue against a generalised accountability regime, having regard to differences in monitoring costs, amongst other factors. So, for example, Ministerial involvement in management may be more necessary in a GC in which the specification and measurement of objectives is more difficult. It is true that there may often need to be differentiation in certain aspects of the GC's governance. However, the case for relaxing the principle of management autonomy is weak. Although monitoring may be harder in some GCs than in others, the Minister's governance powers are not restricted to monitoring. At the margin, the Minister may substitute ex post sanctions, such as removing the board or revising the goals approved for the GC in its official corporate planning process. Likewise, the greater the scope for Ministers to intervene, the harder it is to hold management accountable for the goals set for them.

Similar comments apply to Ministerial influence in relation to, say, complex CSOs. Where Ministers are capable of informally directing the

118   *Corporate Governance in Government Corporations*

board as to methods that are *both* more efficient and social-welfare-enhancing, the board would undoubtedly welcome such advice. Where, however, the Minister's view of CSO delivery is at odds with the commercial objectives of the firm, the appropriate resolution should be against Ministerial involvement. First, there is no simple means of limiting Ministers to involvement that enhances community welfare, rather than minorities that are politically influential. Second, the iterative process of negotiating CSOs and GC objectives, like any repeated game, discourages short-term opportunism by the board. This in turn suggests managerial autonomy is most likely to be asserted where there is a genuine policy dilemma that warrants greater public scrutiny. This problem is another example of the impossibility of selective intervention. That is, the creation of management autonomy and an arm's length interface with the government is inconsistent with a mechanism for low-cost government intervention, as ex post adaptation is inconsistent with market contracting.

If we agree that a governance/management division of powers in GCs is desirable, the more complex question is how this allocation of powers can be enforced. Can Ministers exceed their identified governance parameters? There are three circumstances in which this may occur.

First, as foreshadowed above, there are more issues than just competence and ethics in relation to board appointments. A director may be competent and ethical (in the sense of avoiding personal impropriety), but also be highly partisan. GC boards may be made up of persons who share the Minister's objectives and will act in ways he cannot mandate — so allowing the Minister an indirect role in micro-management. I call this the *simpatico board* scenario. It depends on how directors and CEOs are appointed, and qualifications and preconditions for appointment. For instance, if the Minister is responsible for recruitment, and there are few or no preconditions to board membership, the likelihood of a simpatico board is greater.

Second, the Minister is able to intervene in management in the shadow of a credible threat (see generally Dixit and Nalebuff 1991, pp. 120–126). That is, a Minister can threaten to use his extensive reserved powers or power deriving from some other source (*i.e.*, not arising from the position as a Ministerial shareholder) if the CEO or the board manage contrary to his desires. What credible threats might be made? The roles that are reserved for the Minister under the legislative schemes have been noted above. These include the power to issue directives, the power to influence appointments to the board of directors, the power to impose CSOs, and so on. The Minister may also be a customer of the GC, a financier, or a regulator. In at least some cases, these capacities may accord the Minister

The Government as Shareholder   119

considerable power to make a credible threat, beyond explicit governance entitlements.

However, it does not follow that the Minister can always *credibly* threaten to use these powers — a declaration of an intention to exercise a power conditionally may neither be a threat, nor credible. To be a threat, the directors or CEOs must actually be worse off. Two cases must be distinguished here. The threatened action may make the GC worse off. However, this may not be a threat if the directors and the CEO do not internalise the wealth effects of the threatened action. This depends on officer compensation and performance incentives. In a sense, the weakness of property rights in the GC actually limits the range of possible threats the Minister can make against directors and managers. Alternatively, the threat may affect the director directly. An example is a threat to sack the director. This is credible where the opportunity cost of the director's time spent on the board is relatively low. This will differ between directors. 'Professional' directors, such as those with experience in listed corporations, will not find this a threat, since they are likely to find replacement directorships easy to procure, and they may value a reputation for standing up for the business. Representative appointments (such as community and labour representatives) are more likely to be threatened by such an intimation, because there are far fewer directorships available to such persons in private firms.

Which threats are credible? It must be rational for the Minister to impose the threatened action. A Minister cannot be worse off for doing so. Some threats such as changing appointments to the board or limiting the availability of finance are usually credible. Other threats may not be. For example, where the Minister seeks to influence management in a way that would redistribute wealth to a well-organised interest group, a threat to impose that obligation by way of a directive may not be credible because it may trigger significant opposition from other interest groups that would not occur if the GC had 'gone quietly' (Becker 1983). A threat to change the structure of the market, for instance, increasing the scope for competition, may not be credible for the same reasons (Zeckhauser and Horn 1989, p. 40). Finally, a threat that jeopardised the solvency of the GC is unlikely because of political damage.

Third, the Minister may 'cut a deal' with GC management by offering a sweetener to operate in a manner they otherwise would not choose to. Examples might include a more relaxed approach to setting goals and targets in SCIs, approving compensation arrangements, or providing further equity funding. Such side-deals are a concern. They suggest that Ministerial objectives are to be achieved either by cutting the organisation greater slack or by offering a personal benefit to the director or CEO. The latter is

120   *Corporate Governance in Government Corporations*

inconsistent with fiduciary concerns; the former throws good money after bad.

As is implicit in the analysis above, the Minister's incentive to rely on a side-deal (as with credible threats) is greatest when the end he seeks is least likely to be public-regarding. That is because he has extensive reserved powers to achieve other types of ends, such as the CSO and directive mechanism, which will be preferred when the end sought will withstand public scrutiny.

Since the premise of the corporatisation regime is that Ministers should not have a role in the operation or the management of the GC, are these forms of intervention undesirable? Not necessarily — the Minister may sometimes be acting to reduce excessive agency costs of management. This should be self-evident. There is no hermetic seal between the functions of governance and management. Fama and Jensen (1983) suggest decision management involves initiating business proposals and implementing approved proposals, whereas the function of decision control involves ratifying proposals and monitoring performance of implemented proposals. However, there is an overlap between the two so that the governance functions implicit in decision control partake of managerial elements. In the context of GCs, for example, consider the imposition of a CSO. As Quiggin (2003) notes, a CSO can only be specified in terms that are insufficiently state-contingent — that is, it will lack specification for certain future states of the world. In those circumstances, the Minister's involvement may be important if the community service is to be delivered appropriately, although the comments made above remain valid where the Minister's involvement would endanger commercial objectives. Likewise, the involvement of the Minister's department for regulatory reasons can have a substantial impact at the managerial level. Thus, in practice, the governance-management distinction breaks down. In theory, then, the Minister may take a more active role in reducing certain forms of agency costs — such as overreaching by directors and senior managers, or urging higher levels of effort and receptivity to customer needs. So, the total level of agency costs is likely to be inversely U-shaped, with respect to the degree of discretion the Minister has in relation to management. Figure 4.1 illustrates this point.

Figure 4.1 Total Agency Costs in Government Corporations as a Function of Ministerial Discretion

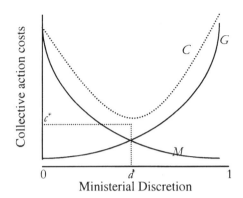

In Figure 4.1, the x-axis graphs the degree of ministerial discretion, D, on a scale from 0 to 1, where 0 is a total lack of discretion to become involved in management, and 1 is complete discretion to do so. The agency costs of management, denoted by the curve, M, are decreasing in ministerial discretion, because of the greater range of responses the Minister may employ in dealing with impropriety, inadequate motivation, and so on. The agency costs of governance, denoted by the curve, G, are increasing in discretion. This reflects the Minister's weaker information, and his incentive to act politically. It follows that the total agency costs, mapped by the curve, C, should have a minimum, c^*, so that $dC/dD=0$, $d^2C/dD^2>0$ at the point $D=d^*$, where $0<d^*<1$.

The question, which is ultimately empirical, is whether corporatisation regimes impose governance parameters on a Minister's discretion that approach d^*. Where $D<d^*$, surpassing the established parameters may increase social welfare. In other circumstances, the reverse should be true.[9] The next part attempts to provide evidence on these questions. Initially, it examines the role of the Minister. It then moves on to consider the interaction between the GC and the Minister's departments, in order to complete the picture.

Evidence on the Minister's Role in Corporate Governance

Hypotheses

The examination in Chapter 3 was a comparison between the devices that control agency costs of management in BCs. However, the concept of agency costs of governance is not well-developed. In order to provide some basic guidance for the analysis, I postulate three generalised null hypotheses for empirical testing:

H1	The Minister restricts interaction with the GC's board and its senior management to the governance functions explicitly reserved in the GC legislation.
H2	Non-standard Ministerial involvement increases the value of the corporation.
H3	The extent of non-standard Ministerial interaction with GCs does not vary between Ministerial portfolios.

H1 is a test of whether the formal specification of permissible Ministerial functions has been effective. H2 seeks to test the motivations and effects of Ministerial involvement in corporate governance, in order to gain some insight into the existence of agency costs of governance — more generally, to suggest the nature of the relation between d and d^*. H3 examines inter-portfolio differences to shed light on whether the Minister-GC 'game' is played differently in different portfolios. If it is, it would provide some evidence on how the corporate governance parameters established by corporatisation regimes are affected by political imperatives and personalities.

Again, it is important to note a possible sampling bias affecting these results. Also, the hypothesis tests can only permit inferences in relation to H2, regarding the maximisation of value.

Appointment Processes

Board appointments influence the capacity for Ministerial intervention by way of credible threats, and determine the existence of a *simpatico* board willing to act in the manner the Minister would prefer. It follows that the nature of the appointment process and of the appointees is a matter of great significance. We therefore asked directors, in relation to seven specified alternatives, 'Which of the following best describes the circumstances in which you came to be considered as an appointee to the board of the GC?'

One of the options, 'I actively solicited the GC to propose my appointment', attracted no responses. Table 4.1 summarises responses.

Table 4.1   Basis for Consideration as an Appointment

	Number	%
I actively solicited the relevant Minister to appoint me.	1	1
Industry or community groups proposed my appointment.	8	8
I was approached by a Minister or department to consider appointment.	84	81
I responded to a public advertisement calling for nominations.	1	1
I placed my name on a register of willing and qualified persons.	6	6
My appointment carried over from earlier involvement with GC.	4	4
Total	104	100

The government functions in the manner of a controlling shareholder, by making necessary appointments. The answers indicate that industry has little direct involvement in appointments, which is desirable as it suggests that interest groups have only indirect influence on the appointment process. We see, in the next chapter, however, that interest groups do lobby board members. Finally, the absence of active solicitation of appointments is desirable, since it suggests that appointees are less likely to seek to further political or social causes.

In order to shed light on which *part* of government was influential, we asked respondents to answer the question, 'With whom did you have *most* of your dealings regarding your appointment? Your answer should be based on events up until the time you were appointed, *not after.*' (emphasis in original) Two of the options — directors other than the chairman, and political party representatives — attracted no responses. Table 4.2 summarises responses. It indicates Ministers (and less often their departments) take the major initiative on appointments. The portfolio Minister dominates the appointments. The portfolio Minister, who will be the subject of lobbying principally by interests within the portfolio, is more likely to favour these sectional interests, vis-à-vis the Treasurer, whose responsibility is for the economy as a whole and is defined along whole-of-government lines. The data indicate that GCs are *unlike* listed companies lacking a controlling shareholder, in which the board (through a nomination committee) is a principal influence on new appointments (Bacon 1993).[10]

124   *Corporate Governance in Government Corporations*

Table 4.2   Major Contact Regarding Appointment

	Number	%
GC chief executive	4	4
GC chairman	3	3
The Treasurer (either personally or his/her office)	14	13
Queensland Treasury	8	7
The Premier (either personally or his office)	4	4
Department of Premier and Cabinet	1	1
The Portfolio Minister (either personally or his/her office)	57	53
The Portfolio Department	7	7
My local member of parliament	7	7
Other person representing an industry or community group	2	2
Total	107	100

Expectations Regarding Intervention

What are the expectations of directors regarding the extent of Ministerial intervention in the governance and management of a GC, and how if at all do these expectations affect the decision to accept a GC directorship? The former question is obviously important, since those who accept directorship may have reasonably accurate expectations regarding Ministerial intervention, based on observations and hearsay from informed sources. The latter question, regarding the effect of intervention on the decision to accept an appointment, is also significant since, taken in conjunction with information regarding expectations as to the circumstances in which it would occur, it provides information about the dispositions of directors, and their '*simpatico*' characteristics. I call the former question the expectations question and the latter the effects question. To address the expectations question, directors were asked to select a response to the following question, 'I thought the Minister, Treasurer and other politicians would become involved in management', from five designated options.

The options are set out in Table 4.3, together with the responses each attracted. Around 34% thought that ministers would rarely intervene — a surprising result, unless good corporate governance practices are, contrary to our expectation, wholly self-enforcing. Because GCs lack the principal market pressures thought to encourage maximisation of value by managers, such as takeovers and the capital market, one would expect a controlling shareholder to be more active in governance than 'rare' involvement. Thus, in a sense, the 'major governance issues' response, selected by around 36% of the sample, is the response expected if the government was seeking to maximise efficiency. Further, 20% of the sample expected intervention of kinds that exceeded the parameters set by the corporatisation regime, inconsistently with H1.

The Government as Shareholder

There is no significant portfolio effect. However, the responses take a surprising turn when they are related to the experience of the director in public companies. Table 4.4 indicates that those with public company experience tended to form different opinions to those without such experience.

Table 4.3   Circumstances of Ministerial Involvement in Management

	Number	%
Rarely, if ever (*i.e.*, they would permit the board maximum freedom to manage efficiently)	41	34
Only in the case of major governance issues (such as bad financial performance)	43	36
Only when political issues arose	12	10
Whenever it suited them	13	11
I didn't have any expectations	11	9
Total	120	100

Table 4.4   Relation between Expectations of Political Intervention in the GC and Public Company Experience

	No public company experience	Public company Experience	Total
Rare involvement	30	11	41
Major governance issues	27	16	43
Political issues	11	1	12
When it suited	10	3	13
Didn't have expectations	11	—	11
Total	89	31	120

The chi-square statistic is weakly significant ($p<0.1$). This indicates that directors with governance experience in public companies all had expectations, and these tended to the belief that Ministers would become involved on major governance issues or not at all. This may reflect experience with institutional investors, or, perhaps, a different (and not necessarily more realistic) view of the significance of political constraints on Ministers. Those without public company experience were more likely to have no opinion, and estimated that Ministers were relatively more likely to become involved in political issues compared to more experienced officers. An alternative explanation of the results is that directors with public company experience hold rather less politicised positions than other directors, as we saw in Chapter 3, and this affects their ex ante expectations of political involvement.

126   *Corporate Governance in Government Corporations*

Directors were asked about influences on their decision to accept an appointment, and whether these factors encouraged them, discouraged them, or had no influence. This was in the same section of the survey that examined other supply-side influences on directorship that we analysed above in Chapter 3.[11] The specific question was 'expectations [at the time of the appointment] as to the extent of involvement of Ministers or other politicians in corporate governances', to be scored on a scale of 1 to 5, where 5 was strong encouragement, 3 was no influence, and 1 was strong discouragement. The results are variable — more were discouraged (32 in total, of which 7 were strongly discouraged) than encouraged (16 were slightly encouraged, 1 was strongly encouraged), although a majority (64) were not influenced. The mean is 2.81, which a one-sample t-test indicates as being significantly different from the mean value, 3, reflecting no influence, at $p<0.05$ ($t=2.515$, $df=112$). So a substantial minority of directors considers that politics in GCs discourages board service. A sample of GC directors will inevitably be biased *against* a finding that directors are discouraged by politics from joining boards, in a self-selecting manner, vis-à-vis the total population of eligible directors.

When these results on encouragement are related to other factors, portfolio seems to be a matter of more explanatory significance than of public company experience. Directors with experience in public companies do not appear to be more discouraged. But our earlier evidence suggests a reason for that — they anticipate interference to be less likely, so the extent to which they are discouraged should be reduced at the margin, which may compensate for the fact that they are presumably more easily discouraged, other things being equal, since they should have more market opportunities. Their lower likelihood of termination or non-reappointment may also decrease their views on the incidence of government interference.

A one-way ANOVA indicates that there is variation between the means for portfolios, the F-statistic being significant at $p<0.05$. Post-hoc comparison of means indicates that directors in Portfolio A were more likely to be discouraged by intervention than the directors in the other GCs (the means were: Portfolio A, 2.6; Portfolio B, 2.98; Portfolio C, 3.0). It may be that these results involve retrospective updating of initial expectations, based on actual experiences, since we will demonstrate in later sections that political intervention occurs most in Portfolio A. The opinions may also reflect observation of the high levels of politically-related takeover in Portfolio A.

Closely related to these questions is the directors' expectation relating to whether the government will constrain the efficient management of the GC. We asked directors the following question:

The Government as Shareholder 127

I thought it likely that the GC's operations and governance would be substantially constrained by the government in inefficient ways (a) True; (b) False; (c) I never considered the matter.

The numbers for the three responses are: 38 thought it true, 54 thought it false; an astonishingly large 28 directors did not consider it. The results are similar to the results for the question in relation to when directors thought Ministerial shareholders would intervene, in the sense that public company directors were much less likely to have formed no opinion — they make up only three of the 28 undecided respondents. However, the differences are not great between the other two category of responses. The responses for Portfolios A and B are not significantly different; however, the proportion of directors *not* believing that government would constrain operations and governance is much higher in the Portfolio C GCs (73%) than in the other two portfolios (an average of 41%).

Regarding the related question of the effect of a change of government, we asked directors to select the best response to the following statement:

I thought that if there was a change of State government, it would;
(a) Cause major change to operations and governance of the GC;
(b) Cause minor change to operations and governance;
(c) Have no effect on operations and governance.

Thirty-nine respondents thought there would be major change; 60 thought there would be minor change, and 21 thought there would be no effect. This suggests that to the extent that directors prefer the status quo and dislike change, service on a GC is likely to impose an element of disutility, given the high expectations of change. There are, once more, differences between directors with public company experience and directors without that experience. Table 4.5 demonstrates this. The chi-square statistic is statistically significant at the $p<0.05$ level. This indicates that directors with experience in public companies took a more blasé attitude towards a change of government. This could be for two reasons — it could be a genuine belief about the resistance of GC management processes to genuine change, or it could be a greater indifference if change did occur, since the cost imposed by the termination of their directorship is bound to be lower, given both *more* market opportunities and *lower* probability of being affected.

128   *Corporate Governance in Government Corporations*

Table 4.5   Relation between Expectations of the Effect of Change of Government and Public Company Experience

	No public company experience	Public company Experience	Total
Major change	32	7	39
Minor change	46	14	60
No effect	11	10	21
Total	89	31	120

The effect of change of government, as between the portfolios, is similar to the response to the question regarding whether the government would constrain the management of the GC in substantially inefficient ways. Portfolios A and B are very similar, but those in Portfolio C are much more likely to believe that change will be minor, if it happens at all. The chi-square for the (unreported) crosstabulation is significant at the $p<0.05$ level.

We then asked directors how the effect of a change of government would impact on their decision to accept appointment as a director. Directors were asked in the section on the effect of various factors on appointment to analyse the proposition, 'Expectations as to the effect of a change of government on the GC or my own position', on the 1–5 scale used in earlier questions. We find three directors were strongly discouraged, 15 slightly discouraged (strongly), two directors slightly encouraged, and 2 directors strongly encouraged. The bulk of respondents — 91 in all — were uninfluenced. The mean response, 2.87, is statistically significantly different from the null mean, 3.00, reflecting no influence, at $p<0.05$. What is significant about these data is that many of the directors professing to be uninfluenced by a change in government nonetheless thought that there would be either major change or minor change. This suggests that the directors are willing to work with both sides of politics, and that they do not internalise any significant costs from change in government policy. Also, of the handful of directors professing to be encouraged by change in government, none have experience in public companies. There are no significant portfolio effects.

To conclude, political costs do appear to create disincentives for directors to become GC directors, even though the selection bias should tend to run in the opposite direction. The most significant factor appears to be the willingness of the government to intervene in the governance and management of the GC. A majority, however, claim not to have been influenced, at the time of their appointment. We consider the nature of such intervention below. Such factors as change of government appear to be less

The Government as Shareholder 129

influential — a matter which contrasts interestingly with the results of our study of director turnover, reported in the last chapter.

Statements of Corporate Intent

A Minister has governance power to formulate goals and objectives for the GC. These are renegotiated annually in the Statement of Corporate Intent (SCI). These goals include, but are not limited to, financial targets, since they may also include aspects of customer service and other community concerns. The SCI operates as a performance agreement. Performance falling below the targets therein provides a clear basis for more active intervention in the GC.

It is important to examine the role the Minister actually takes in the formulation of the SCI and the Corporate Plan, and the perceived consequences for failing to meet those consequences. There are two principal scenarios. The first is that the Minister sets appropriate goals, presumably by negotiation, and takes suitable action where those goals are not achieved, such as seeking explanations or commitments, modifying the content of future SCIs, or by changing the management team. The second is that the Minister is indifferent to the entire process, and uses what sources of informal power he has to affect the conduct of the GC in ways that may not be authorised. There are, however, a range of variations on each of these scenarios.

To judge the role of the Minister in formulating SCIs, we asked directors the question, 'What best describes the process by which the content of the SCI and Corporate Plan are determined?', and gave them eight possible responses. No respondents selected the eighth, namely, that the director did not know the process. The other responses and their frequencies appear in Table 4.6.

130 *Corporate Governance in Government Corporations*

Table 4.6 Nature of SCI and Corporate Plan Formulation

	Number
Actively negotiated between the board and the Ministers	47
	42
Negotiated between the CEO and the Department(s), and rubber-stamped by everyone else	10
Mostly dictated by the CEO, and rubber-stamped by everyone else	2
Mostly dictated by the Portfolio Department or Treasury	2
Negotiated only as a formality, with little relation to actual performance goals	1
Usually a copy of last year's documents, with a few minor or cosmetic changes	4
Total	108

Although there is much variation, the results mainly fall into two major categories — active board-Minister negotiation, and determination by the board with Ministerial rubber-stamping. The former response is consistent with the ideal picture of the Minister as taking an active role in corporate governance. It need not, however, be consistent with the use of the SCI process to pursue only suitable goals. The second is at odds with that image, since the Minister is neglecting the authorised process. The answers may vary because directors have different experiences. However, a cross-tabulation of responses for specific GC identities (not reported) indicates that in some companies active negotiation was clearly dominant, while in others, 'endogenous' formulation at the board level was dominant. What is important is that a chi-square test rejects the proposition that there are differences in responses between portfolios, suggesting that Ministers may not behave consistently in their dealings with all of the companies within their portfolios. The bargaining power of the Minister may vary with respect to different boards or different CEOs, or political sensitivity varies between companies, which would in turn significantly affect the effectiveness or degree of ministerial intervention.

The second question is to what extent the achievement of SCI goals is monitored by the board of directors? This question sheds light on several issues. It indicates something about the relative significance of the goals in the SCI — if the board does not bother to monitor them, the SCI would be difficult to take seriously. It also indicates something about the operation of the board itself. To examine this question, we asked directors the following question, the results to which are set out in Table 4.7:

The Government as Shareholder 131

How does the board monitor whether it is achieving the goals in the SCI?

(a) Progress towards the SCI and Corporate Plan goals are considered at every board meeting.
(b) Monitoring is delegated to the Audit Committee.
(c) Individual directors take it on themselves to monitor but there is no official consideration.
(d) No monitoring occurs.

Table 4.7 Monitoring of SCI Goal Achievement (by Portfolio)

	Portfolio A GCs	Portfolio B GCs	Portfolio C GCs	Total
Progress is considered at each board meeting	35	38	9	82
Monitoring is delegated to the Audit Committee	9	3	1	13
Individual directors monitor unofficially	2	2	—	4
No monitoring	—	2	—	2
Total	46	45	10	101

There are no statistically significant portfolio effects. The board seems to be doing its job. Nonetheless, there is a highly significant correlation between whether or not the board monitors SCI goals and whether or not the Minister negotiates the SCI, as Table 4.8 reveals. It appears to be the case that the board is less likely to monitor, the less active a role the Minister takes in the negotiation of the SCI, which suggests, perhaps, that the Minister's proper exercise of his governance powers can have a significant effect on the commitment with which the board discharges its governance functions related to the SCI. The chi-square statistic is significant at $p<0.01$.

132 *Corporate Governance in Government Corporations*

Table 4.8 Relationship between Minister's Active Negotiation of SCIs and Board Monitoring of SCI goals

	Board does monitor SCI goals	Board does not monitor SCI goals	Total
Minister actively negotiates SCI	38	3	41
Minister does not actively negotiate SCI	40	16	56
Total	78	19	97

Note: The cross-tabulation aggregates the responses for the determination test other than active Ministerial negotiation, and also the responses for the monitoring of SCI objectives other than monitoring at board level.

Finally, the consequences where the GC does not meet SCI goals help us to understand the nature of ministerial intervention in corporate governance. We asked directors, 'What are the consequences of not meeting SCI goals?'. The possible responses and the frequency of their selection are set out in Table 4.9.

Table 4.9 Consequences of not Meeting SCIs

	Portfolio A GCs	Portfolio B GCs	Portfolio C GCs	Total
Government (Ministers or departments) seek explanations for the failure	30	25	6	61
Government seeks commitments from the board to ensure failures do not occur again	5	5	—	10
Government considers changing management team or directors	1	3	—	4
I did not detect there were any consequences	13	11	5	29
Total	49	44	11	104

Hard-line consequences — explicit commitments or changing the management team — are least likely to be imposed, suggesting that the SCI is rarely treated as a formal contract, but simply as a benchmark for future action. Seeking explanations is the most likely response, but a quarter of respondents detected no consequences of any form. The latter conclusion is inconsistent with the expectation that Ministers will function as active investors, aiming to maximise the value of the corporation. Is there a relation between the consequences of not meeting SCIs and whether or not the Minister actively negotiates the SCI?[12] Table 4.10 indicates that active

The Government as Shareholder 133

Ministerial negotiation is related to more serious SCI consequences. The chi-square statistic is statistically significant at $p<0.001$. The only puzzling result is why a Minister who does not actively negotiate SCI goals would be more likely to seek commitments from management.

Table 4.10 Relationship between Active Negotiation of SCIs and Consequences of not Meeting SCI Goals

	Explanation sought	Commitment sought	Management change considered	No consequence	Total
Minister actively negotiates SCI	32	3	3	4	42
Minister does not actively negotiate SCI	23	7	1	23	54
Total	55	10	4	27	96

On balance, although directors took up their appointments expecting a substantial level of intervention by the Minister, there is evidence that Ministers don't exercise the full range of governance roles that are explicitly reserved for them.

The Governance Roles of Ministers and the Treasurer

Having considered the pre-appointment expectations of GC directors regarding managerial intervention by Ministers, we now examine actual experiences and post-appointment impressions. Our evidence relates to how Ministers and directors communicated with each other, the issues that were the subject of communications, the incidence of informal intervention, the means by which informal intervention is credible, the costs of intervention to the GC, and the resolution of conflict between portfolio Ministers.

In the GCs sampled, the 'voting' shares, with applicable governance entitlements, are allocated to two cabinet Ministers. These are the Treasurer, who represents a 'whole-of-government' interest in economic and financial matters, and the Minister into whose portfolio the GC's business falls (and, in the main, the Minister out of whose portfolio the GC was created). This is not of course the only conceivable model, as we saw in Chapter 2, but it raises interesting comparative issues regarding the different incentives of the two Ministers.

We asked directors to describe how often ministers used particular means to communicate with the GC board. The governance functions reserved for the Minister under the legislation are most appropriately served

134   *Corporate Governance in Government Corporations*

by formal communications between the Minister and the chairman, and, for certain matters (for example, operational issues regarding particular contracts or CSOs) the CEO. Some means of communication are inappropriate. One is communicating with individual directors, in order to lobby them in relation to matters coming before the board. Also inappropriate is where the department acts as the principal conduit of information from the Minister, since this seems to raise risks of collusion either between the department and the Minister, or between the department and the GC. Finally, in interviews with GC directors, one interviewee told us that one Minister sometimes communicated by press release, using media pressure to influence the board or the CEO. Thus, directors were asked in respect of each of a number of forms of communication, whether its use was 'usual' (4), 'occasional' (3), 'rare' (2), or 'never' (1). The questions were posed separately for the Minister and the Treasurer. Table 4.11 summarises the means, and reports whether or not a paired-samples t-test of the difference between the means is significant.[13]

We may draw several inferences from these results. First, portfolio Ministers are more frequent communicators than Treasurers. Second, in the case of the Treasurer, communication via Treasury is a relatively more important means than informal communications by the Treasurer to the chairman or to management, a practice which portfolio Ministers use more often. Third, the least desirable communications — direct lobbying of board members, communication by media, and the use of inflexible gazetted directions — are observed rarely but were employed more often by portfolio Ministers.

Are these results driven by portfolio, or by the specific relation between Ministers and boards? The answer is mostly negative based on a one-way ANOVA comparing means for the three portfolios. However, there are two significant exceptions. The first was the use of indirect communications, such as via the media. The mean for the use by portfolio ministers of this communication form, for companies in Portfolio A was 2.10, for companies in Portfolio B 1.60, and for companies in Portfolio C 1.00. That difference is significant at $p<0.001$. The second is the use of gazetted directions, where the equivalent means are 2.02, 1.63, and 1.21, the difference being significant at $p<0.001$. The latter, but not the former result recurs, in the case of the Treasurer, at conventional levels of statistical significance.

Table 4.11 Frequency of Using Particular Means of Communication

	Portfolio Minister	Treasurer	Significant at:
The Minister communicated formally with the board by routing communications through the Chair	3.44 (0.75)	3.27 (0.96)	$p<0.05$
The Minister communicated informally with the Chair who then passed this communication on to the board	2.89 (0.86)	2.34 (1.04)	$p<0.001$
The Minister communicated with management (*e.g.* the CEO) who then relayed this to the Chair and board	2.76 (0.90)	2.40 (1.06)	$p<0.001$
Communication from the Minister came via the Department, directly to the Chair and board	2.70 (0.95)	2.78 (0.94)	NS
Communication from the Minister came via the Department to GC management, and then to the board	2.75 (1.01)	2.76 (1.07)	NS
The Minister communicated with directors personally	1.72 (0.76)	1.39 (0.57)	$p<0.001$
The Minister communicated with the GC indirectly, *e.g.* through comments in the media	1.79 (0.85)	1.28 (0.45)	$p<0.001$
The Minister issued the GC with a formal, gazetted direction	1.78 (0.84)	1.62 (0.81)	$p<0.05$

Note: The first number in the column is the mean, the number in parentheses is the standard deviation. A paired-samples t-test is used for the test of significance.

We next surveyed directors on the issues raised when Ministers communicated with directors. This helps us to understand the issues most important to Ministers, and, by implication, the ones where the Minister is most likely to want to intervene. The question used the same format as the one reported in Table 4.11, involving a number of specified issues, and the same 1-4 scale. Table 4.12 summarises the frequency with which particular issues were raised by the Minister and the Treasurer, and reports whether or not a paired-samples t-test of the difference between means is significant.[14]

The results show that, first, financial performance issues (predictably) concern the Treasurer most, but clearly both are strongly interested. Second, infrequent communications on pricing issues suggest a reasonable degree of latitude being afforded to the board to make managerial decisions. Third, corporate governance issues are raised less than 'rarely' by both Ministers. This is somewhat surprising, since corporate governance ought to be one of the principal subjects of communication — the fact that it is less frequent than management issues is inconsistent with the aspirations of

136 *Corporate Governance in Government Corporations*

corporatisation. Fourth, the Minister is more likely to intervene in matters which lie within the supposed remit of GC — industrial relations, and management and operational issues. Fifth, the Minister seems much more likely than the Treasurer to intervene on the basis of interest groups considerations, which result is mirrored by the responses on industrial relations and interest group concerns. The Minister evidently perceives that his political interests are more directly affected by the GC in light of his more frequent communications on media issues.

Table 4.12 Frequency with which Ministers Raise Particular Issues

	Portfolio Minister	Treasurer	Significant at:
Financial performance issues	2.80 (1.02)	3.30 (0.89)	$p<0.001$
Community service obligations	2.22 (1.07)	2.34 (1.16)	NS
Pricing of GC services	2.16 (0.98)	2.22 (1.12)	NS
Industrial relations issues	2.62 (1.06)	1.66 (0.85)	$p<0.001$
Management issues (*e.g.*, remuneration)	2.72 (1.04)	2.12 (0.95)	$p<0.001$
Operational issues (*e.g.*, travel expenses)	2.44 (1.14)	1.84 (0.96)	$p<0.001$
Other corporate governance issues (including ethics)	1.97 (0.83)	1.89 (0.89)	NS
Major investment issues	3.11 (0.97)	3.10 (1.03)	NS
Interest group or constituency concerns	2.41 (1.04)	1.48 (0.73)	$p<0.001$
Issues concerning the GC raised in media	2.52 (1.03)	1.65 (0.78)	$p<0.001$
Conflicts between the GC and the department	2.03 (0.98)	1.92 (1.03)	NS

Note: The first number in the column is the mean; the number in parentheses is the standard deviation. A paired-samples t-test is used for the test of significance.

Are these differences driven by portfolio? There are some important differences between the portfolios. These shadow the earlier differences we saw regarding the means of communication. ANOVA tests indicate that the minister for Portfolio A is significantly more likely to raise industrial relations, operational, investment, interest group, and media-relevant issues and conflicts between the department and the GC than portfolio ministers in the other GCs. Running the same tests for the Treasurer, we find that the Treasurer was more likely to raise issues connected with community service obligations in GCs in Portfolio A,[15] but less likely to raise managerial[16] or operational[17] issues, than in other GCs. The results by portfolio for the Portfolio Minister are set out in Table 4.13. Those for the Treasurer are set out in Table 4.14.

The Government as Shareholder 137

Table 4.13 Frequency with which Portfolio Ministers Raise Particular Issues (Means by Portfolio and ANOVA)

	Portfolio A GCs	Portfolio B GCs	Portfolio C GCs	ANOVA
Financial performance issues	2.62	2.88	3.23	NS
Community service obligations	2.17	2.37	1.31	$p<0.005$
Pricing of GC services	2.08	2.29	1.69	NS
Industrial relations issues	2.92	2.47	1.54	$p<0.0001$
Management issues	2.85	2.57	2.64	NS
Operational issues	2.75	2.13	1.85	$p<0.005$
Other corporate governance issues	1.79	2.07	2.00	NS
Major investment issues	3.06	3.17	2.31	$p<0.05$
Interest group or constituency concerns	2.64	2.29	1.62	$p<0.005$
Issues concerning GC raised in media	2.91	2.23	1.79	$p<0.0001$
Conflicts between GC and department	2.31	1.91	1.23	$p<0.001$

Table 4.14 Frequency with which Treasurers Raise Particular Issues (Means by Portfolio and ANOVA)

	Portfolio A GCs	Portfolio B GCs	Portfolio C GCs	ANOVA
Financial performance issues	3.24	3.29	2.92	NS
Community service obligations	2.62	2.34	1.50	$p<0.05$
Pricing of GC services	2.23	2.22	1.90	NS
Industrial relations issues	1.62	1.64	1.80	NS
Management issues	1.89	2.26	2.58	$p<0.05$
Operational issues	1.53	2.08	1.89	$p<0.05$
Other corporate governance issues	1.84	1.84	2.10	NS
Major investment issues	3.20	3.02	2.33	$p<0.1$
Interest group or constituency concerns	1.39	1.58	1.60	NS
Issues concerning GC raised in media	1.55	1.69	1.91	NS
Conflicts between GC and department	1.95	1.93	1.40	NS

We next asked directors whether they would initiate communications with the Minister and with the Treasurer in respect of five specified issues. The issues and frequencies are set out in Table 4.15, which also reports the result of a paired-samples t-test comparing the results for the Portfolio Minister and the Treasurer. Percentages do not add to 100% because directors could cross as many boxes as they thought appropriate:

138 *Corporate Governance in Government Corporations*

Table 4.15 Circumstances Where the Board would Initiate Communications with a Minister Regarding Particular Issues

	Portfolio Minister	Treasurer	Significant at:
When the board thought a decision might raise political controversies	0.70 (0.46)	0.53 (0.50)	$p<0.001$
When the GC sought legislative action or change in government policy	0.70 (0.46)	0.67 (0.47)	NS
When significant management decisions were to be made	0.58 (0.50)	0.54 (0.50)	NS
When service levels or pricing were being revised	0.27 (0.45)	0.23 (0.42)	NS
When human resource arrangements (*e.g.*, salary levels) were being revised	0.48 (0.50)	0.26 (0.44)	$p<0.001$

Note: The first number in the column is the proportion of respondents indicating agreement with the particular response, the number in parentheses is the standard deviation. A paired-samples t-test is used for the test of significance.

There are no significant differences amongst the portfolios. There are some statistically significant differences between the responses of past and current directors in three cases for portfolio Ministers. First, as regards significant management decisions, the mean for current directors is 0.68 and for past directors it is 0.49 ($p<0.05$). Second, as regards human resource arrangements, the mean for current directors is 0.64 and for past directors it is 0.32 ($p<0.001$). For Treasurers, there is a similar, but much weaker result for human resource arrangements: the mean for current directors is 0.33 and for past directors it is 0.19 ($p<0.1$). These results all suggest increased Ministerial expectations that they be contacted regarding these issues.

These results suggest that a GC must tread with caution in political matters, to the extent it feels the need to initiate communications when issues have potential political content.[18] The finding that the Portfolio Minister is contacted more frequently is consistent with the earlier findings regarding the Portfolio Minister's higher profile in political and interest group concerns. The high proportions on such items as significant management decisions and the revision of human resource arrangements are inconsistent with the managerial and operating freedom the GC is supposed to have.[19]

We asked directors questions to shed further light on the circumstances and effects of the involvement of ministers in the GC as a test of H2. Initially, we posed a question which referred to the involvement of ministers, which did *not* presuppose that their involvement exceeded the parameters established by the GC regime.[20] This question asked the respondents to describe the effects of ministerial involvement in GC business, with reference to seven specific statements. The answers are set out in Table 4.16.

Table 4.16 Effect of Ministerial Involvement in the Business of the GC

Involvement by the Minister ...	Portfolio Minister	Treasurer	Significant at:
Increased GC efficiency	0.16 (0.37)	0.26 (0.44)	$p<0.05$
Led the GC to adopt more sound business practices	0.19 (0.40)	0.30 (0.46)	$p<0.005$
Prevented the GC from making substantial errors with markets or consumers	0.04 (0.20)	0.06 (0.24)	NS
Prevented the GC from divesting uncommercial business elements or practices	0.22 (0.42)	0.11 (0.32)	$p<0.01$
Resulted in unnecessary and more expensive operating procedures	0.43 (0.50)	0.24 (0.43)	$p<0.001$
Led to the GC losing opportunities to make good investments	0.33 (0.47)	0.27 (0.45)	$p<0.1$
Caused the GC to lose good management staff	0.19 (0.40)	0.05 (0.22)	$p<0.0001$

Note: The first number in the column is the proportion of respondents indicating agreement with the particular response, the number in parentheses is the standard deviation. A paired-samples t-test is used for the test of significance.

Table 4.17 Effect of Portfolio Minister's Involvement in the Business of the GC (Means by Portfolio and ANOVA)

Involvement by the Minister ...	Portfolio A GCs	Portfolio B GCs	Portfolio C GCs	ANOVA
Increased GC efficiency:	0.07	0.24	0.21	$p<0.05$
Led the GC to adopt more sound business practices	0.09	0.29	0.21	$p<0.05$
Prevented the GC from making substantial errors with markets or consumers	0.06	0.02	0.00	NS
Prevented the GC from divesting uncommercial business elements or practices	0.25	0.24	0.07	NS
Resulted in unnecessary and more expensive operating procedures	0.49	0.41	0.07	$p<0.05$
Led to the GC losing opportunities to make good investments	0.40	0.29	0.14	$p<0.05$
Caused the GC to lose good management staff	0.38	0.02	0.00	$p<0.0001$

140   *Corporate Governance in Government Corporations*

There is, once again, a clear (and, in places, dramatic) portfolio effect, which Table 4.17 documents.[21] A one-way ANOVA indicates that the mean proportions for the Portfolio Minister for Portfolio A, are significantly lower than for other portfolios in the case of increased efficiency and sound business practices, and significantly higher for unnecessary operating procedures, losing good investments, and, in particular, losing good managers. There are no analogous differences for the Treasurer.

We then changed the word *involvement* to *intervention*. We asked the respondents separately for both Treasurer and portfolio Minister:

> In your experience, do Ministers ever intervene informally in the management or governance of the GC (*i.e.*, other than by means of legislation, published policy, formal direction or terminating director appointments)?

Just over 50% (59 out of 117) said portfolio Ministers intervened, compared to 23% (26 out of 114) for Treasurers, a difference significant at $p<0.0001$.[22] The former result is dominated by the GCs in Portfolio A: 71% (37 out of 52) of GC directors in this portfolio said that there was informal intervention by the portfolio Minister, compared to 38% and 20% in Portfolios B and C respectively. An intriguing analysis is to partition the results by portfolio and whether or not the director is currently serving. Table 4.18 implies that the level of intervention has increased in Portfolio A from 66% to 77%, but, strikingly, has fallen in Portfolio B from 46% to 29%. The percentage is consistently low in Portfolio C.

Table 4.18 Ministerial Intervention in GC Management or Governance (broken down by Director Status and Portfolio)

		Portfolio A GCs	Portfolio B GCs	Portfolio C GCs	Total
Past directors	Ministers do intervene	20	12	1	33
	Ministers don't intervene	10	14	5	29
Current directors	Ministers do intervene	17	7	2	26
	Ministers don't intervene	5	17	7	29
	Total	52	50	15	117

We then asked directors who thought Ministers *did* intervene in GC management to specify the circumstances in which intervention was most likely. Table 4.19 sets out these responses for the Portfolio Minister and for the Treasurer.

The Government as Shareholder   141

The first possible response is the ideal case where the Minister functions as an active shareholder. The second possible response is more contestable, since it assumes that the Minister should maximise social welfare, broadly defined, rather than the value of the GC. The third and fourth indicate politically motivated behaviour. The results indicate intervention by portfolio ministers is unlikely to increase welfare. A test of significance has not been calculated, but there is a clear difference. The case for the Treasurer is more favourable, in so far as there is a lower incidence of political motivation and the smaller number of cases.

Table 4.19 Motivations and Circumstances in which a Minister Will Intervene in Management under Particular Circumstances

The Minister is likely to intervene in GC management	Portfolio A GCs	Portfolio B GCs	Portfolio C GCs
Only when it will improve GC financial performance	0 (0%)	1 (5%)	1 (33%)
Only after balancing the impact of intervening with the benefit to social welfare	3 (6%)	3 (16%)	—
In any case or issue which has a high public profile	16 (44%)	8 (42%)	—
Whenever it serves his or her political interests	14 (39%)	7 (37%)	—
The Treasurer is likely to intervene in GC management			
Only when it will improve GC financial performance	1 (8%)	2 (18%)	1 (33%)
Only after balancing the impact of intervening with the benefit to social welfare	3 (25%)	2 (18%)	—
In any case or issue which has a high public profile	3 (25%)	3 (27%)	—
Whenever it serves his or her political interests	4 (33%)	2 (18%)	—

Note: The first number in the column is the proportion of respondents indicating agreement with the particular response, the number in parentheses is the proportion of respondents selecting this response out of the total number considering that there had been intervention. Given missing responses the proportions do not add to 100%.

To shed further light on this question we asked directors to tell us how often Ministerial intervention could be characterised as political interference. Table 4.20 sets out these responses. The results suggest that the portfolio minister's interventions often constitute political interference in management.

142   *Corporate Governance in Government Corporations*

By what means do Ministers intervene without invoking their formal governance powers? This was discussed above by reference to the credibility of a minister's threat. To determine the sources of credibility we permitted directors to choose up to three out of seven possible explanations which attempt to encapsulate both formal powers explicitly reserved under the legislation as well as more informal sources of power that create leverage if a relation becomes uncooperative which. Table 4.21 sets out these explanations and reports the results for Portfolio A separately, since it is the principal focus of Ministerial intervention in the above evidence. Portfolios B and C are combined, although there are only a very small number for Portfolio C.

Table 4.20 Circumstances where Intervention by the Portfolio Minister is Political Interference

	Portfolio A GCs	Portfolio B GCs	Portfolio C GCs
Intervention by the Portfolio Minisrer ...			
Rarely or never amounts to political interference	5 (14%)	1 (5%)	2 (67%)
Sometimes amounts to political interference, but usually only on trivial issues	5 (14%)	—	1 (33%)
Sometimes amounts to political interference, and on major issues	20 (54%)	13 (68%)	—
Usually or always amounts to political interference	6 (16%)	4 (16%)	––
Intervention by the Treasurer ...			
Rarely or never amounts to political interference	3 (25%)	3 (27%)	2 (67%)
Sometimes amounts to political interference, but usually only on trivial issues	1 (8%)	1 (9%)	1 (33%)
Sometimes amounts to political interference, and on major issues	7 (58%)	3 (27%)	—
Usually or always amounts to political interference	1 (8%)	1 (9%)	—

Note: The first number in the column is the number of respondents agreeing with the particular response, the number in parentheses is the proportion of respondents opting for this item of those who thought Ministers intervened informally. The proportions do not add to 100% as there are missing responses.

Table 4.21 Attribution of Minister's Credibility to Particular Sources of Power

| | Portfolio Minister: | | Treasurer |
	A	B and C	
The Minister's reasons for intervening are usually well-based, logical and persuasive	6 (16%)	8 (36%)	13 (50%)
The Minister's threat of issuing a formal directive makes opposition fruitless	16 (43%)	5 (22%)	10 (38%)
The Minister's threat of terminating a director's appointment makes his wishes authoritative	3 (8%)	2 (9%)	1 (4%)
The Minister controls resources, customers or suppliers on which the GC depends	3 (8%)	1 (5%)	3 (12%)
The Minister can create a political environment which is adverse to GC business	14 (38%)	6 (27%)	9 (35%)
The Minister can threaten to retaliate by legislative means (*e.g.*, imposing a stricter regulatory regime)	5 (14%)	2 (9%)	1 (4%)
The Minister can generally make a major nuisance of himself	16 (43%)	6 (27%)	2 (8%)

Note: The first number in the column is the number of respondents agreeing with the response, the number in parentheses is the proportion of the respondents opting for this item of whose who thought Ministers intervened informally. The proportions do not add to 100% because more than one option could be chosen.

The results are ambiguous. Clearly, the Treasurer is more likely to be persuasive than forceful, but the source of power backing the Minister is not very clear. The threat of a directive appears significant, suggesting that there is significant scope for power within its shadow. The other item emerging with consistent support across all categories is the capacity of the Minister to create an adverse political environment. The threat to retaliate legislatively appears ineffective, which may reflect concentrated interest group opposition to changes. The results do not indicate that the threat of termination is very effective, nor that the Minister controls essential resources.

The final aspect of the survey reported here involved questions relating to conflict between the Minister and the Treasurer. Conflicts can impede the making of decisions reserved to Ministers in GCs, such as the setting of objectives. This increases costs. However, the presence of two equal shareholders can reduce the capacity of a single Minister to pursue the agenda of a particular interest group, if that agenda is opposed by the other Minister (especially where the GC opposes it). We asked directors whether the Treasurer and the Portfolio Minister have different objectives with respect to the GC. The three possible answers and the frequency with which

144   *Corporate Governance in Government Corporations*

they were selected are set out in Table 4.22, which is crosstabulated by portfolio.

Table 4.22 Differences in Objectives between the Portfolio Minister and the Treasurer

	Portfolio A GCs	Portfolio B GCs	Portfolio C GCs	Total
Their objectives are the same	11	21	11	43
Their objectives are different but those objectives don't conflict	24	19	—	43
Their objectives conflict	17	10	1	28
Total	52	50	12	114

Thus, a minority overall thought the two had the same objectives, but only a minority thought that the objectives actually conflicted. The greatest degree of unanimity is in Portfolio C. The chi-square test indicates that the null hypothesis of no association between response and portfolio is rejected at $p<0.01$. Directors who thought that there were conflicting objectives were then asked how these were resolved in practice. There were seven possible responses. One — that the opinion of the GC board breaks the deadlock — attracted no responses. The rest are set out in Table 4.23. I have limited it to Portfolios A and B for obvious reasons.

Table 4.23 Resolution of Conflicting Objectives by the Portfolio Minister and the Treasurer

	Portfolio A GCs	Portfolio B GCs	Total
The Treasurer always wins	1	2	3
The Minister always wins	2	—	2
Whichever is the most senior figure in the government wins	3	1	4
The opinion of the GC board breaks any deadlock	—	—	0
The Treasurer and the Minister log-roll (*i.e.*, they trade support from issue to issue)	1	2	3
The Treasurer and the Minister negotiate the conflict with the assistance of GC officers	2	—	2
The conflict is not resolved and the GC must steer a path between the two as best it can	7	4	11
Total	16	9	25

The Government as Shareholder

Table 4.23 records the results. The only marked impression from these responses is that conflicts are frequently *not* resolved. Otherwise, the results demonstrate much variation, suggesting that the resolution of issues varies from case to case, and company to company. There is no significant portfolio effect.

Results of Hypothesis Tests

I specified three hypotheses at the outset of this paper. H1 proposed that Ministers restrict interaction with the board and senior management to the governance functions explicitly reserved in the GC legislation. There is evidence that Ministers do intervene in various areas supposed to lie within managerial discretion. H2 proposed that non-standard Ministerial interaction increases the value of the corporation. This is a much harder hypothesis to prove or disprove. Having regard to the nature of our evidence, most directors seem to regard Ministerial interaction as being value-decreasing, and that it is sometimes motivated by political considerations. H3 proposed that non-standard Ministerial interaction with GCs does not vary between Ministerial portfolios. This is rejected by the evidence. The Treasurer is the least likely to interfere politically and is the most likely to interact beneficially and with respect to legitimate areas of concern. Amongst the portfolio Ministers, we also saw evidence of significant variation, between portfolios. This suggests that the demarcation between governance and management in GCs is not self-enforcing. It requires further reinforcement if it is to diminish non-standard Ministerial intervention.

The evidence reviewed so far in this chapter suggests that the ideal-type that is projected by the corporatisation models, in which Ministerial shareholders have defined roles in governance and in the determination of CSOs, and the board and the management are responsible for managerial and operating matters, breaks down in a range of ways. Although questionnaire evidence can only ever be suggestive, the agency costs of governance seem significant, and that the substantial intervention by ministers is unlikely to have reduced the agency costs of management.

This in turn suggests, in light of the graphical representation in Figure 4.1 of ministerial discretion and its relation to both forms of agency costs, that, first, the true level of that discretion is different to the formal level of that discretion. Second, the evidence suggests that the true level of discretion is unlikely to be set at less than the optimal level of discretion, d^*, and that it is probably also true that the formal level of discretion is not less than d^*, making the efficiency case for informal intervention weak.

146   *Corporate Governance in Government Corporations*

We turn in the next section to examine in more detail questions that extend the analysis of the relation between the Minister and the GC. The extensions consider the relation between the Ministers' departments and the GC, and then to examine a cognate question associated with the application of general government policy to GCs.

Government Corporations and Government Departments

The establishment of a GC represents a major and deliberate restructuring of a government department. One common purpose of that restructuring is to separate regulatory and policy functions from other functions which may be run as businesses. Although it will usually be the aim to establish GCs in such a way as to minimise mutual interdependencies between the GC and the government department, it is impossible for the GC and the department not to have extensive interactions over time. The department will continue to function as a regulator and often as a purchaser of services, and will provide a great deal of assistance and direction to the Minister in her direction and governance of the GC. It follows that examining how the departments and the GCs interact is a matter of primary importance to a study of corporate governance of GCs, and of the agency costs of governance.

It is difficult to predict the actual dynamics of the relation between the GC and the department. There are theories of bureaucratic behaviour that offer quite different predictions for how these competitions might be expected to be resolved. Niskanen (1971), for example, suggests that the GC CEO and the department head will both seek to maximise their budgets. Dunleavy (1991) outlines a 'bureau-shaping' theory where heads do not want larger budgets or departments per se, but prefer to build a bureaucracy that involves more discretionary activities, more responsibility for the formulation of policy, and so on. Under this theory, by contrast to Niskanen's, heads may be quite willing to get rid of cost centres to GCs, especially those generating little or no discretionary income. What is more important to the head is the capacity to build a bureau that has stronger policy influence, including influence over the activities of the GC, and greater discretion in the allocation of funds.

There is the potential for significant strategic behaviour as between the GC, the Minister and the department, as each competes for resources and responsibilities. The most likely possibility is that the department and the Minister influence the management of the GC to deliver the quantity and the price of services that maximises political support. This outcome serves a Minister's political aspirations. It also serves the Department, since it

The Government as Shareholder 147

increases its influence over the GC in the manner Dunleavy suggests. To reach this outcome, various strategies might be employed in relation to the GC, such as tying funds to particular programs, limiting either divestment or competition in certain areas, and so on. Alternatively, the GC and the Minister might form an alliance at the expense of the department. This could be done by relocating services from the department to the GC that the department might wish to retain. The Minister may do that in order to maximise microeconomic efficiency, or to shield the process from public law review. Finally, the GC and the department may collude at the expense of the Minister. Although the two may often be budget competitors, a GC which is substantially self-funding may not be a competitor. Such an alliance might involve an agreement not to expose areas of inefficiency or financial slack in the other. In light of these risks, it is important to examine how departments and GCs interact.

GCs may have to relate not to one government department, but to several. In our sample, GCs must respond to a portfolio department and to Treasury.[23] The incentives of the two departments, with respect to the GC, will presumably reflect the differences between the Ministers. We have already seen that there are substantial differences between the incentives of the Ministers. The Treasurer's interventions are more likely to align with the governance purposes envisaged by the legislation, whereas the Minister's interventions are often more explicitly political. Thus, we might expect the GC to experience greater frictions with the portfolio department than with Treasury. The result of this friction is an empirical question. It may make governance more complex because of the likelihood of unresolved issues, as we saw with inconsistencies between Ministers; on the other hand, it may limit some of the more naked forms of opportunistic governance by reason of the limit on any one Minister's control in the GC.

Evidence on Relation to Departments

We asked directors questions in separate sections regarding the GC's relations to the portfolio department and Queensland Treasury. Many of these questions have been phrased in identical terms in order to facilitate comparison by paired sample t-tests. We asked questions in relation to the portfolio department initially. The first question asked directors, 'How would you describe the nature of the working relationship between the GC and its portfolio department?' Nine statements regarding the working relation were posed, to which directors were asked to indicate the extent of their agreement on a scale of 1–5, where 5 was strong agreement and 1 was strong disagreement. We then asked eight of these nine questions about the working relationship between the GC and Treasury, excepting the statement

148 *Corporate Governance in Government Corporations*

regarding the extent to which the department viewed the GC as remaining a part of the department. Table 4.24 indicates the mean response by portfolio for the questions on the portfolio department.

Table 4.24 Aspects of the Working Relationship between GCs and the Portfolio Department (Means by Portfolio)

	Portfolio A GCs	Portfolio B GCs	Portfolio C GCs	ANOVA
Relations between GC management and the department are generally cooperative	3.85	3.94	4.21	NS
The department sometimes restricts the flow of relevant information to the GC	2.86	3.08	2.46	$p<0.1$
The department sometimes distorts relevant information between the GC and Minister	2.94	3.14	2.23	$p<0.01$
GC management sometimes withholds relevant information from the department	2.41	2.18	2.00	NS
The Minister often arbitrates disagreements between GC management and the department	2.35	2.30	2.08	NS
In disagreements, the Minister always sides with the department	3.22	2.83	2.08	$p<0.005$
The department has a good understanding of the GC's commercial environment	3.02	3.12	3.69	NS
The department has the correct understanding of the level of autonomy needed by the GC	2.73	2.82	3.62	$p<0.1$
The department considers the GC to still be largely a part of the department	3.35	3.66	1.92	$p<0.001$

Table 4.25 indicates the equivalent statistics for Treasury. Both Tables indicate whether or not an ANOVA indicates a statistically significant difference between the means. Table 4.26 summarises the results of an independent samples t-test comparing the means for Treasury and the portfolio department.

Relations between management and both Treasury and the portfolio department seem to be generally cooperative. The mean score for agreement with this statement is 3.93 (for the portfolio department) and 4.09 (for Treasury), both of which are significantly above the mean of 3 at any conventional level of significance. There are no significant differences between the portfolios.

Table 4.25 Aspects of the Working Relationship between GCs and Treasury (Means by Portfolio)

	Portfolio A GCs	Portfolio B GCs	Portfolio C GCs	ANOVA
Relations between GC management and Treasury are generally cooperative	4.09	4.02	4.33	NS
Treasury sometimes restricts the flow of relevant information to the GC	2.64	3.14	2.36	$p<0.005$
Treasury sometimes distorts relevant information between the GC and Minister	2.62	2.90	2.21	$p<0.05$
GC management sometimes withholds relevant information from Treasury	2.10	2.08	2.00	NS
The Minister often arbitrates disagreements between GC management and Treasury	2.20	2.46	2.00	NS
In disagreements, the Minister always sides with Treasury	3.04	2.85	2.62	$p<0.005$
Treasury has a good understanding of the GC's commercial environment	3.54	3.26	3.57	NS
Treasury has the correct understanding of the level of autonomy needed by the GC	3.29	2.74	3.14	$p<0.05$

However, there does seem to be evidence of uncooperative and perhaps strategic behaviour when we examine the items for restricting the flow of information. The mean value for restricting the flow of information to the GC and the mean value for restricting the flow of information between the GC and the Minister are, for the portfolio department, not significantly different from the undecided mean, 3. Moreover, the ANOVA test shows that there are differences between the portfolios. The case for information distortions seems most strongly supported for Portfolio B GCs, where the response is slightly higher than 3, and much lower for Portfolio C. By contrast, Treasury performs better. Its means across all of the portfolios are 2.82 and 2.69, both significantly different from the undecided mean of 3 at $p<0.05$ and $p<0.001$, and lower than the means for the comparable portfolio department at $p<0.1$ and $p<0.001$. The responses for Treasury continue to be lowest for Portfolio C GCs. It is predictable that the GC directors would deny withholding information from the department.

150 *Corporate Governance in Government Corporations*

Table 4.26 Differences Between the Working Relationship with the Portfolio Department and Treasury (Means by Portfolio)

	Portfolio department	Treasury	Significant at:
Relations with the department are generally cooperative	3.89 (0.82)	4.07 (0.58)	$p<0.05$
The department sometimes restricts the flow of relevant information to the GC	2.95 (0.92)	2.81 (0.89)	$p<0.1$
The department sometimes distorts relevant information between the GC and Minister	3.00 (0.95)	2.73 (0.83)	$p<0.001$
GC management sometimes withholds relevant information from the department	2.31 (0.94)	2.11 (0.74)	$p<0.05$
The Minister often arbitrates disagreements between GC management and the department	2.38 (0.96)	2.34 (0.93)	NS
In disagreements, the Minister always sides with the department	2.91 (1.07)	2.88 (0.98)	NS
The department has a good understanding of the GC's commercial environment	3.10 (1.15)	3.39 (1.07)	$p<0.01$
The department has the correct understanding of the level of autonomy needed by the GC	2.83 (1.20)	3.00 (1.09)	NS

The next two questions continued to probe issues of strategic interaction by asking directors about the role Ministers play in disagreements between the GC and the portfolio. In general, the responses indicate that neither the Minister nor the Treasurer often arbitrates disagreements between GC management and the department, and that there are no significant differences between the portfolios. The next question asked whether the Minister always sided with the department. Here, the differences are clearer. For the portfolio department and Minister, the overall mean was 2.93 — a value not significantly different from the undecided mean of 3. However, it is clear that this mean varies substantially between the portfolios, being highest for Portfolio A (3.22) and lowest for Portfolio C (2.08). The overall mean for this question for Treasury is also not significantly different from the undecided mean of 3, but there are no significant differences between the portfolios.

The final group of questions examined how the department responds to the commercial environment of the GC, and the autonomy required by commercial management. The first question was whether the department had a good understanding of the GC's commercial environment. For the portfolio departments, the mean was 3.14 — not significantly different from the undecided mean of 3. The highest portfolio mean is in Portfolio C (3.69 versus 3.12 and 3.02). Treasury's performance is considerably better. Its overall mean is 3.39, which is significantly different from both the undecided mean of 3 (at $p<0.001$) and from the mean for the portfolio departments for this question (at $p<0.01$). These results recur in the next two questions. Directors were asked whether the department has the correct understanding of the level of autonomy needed by the GC. The global mean does not vary from the undecided mean, but there is sharp variation (significant at $p<0.001$) between the portfolio means — Portfolios A and B are below the mean but Portfolio C GCs are substantially above it. Treasury's performance is not significantly different. The final question, asked only in relation to the portfolio department, was whether the department considered the GC to be still part of the department. The mean response, 3.32, is significantly above the undecided mean of 3 ($p<0.005$), and is high for Portfolio B (3.66), but very low for Portfolio C (1.92).

There are relatively few differences between the responses of current and past directors. Former directors were slightly more likely to agree that the portfolio department still considered that the GC was part of it: the mean for former directors was 3.51, and current directors 3.11, a difference significant at $p<0.1$. Current directors were more likely to agree that the Treasury understands the autonomy the GC requires: the mean for current directors was 3.24, and former directors 2.85, a difference significant at $p<0.1$.

There are, however, more differences between the responses of directors who have corporate governance experience in a listed public company. All of the t-tests producing significant results related to the portfolio department — there were none for Treasury. The results are set out in Table 4.27. They indicate that directors with listed public company experience tend to take a generally more negative view of the portfolio department. They regard the relation as less cooperative, the GC as more likely to withhold information, the Minister as more likely to side with the department, and the department less understanding of the commercial environment, the need for commercial autonomy, or its own organisational relation to the GC. As highly experienced directors, this negative view of the portfolio department is important, especially since the same respondents had a sanguine view about the effect of political change.

152 *Corporate Governance in Government Corporations*

Table 4.27 Difference in the Perception of Directors with Listed Public Company Experience of the Working Relationship between GCs and the Portfolio Department (Means by Portfolio)

	Listed experience	No Listed experience	Significant at:
Relations with the department are generally cooperative	3.48	4.09	$p<0.001$
The department sometimes restricts the flow of relevant information to the GC	3.13	2.83	NS
The department sometimes distorts relevant information between the GC and Minister	3.06	2.90	NS
GC management sometimes withholds relevant information from the department	2.58	2.14	$p<0.05$
The Minister often arbitrates disagreements between GC management and the department	2.39	2.27	NS
In disagreements, the Minister always sides with the department	3.23	2.80	$p<0.1$
The department has a good understanding of the GC's commercial environment	2.77	3.27	$p<0.05$
The department has the correct understanding of the level of autonomy needed by the GC	2.52	3.00	$p<0.1$
The department considers the GC to still be largely a part of the department	3.71	3.18	$p<0.05$

What are we to make of these findings? Relations seem cooperative, and Treasury's performance is on average better than the portfolio department, perhaps because there are fewer explicit areas of conflict. This may explain the unexpected finding that Treasury better understands the commercial environment than the department, despite the greater operational and technical familiarity that the latter presumably has. The results indicate that Portfolio B presents the most problematic set of GC-department relations. Here, the department is most likely to distort information and to treat the GC as remaining part of the department. This is surprising, in a sense, as one may have expected relations to be most problematic in Portfolio A where intervention by the Minister was most problematic. It shows that the department is by no means isomorphic with the Minister.

Government Corporations and Government Policy

GCs operate in a framework partially determined by the government at two levels — first, through the formulation of the specific corporate plan and the SCI, and second, through the decision of the government to apply its policies to GCs. In the first, government is acting as a shareholder, in the second, its role is regulatory. Nonetheless, the formulation of policy does influence the structure of governance in the GC. For example, policy may impose unnecessary restrictions on the management of the GC that inhibit optimal management or investment decisions. So, it remains to be seen how policy influences the overall level of agency costs in GCs.

Government policy may be specifically applied to GCs by legislation. Alternatively, it may be a policy applicable generally to government, which the GC complies with, either by directive or a choice to accede to an informal Ministerial request. Policy may range across a number of subjects — from matters of operation, such as policy on travel expenditure, to matters of pricing, to investment issues. When a corporation is required to comply with a policy, it may be the case that the government pays the marginal costs of compliance in a manner similar to the one used for CSOs. There is, however, no guarantee of that, and the GC may be required to bear the deadweight costs of the policy.

Subjecting the GC to general government policy should be a matter of potential concern in a number of respects. First, if the policy is directed to managerial issues, it would seem to abrogate the key principle of corporatisation regarding the conferral on the board of autonomy and authority to make commercial decisions within areas of responsibility defined by the corporatisation framework. Second, some policies may raise concerns connected with interest group politics, but without the safeguards associated with the application of public law to administrative discretions. This in turn raises issues associated with the transparency and visibility of the formulation of policy — it can be difficult to distinguish 'policy' from the sorts of informal influence exercised by Ministerial shareholders over the board that we studied above.

The Scope of Freedom and Informal Policy and Intervention

Before specifically examining policy, we asked directors a question designed to gauge the effective scope of their discretion. Policy is an explicit set of restrictions on the corporation, but there may be implicit restrictions as well, which raise transparency and accountability concerns. We asked, 'Did the GC have sufficient freedom over the services it offered and the prices it set?'. This is a fundamental issue in determining the actual degree of managerial discretion. This was asked in a section dealing with the services offered by the GC, which also dealt with CSOs. Three responses were possible:

154   *Corporate Governance in Government Corporations*

(a)   Yes, within the limitations of market competition.
(b)   The GC had sufficient freedom in theory, but exercising it was politically unrealistic.
(c)   No, the GC had insufficient freedom in both theory and practice.

Table 4.28 sets out the responses to this question (by portfolio). The chi-square is significant at $p<0.05$. Two things are notable about this table. The first is that almost 40% of the sample thought there was insufficient freedom, either in practice or at the formal policy level. This is a high percentage, and if their opinions are accurate, the deadweight costs of the corporatisation regime may be substantial. Second, it is notable that the responses for the Portfolio C are dichotomised — there are no responses in the intermediate category, whereas a quarter of the responses in the other portfolio fall into this category. It implies that Portfolios A and B are the portfolios where there is likely to be substantial informal authority exerted that limits the effective scope and authority of the management and the board. This is consistent with the results above, regarding the incidence of informal intervention in the management and governance of the GC.[24] Concerns about insufficient managerial freedoms varied substantially between the different GCs, perhaps reflecting different interest group pressures. It seems that policy can be a major imposition on the operations of the GC, and that it can be both implicit and explicit.

Table 4.28 Freedom in Relation to Services and Prices (by Portfolio)

	Portfolio A GCs	Portfolio B GCs	Portfolio C GCs	Total
Sufficient freedom	24	35	8	67
Freedom in theory only	13	12	—	25
Insufficient freedom	13	4	4	21
Total	50	51	12	113

Deadweight Costs of Government Policy

The government may often have the power to impose policy on GCs. That is true in Queensland, which incorporates a directive mechanism, by which policy can be mandated. The government may do this for reasons that are not necessarily consistent with the commercial motivation the GC's board is expected to pursue. We surveyed directors on the question, 'Did other government policies generally represent a constraint on corporate management policies (such as local industry content, travel and entertainment expenses)?'. Directors were given four possible responses:

The Government as Shareholder 155

(a) Yes, government policies were a major constraint on such corporate policies.
(b) Government policies were a constraint, but not much more than in the private sector.
(c) We were aware of, but generally did not worry about, these government policies.
(d) We weren't aware of the government's policies.

Table 4.29 indicates the responses by portfolio. More than a quarter of the sample regarded policies as a major constraint on corporate policies, and only a handful of respondents fell into the 'did not worry' or 'were not aware' categories. Although the effect is not significant, the incidence of respondents regarding policies as being a major constraint was lowest in Portfolio C — less than 7%, compared to 30% in Portfolio B.

Table 4.29 Effect of Government Policies (by Portfolio)

	Portfolio A GCs	Portfolio B GCs	Portfolio C GCs	Total
Policies a major constraint	17	15	1	33
Not much different to private sector	32	28	13	73
Did not worry about policies	3	4	1	8
Weren't aware of policies	1	3	—	4
Total	53	50	15	118

Table 4.30 crosstabulates the responses according to whether or not the directors are current or former directors. The results are striking and important — they reveal that current directors are *more* likely to regard government policies as a major constraint than former directors. The latter were, for their part, more likely to ignore the content or the existence of the policies. This result is highly significant ($p<0.001$). It is common, in other results, for current directors to take a more favourable view of the GC or of the government than past directors. For this result to run in the opposite direction suggests that problems with the present application of government policy to GCs had increased over time.

156 *Corporate Governance in Government Corporations*

Table 4.30 Effect of Government Policies (by Director Status)

	Current directors	Former directors	Total
Policies a major constraint	23	10	33
Not much different to private sector	30	43	73
Did not worry about policies	–	8	8
Weren't aware of policies	1	3	4
Total	54	64	118

Table 4.31 reveals that this effect is pronounced in Portfolios A and B, but is not apparent in Portfolio C. The responses of directors with listed public company experience are practically identical to the responses of the other directors.

Table 4.31 Effect of Government Policies (by Portfolio and Director Status)

		Current director	Former director	Total
Portfolio A	Policies a major constraint	11	6	17
	Not much different to private sector	11	21	32
	Did not worry about policies		3	3
	Weren't aware of policies		1	1
Portfolio B	Policies a major constraint	11	4	15
	Not much different to private sector	11	17	28
	Did not worry about policies		4	4
	Weren't aware of policies	1	2	3
Portfolio C	Policies a major constraint	1		1
	Not much different to private sector	8	5	13
	Did not worry about policies		1	1
	Weren't aware of policies			
	Total	54	64	118

If government policies do impose excessive deadweight costs on the GC, how do GCs respond to these policies? The GC may choose to submit, or to try to have the policy changed. If it chooses the latter, it may succeed or it may fail. We therefore asked directors to tell us how they responded. The question we asked was, 'Where government policies represented a constraint, how was this handled?'. We gave directors five choices:

The Government as Shareholder 157

(a) The GC adopted the policy without complaint.
(b) The GC tried to negotiate a more appropriate policy, without success.
(c) The GC succeeded in negotiating a more appropriate policy.
(d) We tried to get government to pay the compliance costs of the policy like a CSO, but without success.
(e) We succeeded in getting government to pay compliance costs as if it were a CSO.

The responses reflect the fact that the GCs attempt to renegotiate the policy may have two different aims — either change to the substantive policy, or seeking funding for marginal compliance costs. Table 4.32 sets out the responses to these questions. It shows that attempts to seek incremental funding for policies are infrequent and rarely successful. Otherwise, three quarters of the respondents indicated that they sought to renegotiate the policy — acquiescence is relatively infrequent, but for every success in renegotiation there are two failures. The GCs in Portfolio C are again different from Portfolio A and B, in so far as renegotiations there were far more successful.[25]

Table 4.32 Response to Government Policies (by Portfolio)

	Portfolio A GCs	Portfolio B GCs	Portfolio C GCs	Total
GC adopted policy without complaint	4	13	3	20
GC tried to negotiate policy without success	28	19	3	50
GC succeeded in negotiating policy	12	10	6	28
Tried to get government to pay compliance costs without success	3	3	–	6
Got the government to pay compliance costs	–	1	–	1
Total	47	46	12	105

What is the relationship between the perception of how constraining government policies were, and the response to government policies? In order to reduce the degrees of freedom, and to permit a more reliable test, the data were recoded. First, the effect of the policy was recoded either as a major constraint, or not — those saying they ignored or weren't aware of the policies were treated as not regarding the policy as a major constraint. Second, the response to the policy was recoded into three categories — adoption without complaint, successful renegotiation, and unsuccessful renegotiation. The latter two categories included attempts to change the

158   *Corporate Governance in Government Corporations*

substantive policy or to seek compliance cost funding. The results of the crosstabulation are set out in Table 4.33.

Table 4.33 Relation Between Effect of and Response to Government Policies

	Adopted without complaint	Unsuccessful renegotiation	Successful renegotiation	Total
Policies a major constraint	3	25	3	31
Policies not a major constraint	17	31	26	74
Total	20	56	29	105

The results indicate that when policies are thought to be a major constraint, the most common reaction is to seek to renegotiate them, but success in doing so is very rare. For other policies, the GC sometimes acquiesces, but more often it seeks renegotiation. What is important is that successful renegotiations are concentrated in those cases where policies are *not* major constraints. The chi-square statistic for the crosstabulation is significant at $p<0.001$.

In the following chapter, we shall return to examine other issues connected with the interface between government policy and interest group politics, with particular reference to industrial relations. For now, though, we may conclude that the formulation of policy is likely to be attended by substantial agency costs of governance. The evidence on policy is consistent with the earlier evidence of Ministerial intervention, and shows how the corporatisation parameters can be circumvented in a range of complex ways that are not wholly transparent.

Conclusion

Five points can be made in conclusion. First, the analysis in this chapter shows why the governance structures of GCs may not and often should not emulate those of listed public companies. The governance problems are different, and there are no markets to discipline GC governance structures which generate excessive agency costs of governance. The need to control *two* sets of agents limits the norms capable of transplantation from private companies to GCs.

Second, corporatisation regimes have started from a sound premise of defining the roles and responsibilities of the ministerial shareholder and the

The Government as Shareholder 159

management. However, the parameters embodying those delineations are not self-enforcing. There are a range of ways by which a minister may exceed those parameters. The introduction of government departments creates new possibilities of strategic behaviour.

Third, empirical evidence confirms that Ministers do exceed governance parameters, and some of this behaviour is likely to lead to high levels of agency costs of governance. What, however, is less clear is the precise source by which they are capable of exceeding these parameters — it seems to have less to do with threats made in the shadow of formal authority than one might perhaps expect.

Fourth, government departments interact in a complex way. There is evidence of uncooperative and strategic behaviour, including the distortion of information and evidence of recurring 'turf wars'. These are likely to contribute to the agency costs of governance.

Fifth, there is evidence that the application of government policy to GCs increases the agency costs of governance. The evidence is consistent with the suggestion that policy is formulated for reasons that are not consistent with minimising the agency costs of management, but are instead motivated by political considerations. In the next chapter, we examine some of these issues in more detail by examining the role of stakeholders in the GC, and their impact on the management and governance of the firm.

Notes

1. This claim is also consistent with economic theories of property rights (Alchian 1965; Demsetz 1967; De Alessi 1969, 1973).
2. For full legislative references, see Chapter 2, note 2. NSW: ss. 20H-20I; Qld: ss. 71, 76, 77. In Tasmania, the second Minister is the Minister responsible for administering the Act: Tas: s. 3. In other jurisdictions, no explicit bi-Ministerial governance structure is provided for, rather, the Act refers in a general fashion to both the Treasurer and the responsible Minister. The ACT legislation provides for multiple shareholders, all of whom must be Ministers: ACT: s. 13(1)(a).
3. Qld: s. 96; NSW: s. 20J (for statutory SOCs only); Vic: s. 25; Tas: s. 11 and Sch. 5; in the ACT, appointments are made by the voting (minister) shareholders: s. 12, Sch. 3, Pt II, s. 3.
4. Qld: ss. 106–108 (Corporate Plan), 116–120 (SCI); NSW: ss. 21, 22 (SCI); Vic: ss. 41 (CP), 41 and 42 (SCI); SA: ss. 12 (CP), 13 (SCI); Tas: ss. 39–40 (CP), ss. 41 (SCI); ACT: ss. 19, 20 (SCI); and Cth: s. 17 (CP).
5. Qld: ss. 95, 98.
6. Qld: ss. 121, 122; NSW: ss. 11, 20N(3); SA: s. 12; Tas: Pt 9; Vic: s. 45.

160 *Corporate Governance in Government Corporations*

7. Qld ss 123–124. Other jurisdictions provide the Minister power to issue directions in the public interest: NSW: ss. 20O, 20P; Vic: s. 16(c); Tas: s. 65; ACT: s. 17; Cth: ss. 28 and 43.
8. We shall return to side-deals in more detail below.
9. Moreover, even if interventions are undesirable, they do not necessarily involve rent-seeking. One example is where a Minister desires to cultivate an image of political 'toughness' by bringing to heel a substantial organisation. A second example might be the relevance of particular concerns or causes that the Minister has strong private preferences, such as a concern with social justice.
10. Korn/Ferry International (2000) report that 33% of the top 15% of companies (by sales) had nomination committees.
11. See chapter 3, pp. 82–88 *supra.*
12. There is a similar correlation between the consequences of not meeting the SCI goals and the role of the board in monitoring compliance with those goals. The results are not reported.
13. There are statistically significant differences between the responses of past and current directors in three cases for portfolio Ministers. First, as regards communications between Ministers and individual directors, the mean for current directors is 1.96 and for past directors it is 1.51 ($p<0.01$). Given the problems associated with such communication processes — they imply an element of lobbying — this is not a desirable change. Second, as regards indirect communications, the mean for current directors is 1.55 and for past directors it is 1.93 ($p<0.05$) (the reverse of the first result, with more positive implications). Third, as regards gazetted directions, the mean for current directors is 1.6 and for past directors it is 1.88 ($p<0.1$). There are also differences for the Treasurer. First, as regards communications between Ministers to the board routed formally through the chair, the mean for current directors is 3.46 and for past directors it is 3.05 ($p<0.05$). This improvement is appropriate. There is also a weakly significant result for gazetted directions, similar to that for the portfolio Minister.
14. There are some statistically significant differences between the responses of past and current directors in three cases for portfolio Ministers. First, as regards financial performance issues, the mean for current directors is 2.6 and for past directors it is 2.96 ($p<0.1$). Second, as regards CSOs, the mean for current directors is 1.91 and for past directors it is 2.32 ($p<0.05$). Third, as regards management issues, the results go the opposite way: the mean for current directors is 3.14 and for past directors, it is 2.34 ($p<0.001$). Fourth, as regards operational issues, the mean for current directors is 2.8 and for past directors it is 2.02 ($p<0.001$). Fifth, as regards GC-department conflicts, the mean for current directors is 1.81 and for past directors it is 2.17 ($p<0.1$). There are also differences for the Treasurer. There are similar, but weaker differences for management and operational issues, and much the same result for GC-department conflicts. The other significant result is that the mean for current

The Government as Shareholder 161

directors for corporate governance issues is 2.04 and 1.74 for past directors, which is weakly significant ($p<0.1$).

15. The means for the portfolios were: A 2.62, B 2.34, C 1.90. The difference is significant at $p<0.05$.

16. The means for the portfolios were: A 1.89, B 1.84, C 2.10. The difference is significant at $p<0.05$.

17. The means for the portfolios were: A 1.53, B 2.08, C 1.89. The difference is significant at $p<0.05$.

18. There are some statistically significant differences between the responses of past and current directors in three cases for portfolio Ministers. First, as regards significant management decisions, the mean for current directors is 0.68 and for past directors it is 0.49 ($p<0.05$). Second, as regards human resource arrangements, the mean for current directors is 0.64 and for past directors it is 0.32 ($p<0.001$). For Treasurers, there is a similar, but much weaker result for human resource arrangements: the mean for current directors is 0.33 and for past directors it is 0.19 ($p<0.1$).

19. GC legislation constrains human resource policies. A GC Board must have an 'employment and industrial relations plan' which must include remuneration arrangements (including for senior executives') Qld: ss 171(1) and (3)(a)(i). This is included in the SCI which requires Ministerial approval for change. Thus, it is arguable that Ministers are *required* to be contacted where the matter is not consistent with the plan.

20. We used three different words in the course of the survey: involvement, intervention, and interference. Intervention is a subset of involvement, as interference is of intervention.

21. There are some statistically significant differences between the responses of past and current directors, but only for the Treasurer, not for the portfolio Minister. First, as regards the Minister increasing efficiency, the mean for past directors is 0.18 and for current directors it is 0.33 ($p<0.1$). Second, as regards preventing divestiture, the mean for current directors is 0.2 and for past directors it is 0.38 ($p<0.05$). Third, as regards unnecessary operating procedures, the mean for current directors is 0.13 and for past directors it is 0.33 ($p<0.05$).

22. There is no statistically significant difference as between current and past directors' responses.

23. Other departments may also have regulatory responsibility over the GC.

24. It should be noted that, in this respect, there are no significant differences between the responses of either current and former directors or the responses of those who have experience in corporate governance in a listed company, and those who do not.

25. There are no significant differences between the responses of former and current directors.

Chapter 5

Stakeholders and Corporate Governance

The role of stakeholders in corporate governance is one of the essential axes around which have revolved the principal contributions to the literature on corporate governance. The economic literature has been characterised by an emphatic rejection of the proposition that any group of stakeholders, other than equity investors, have a role to play in corporate governance. That proposition follows from the theory of contracting, and the recognition of special difficulties of the shareholders. By contrast, a literature emerged to attack that normative claim which was inspired by communitarian theory (Mitchell 1996). That literature sought to draw attention to the need for the law's agenda to expand beyond a single constituency. The interests of employees, creditors, customers and the community were emphasised in this literature. Blurring the line between these two bodies of theory is the work on comparative corporate governance. Here, scholars working in economic paradigms emphasised the contingency of the Anglo-American model in which equity investors are paramount, by examining the greater importance of employees and other constituencies in other jurisdictions, including Japan and Germany (see, *e.g.*, Gilson and Roe 1993; Macey and Miller 1995; Roe 1993).

How do these literatures fare when they are applied to corporate governance issues in GCs? Two points can be made. First, a distinct class of equity investors no longer exists. As we saw in Chapter 3, that greatly complicates the evaluation of alternative proposals or of action by management, directors or Ministers. Second, the 'publicness' of the corporation arguably endorses the 'public interest' as the criterion for action by, and in relation to, GCs. Because, however, the concept of the public interest is much harder to express than the interests of shareholders, it may give way to an approach that favours a range of stakeholder constituencies. Each constituency represents a part of the public.

Set against this approach is the premise that corporatisation is intended as a means of reforming government and emphasising efficiency in the use of resources. A sophisticated application of this approach is not necessarily

Stakeholders and Corporate Governance 163

inimical to the interests of stakeholders and other public constituencies, since corporatisation should permit means by which those public interests may be served. One such mechanism, much used in the modern corporatisation model is the community service obligation (CSO), which allows the public interest associated with the satisfaction of the needs of particular constituencies to be recognised and fulfilled.

How we resolve issues associated with stakeholders is important at a number of levels associated with the governance of the firm. It influences the content of the standards we apply to determine the legitimacy and appropriateness of action by managers, directors, and Ministers, in GCs. At another level, it determines the need for, and importance of, mechanisms such as the CSO in the governance of the GC, and in the distribution of any profits it makes. The role of stakeholders influences the basic but vital issue of the constitution of governance processes in the firm. We saw in Chapter 3 that the background and experience of directors in GCs is greatly variable. One's view on the role of stakeholders will determine one's view of the backgrounds appropriate or desirable in appointees to the board. The role of stakeholders may also shape substantive law issues associated with the standing of members of the public to invoke any available grounds of judicial review (Stearns 2002).

Below we analyse these questions in more detail, we begin by examining the important issue of interest group politics and its relation to the GC. We then examine some empirical evidence associated with the effect of interest group politics on governance processes in the GC. We focus particularly on the role of employees and their representation in governance. We then examine the role of the CSO and its capacity to intermediate between efficiency and the satisfaction of stakeholders' desires.

Interest Group Politics and Stakeholders

What role do interest groups play in GCs, and how do they affect management and governance? This issue is unfortunately the subject of rather extreme views. On the one hand, advocates of privatisation take the view that the only means of controlling interest group politics is by taking business enterprises out of government and subjecting them to provision in the marketplace (Shapiro and Willig 1990). This view neglects, of course, a range of interest group issues associated with the process of privatisation, such as the deals that are cut in order to clear the way for privatisation, the distribution amongst interest groups of the proceeds from the privatisation, and the political ends that privatisation serves. By contrast, the more

164   *Corporate Governance in Government Corporations*

enthusiastic endorsements of corporatisation, as an end in its own right, rather than as a halfway house to privatisation, have often neglected to address this issue in full detail.

The role of interest group politics in society is evaluated in different ways. On the one hand, theories of pluralism regard interest group politics as desirable because it provides opportunities for citizens to be represented and to play some role in political processes. Theories of public choice take the opposite view. These theories, which were highly influential in the reorientation of public provision in the 1980s and 1990s, regard success in interest group politics as being determined, in substantial part, by the effectiveness of interest group organisation (Buchanan and Tullock 1965; Stigler 1971). Typically, smaller groups are more effective than larger groups, and the political process is one which enables these smaller groups to engineer the redistribution of wealth in their favour.

How these theories reconcile with corporatisation is not satisfactorily addressed in the literature or in policy documents. It is possible to argue, on the one hand, that conferring a higher degree of management authority on the board of directors of a GC is a way of liberating public provision from the competition for rents between interest groups. Some of the factors which might be thought to support this view are the existence of the CSO mechanism, in order to make explicit the magnitude of a subsidy benefiting an interest group. It is also possible to argue, on the other hand, that GCs are meant to make it easier for interest groups to influence public provision. They do this by extricating the bureaucratic decisions regarding provision from the control mechanisms of public law while ensuring that the Minister has a range of reserve powers which can be invoked to influence the outcome of interest group competition. The analysis below is based on the approach, close to the first argument, that GCs are meant to give primacy to allocative efficiency over redistribution. Although they are not and cannot be immune from interest group politics, they should be subject to governance mechanisms to make subsidies and other interest group benefits explicit. Interest group politics may be expected to affect both the agency costs of management and the agency costs of governance in the same direction. That is, the fewer the constraints on rent-seeking by interest groups, the higher one would expect both forms of agency costs to be. Ministerial shareholders are more likely to make inefficient decisions exercising their governance powers, and managers and directors are more likely to make inefficient decisions that favour interest groups.

A Review of Earlier Evidence of Interest Group Politics

In earlier parts of the book, the empirical evidence has suggested a range of findings which resonate with a model of active interest group politics. These are consistent with interest group politics and related political considerations having some influence on management and governance in GCs. We summarise the most important of these here. First, we have seen that Ministerial shareholders communicate with their boards on political and interest group considerations, that they become involved in the management and governance of GCs in a manner outside the parameters of the legislation, and that these interventions are not regarded as adding value to the GC.

Second, we found a relatively high level of tolerance for directors who deliberate or vote on transactions raising interest group questions. Generally, fiduciary duties are not well-mated to the reduction of interest group activity in the management and governance of the GC, however well-suited they may be to other forms of self-interest seeking.

Third, the portfolio Minister plays the dominant role, vis-à-vis the Treasurer, in selecting and appointing directors to the GC. The portfolio Minister is likely to have closer contact to the interest groups active in the industry. On the other hand, interest groups do not seem to have direct involvement in the appointment process in the vast majority of cases.

Fourth, although in the minority, some directors considered that their political or representative skills were highly relevant or relevant to their appointment. A related group were encouraged by the opportunities to represent sectional interests, and regarded it as their duty to do so. Similarly, a small number of directors indicated that they were encouraged to become directors because of the opportunities for involvement of Ministers.

Fifth, a significant group of directors thought that one of the effects of undercompensating CEOs was to make them more amenable to the making of decisions that improve their political reputation.

Sixth, there is a a high level of director turnover associated with change in the party forming government; that level of turnover is likely to render directors more amenable to responding to political considerations. This is supported by the qualitative evidence that political controversy is likely to result in a director being terminated or not reappointed.

Finally, a substantial minority of directors believe that the Minister and the Treasurer have conflicting objectives for the GC. This is not evidence of rent-seeking per se, but is likely to reflect the influence of different constituencies. Consistent with this finding is the fact that the GC is

166   *Corporate Governance in Government Corporations*

unlikely to have any role in resolving the conflict, which suggests the importance of political considerations to resolution.

Further Evidence of Interest Group Politics

In light of the above evidence, we sought more specific evidence on two issues — the extent and significance of lobbying of directors by interest groups and the extent to which politicians or Ministerial shareholders applied pressure in relation to management decisions for political reasons. To examine the first question, directors were asked, 'In your experience, do customers of the GC actively lobby board members or management in relation to the extent and pricing of services?'. Directors were asked to select one of four responses — (a) frequently; (b) sometimes; (c) only rarely; (d) no, never. Table 5.1 sets out the responses by portfolio. It is apparent that lobbying is common, a result which is a matter of concern since it directly implicates the board in interest group activity. There are no statistically significant differences between the portfolios, but there are differences between some of the GCs within individual portfolios (not reported).

Table 5.1   Lobbying of Board Members or Management by Customers (by Portfolio)

	Portfolio A GCs	Portfolio B GCs	Portfolio C GCs	Total
Frequently	6	11	2	19
Sometimes	21	24	7	52
Only rarely	16	10	3	29
No, never	10	6	3	19
Total	53	51	15	119

There are differences between the responses of current and former directors. If we code the responses on a scale of 1–4, where four is frequently and 1 is never, the mean for current directors is 2.81, and for former directors is 2.35. The t-statistic for that difference is statistically significant $(p<0.01)$. This suggests increased lobbying, a result that is important as one would not expect that current directors should be biased in favour of reporting lobbying.

The next issue, closely connected to lobbying, is the question of whether directors functioned as advocates for different constituencies. We asked directors the following question, 'Did any individual members of the

Stakeholders and Corporate Governance 167

board specifically act as advocates for particular customers or users?'. The three possible responses were:

(a) Yes, some directors always acted as advocates for particular constituents.
(b) Some directors were open to lobbying, but were not natural representatives.
(c) No.

Table 5.2 reports the responses to this question. It shows that directors were the least likely to function as advocates in Portfolio C (although the chi-square statistic is outside the range of statistical significance), but that a quarter of the directors were of the opinion that some board members did function in a partisan way. Again, results by GC show sharply variable patterns in relation to director advocacy.

Table 5.2 Advocacy by Board Members for Customers or Users (by Portfolio)

	Portfolio A GCs	Portfolio B GCs	Portfolio C GCs	Total
Yes, some directors always advocated particular constituents	12	5	1	18
Directors open to lobbying	4	7	–	11
No	38	39	14	91
Total	54	51	15	120

When we relate the responses regarding the prevalence of customers lobbying the board with the existence of directors who advocated sectional interests, we find a predictable coincidence. Directors were most likely to be advocates when customers lobbied more frequently. Table 5.3 shows the crosstabulation. The chi-square statistic is significant at $p<0.01$. The intuition is consistent with the sense of public choice theory — that the best-organised lobby groups are likely to be the most effective in the political process — and demonstrates its application to GCs.

168 *Corporate Governance in Government Corporations*

Table 5.3   Relation between Lobbying and Advocacy by Directors

	Frequently	Sometimes	Rarely	Never	Total
Yes, some directors always advocated particular constituents	5	12	1	–	18
Directors open to lobbying	4	5	2	–	11
No	10	35	26	19	90
Total	19	52	29	19	119

The next question focusing on interest group politics related to the influence brought to bear on directors in determining the services provided by the GC. We have already seen that Ministerial shareholders significantly influence the management and governance of the GC, and that this can occur outside the parameters of the corporatisation model. We can probe therefore the extent to which this influence specifically addresses political issues. We asked directors the question, 'Did your GC ever experience pressure to provide services for political reasons (*e.g.*, extra services or staffing in specific marginal electorates)?'. We offered three responses.

(a)   Yes, irrespective of whether this coincided with commercial objectives.

(b)   Yes, but only if it coincided with commercial objectives.

(c)   No, there was never any issue of political pressure for services.

Before presenting the results, this question is affected somewhat by a low response rate — only 86 directors responded out of the 121 subjects. Obviously, the question is a sensitive one. We can only speculate about what the other respondents would have said. The directors of the Portfolio C GCs were most likely not to respond to this question — only 6 out of 15 responded. From their other answers, it appeared that the level of interest group politics in these GCs was low, so those who did not answer were probably likely to say no as well. By comparison, the response rate of the directors in Portfolios A and B was close to 80%. For the directors in these GCs who did not answer, it is possible that, since they could answer no, the number of persons choosing affirmative answers may understate the actual percentage in the population. The results are presented by portfolio in Table 5.4.

Stakeholders and Corporate Governance

Table 5.4 Political Pressure on Services (by Portfolio)

	Portfolio A GCs	Portfolio B GCs	Portfolio C GCs	Total
Yes, whether commercial or not	11	14	–	25
Yes, if commercial	4	4	–	8
No	23	24	6	53
Total	38	42	6	86

Forty per cent of directors responding to this question reported political pressure, and the large majority of these responses fell into the first category where the pressure was in spite of commercial objectives. Although there are no statistically significant differences between the portfolios, compiling the results by GC indicates that the level of political pressure is very high in some specific, high-profile GCs. These experience a very high level of political pressure, which is likely to be at odds with the proper operation of the corporatisation regime. The response rate was somewhat lower for current directors (34 out of 55, compared to 52 former directors out of 66), but the difference in the political pressure they report is not statistically significantly different. Of the twenty directors with listed public company experience who responded, nine said there was pressure notwithstanding commercial objectives (45%), and the remainder said there was no pressure. By comparison, of the 66 other respondents, only sixteen said there was pressure notwithstanding commercial objectives (24%), but all eight of the directors who said there was pressure if the services were commercial justified came from this category of director (12%). The difference in responses between these director classes is weakly significant at $p<0.1$.

How is the incidence of political pressure regarding services related to the lobbying of board members? One might expect a strong correlation — political pressure is bound to be related to the lobbying of politicians by interest groups, which is simply a slightly less direct form than lobbying the board. When responses are crosstabulated, this expected correlation is strongly supported. The results are set out in Table 5.5. As it shows, there is a clear relation between the extent to which the board is lobbied and the political pressure on services to which the board is subject. The chi-square statistic (19.595, $df=6$) for the differences in response between these director classes is significant at $p<0.005$. To test the association in a slightly different way, Spearman's ρ statistic (a non-parametric coefficient of correlation) is 0.335, which is significant at the same level. The relation between political pressure and the existence on the board of directors who advocated sectional interests is weaker. Table 5.6 sets out the

170 *Corporate Governance in Government Corporations*

crosstabulation. The chi-square statistic (8.689, df=4) is only weakly significant at p<0.1, and Spearman's ρ statistic is not significant.

Table 5.5 Relation between Political Pressure on Services and Lobbying of Board Members

	Frequently	Sometimes	Rarely	Never	Total
Yes, whether commercial or not	12	7	5	1	25
Yes, if commercial		6	1	1	8
No	6	22	16	9	53
Total	18	35	22	11	86

Table 5.6 Relation between Political Pressure on Services and Directors Advocating Interest Groups

	Natural advocates	Open to lobbying	No advocates	Total
Yes, whether commercial or not	5	3	17	25
Yes, if commercial	2	3	3	8
No	9	3	41	53
Total	16	9	61	86

In Chapter 4, we examined the freedom that directors considered they had in relation to the services offered by the GC. Directors could answer that there was sufficient freedom, that there was not, or that the exercise of the freedom was politically unrealistic. How is this variable related to the other interest group considerations examined in this section? First, we can examine its relation to lobbying of the board or management. The crosstabulation is not reported, and the relation is not significant. Second, there is a significant relation between sufficient freedom in relation to goods and services and to the existence of interest group advocates or representatives on the board. This is reported in Table 5.7. The chi-square statistic is significant at the $p<0.05$ level, as is also true of the Spearman's ρ statistic.

Stakeholders and Corporate Governance   171

Table 5.7   Relation between Sufficient Freedom on Service Levels and Directors Advocating Interest Groups

	Natural advocates	Open to lobbying	No advocates	Total
Sufficient freedom	8	5	54	67
Freedom in theory only	3	5	17	25
Insufficient freedom	7	1	13	21
Total	18	11	84	113

Finally, when freedom regarding the services offered by the GC is related to political pressure, we see a very clear result — the more pressure applied to render services for political purposes, the less generic freedom the GC has on its service and price levels. Table 5.8 reports the cross-tabulation. The chi-square statistic for the differences in response is significant at $p<0.0001$. Spearman's ρ statistic is also significant at a similarly high level.

Table 5.8   Relation between Political Pressure on Services and Sufficient Freedom on Service Levels

	Sufficient freedom	Freedom in theory only	Insufficient freedom	Total
Yes, whether commercial or not	4	13	8	25
Yes, if commercial	3	3	2	8
No	38	6	8	52
Total	45	22	18	85

In Chapter 4, we studied factors influencing the decision of directors to accept appointment and the expectations they had at the time. One factor studied, the results of which were reported in Table 4.4 and following, was the expectations regarding the constraints that would be imposed by the government on the operations and governance of the firm. We saw that about a quarter of directors had no expectations; of the remainder about 40% thought operations and governance would be constrained in inefficient ways. How is this factor related to the evidence studied in this section? There is a clear relation between expectations of inefficient constraints and political pressure regarding services. Table 5.9 sets out this relation, the chi-square for which is significant at $p<0.05$. Table 5.10 also shows that expectations of inefficient constraints are also related to the existence of sufficient freedom in the level and price of services offered. Those

172 *Corporate Governance in Government Corporations*

expecting those constraints were slightly more likely to report the lowest level of freedom ($p=0.056$). In this sense, then, expectations regarding political involvement are relatively accurate.

Table 5.9 Relation between Political Pressure on Services and Expectations Regarding Inefficient Constraints by Government

	Expected constraints	Didn't expect constraints	No expectations	Total
Yes, whether commercial or not	8	14	3	25
Yes, if commercial	–	5	3	8
No	23	14	16	53
Total	31	33	22	86

Table 5.10 Relation between Sufficient Freedom on Service Levels and Expectations Regarding Inefficient Constraints by Government

	Expected constraints	Didn't expect constraints	No expectations	Total
Sufficient freedom	16	36	15	67
Freedom in theory only	12	9	4	25
Insufficient freedom	10	5	6	21
Total	38	50	25	113

The final subject of interest is to study the relationship between these interest group variables and the presence of informal intervention by Ministers which we studied in chapter 4. First, there are no significant relations between the degree to which the board is lobbied, or the presence of sectional advocates on the board, and the incidence of Ministerial intervention. There are however significant relations between the incidence of Ministerial intervention and both the incidence of political pressure and the degree of freedom on services and pricing. Table 5.11 records the crosstabulation of the incidence of Ministerial intervention (by the portfolio Minister) and the incidence of pressure to provide services for political reasons. It shows how Ministerial intervention occurs most in the cases where directors reported political pressure. The chi-square statistic is

27.952 (df=2), which is significant at $p<0.000001$. The equivalent crosstabulation for the Treasurer is not significant.

Table 5.11 Relation between Political Pressure on Services and Incidence of Informal Intervention by Ministers in Management and Governance

	Minister intervenes	Minister does not intervene	Total
Yes, whether commercial or not	22	3	25
Yes, if commercial	6	2	8
No	13	37	50
Total	41	42	83

Table 5.12 shows these results in a slightly different way. It divides results by portfolio, and aggregates those directors who said there was no pressure with those who said there was pressure but only where it could be commercially justified (in order to address the relatively small numbers in the latter categories). It shows how these trends carry consistently through Portfolios A and B.

Table 5.12 Relation between Political Pressure on Services and Incidence of Informal Intervention by Ministers in Management and Governance (by Portfolio)

Portfolio		Minister intervenes	Minister does not intervene	Total
A	Political pressure	11	—	11
	No uncommercial pressure	14	11	25
B	Political pressure	11	3	14
	No uncommercial pressure	4	23	27
C	Political pressure	—	—	—
	No uncommercial pressure	1	5	6
	Total	41	42	83

If we then examine the relation between the incidence of Ministerial intervention and the degree of freedom on services and pricing, we see a similar story, although it is not as strong. Table 5.13 shows the crosstabulation. It shows that those companies least affected by Ministerial intervention are the most likely to have freedom in services and pricing. The chi-square statistic is significant at $p<0.05$.[1]

174　　*Corporate Governance in Government Corporations*

Table 5.13 Relation between Sufficient Freedom on Pricing and Services and Incidence of Informal Intervention by Ministers in Management and Governance

	Minister intervenes	Minister does not intervene	Total
Sufficient freedom	27	38	65
Freedom in theory only	17	8	25
Insufficient freedom	13	7	20
Total	57	53	110

This evidence indicates that, for at least some of the GCs in the sample, interest group politics affects the agenda of board deliberations and constrains products offered and levels of service. This shows the significant challenges to a GC regime in insulating the management of the GC from political influence. As we saw in the general analysis of Ministerial shareholders, the governance parameters established by the legislation are often bypassed.

Labour Policies

In this section, we examine the case of a specific interest group, labour, and its involvement in the corporate governance of GCs. Labour is obviously a critical interest group, because of its relatively high degree of concentration in firms and its topicality in analyses of comparative corporate governance. In addition, the role of labour is particularly important in the context of this sample, since the positions of the two principal sides of politics in Queensland (as in Australia generally) are substantially at odds with each other in their relation to labour interests and trade unions. The Australian Labor Party, as the name suggests, is very close to the interests of organised labour, whereas the conservative Liberal and National Parties are historically much less accommodating to labour interests.

In the context of other questions on government policy (with a focus on industrial relations and staffing), we asked directors, 'Did the GC have sufficient liberty to make decisions to maximise the workforce's productivity (*e.g.*, on issues such as retrenchments, enterprise bargains, and equality of employment opportunity)?'. Directors were given three possible responses — yes, no, and 'It depended which party was in government'. The answer to this question is important, as a negative answer is likely to suggest the effectiveness of labour interest groups in maximising the welfare of workers, even at the expense of the operational efficiency of the GC. For the answer to depend on the party in government suggests that

Stakeholders and Corporate Governance 175

labour, as an interest group, is partially successful, but not under all circumstances. Table 5.14 sets out the responses by portfolio.

Table 5.14 Liberty to Maximise Workforce Productivity (by Portfolio)

	Portfolio A GCs	Portfolio B GCs	Portfolio C GCs	Total
Yes	28	30	13	71
No	19	16	2	37
Depended on government	7	5	—	12
Total	54	51	15	120

The results show that 87% of the directors in Portfolio C GCs generally regard themselves as having sufficient liberty to maximise workforce productivity. This may reflect the different workforce composition of these GCs, being more professional and less blue-collar. The situation is different in the other portfolios — that percentage falls to 50–60%, and over 30% say no. There is a relatively small group of about 10% in Portfolios A and B who take the view that it depends which party is in government. There is a slightly higher percentage of former directors opting for the negative or party-dependent answers, but the differences are not significant. There are, however, quite different responses from directors who have had corporate governance experience in a listed public company. As Table 5.15 shows, only 42% of these directors responded affirmatively, compared with 65% of the other directors. The chi-square for the Table is significant at $p<0.05$.

Table 5.15 Liberty to Maximise Workforce Productivity Related to Corporate Governance Experience in a Listed Public Company

	Listed experience	No listed experience	Total
Yes	13	58	71
No	11	26	37
Depended on governmt	7	5	12
Total	31	89	120

Table 5.16 reveals a two-way breakdown of the responses by portfolio and listed company experience. It shows how a majority of directors in Portfolios A and B with listed company experience tend to take a negative view on workforce (sixteen out of 25 said no, or that it depended on the government, compared to 30 out of 79 of the other directors). In view of

176 *Corporate Governance in Government Corporations*

their greater experience, these directors' opinions carry weight. The results suggest that the combination of explicit government policies on industrial relations and the informal intervention of the Minister and other parts of the government are likely to circumscribe the flexibility of the GCs to maximise productivity of the labour force.

Table 5.16 Liberty to Maximise Workforce Productivity Related to Corporate Governance Experience in a Listed Public Company (by Portfolio)

		Portfolio A GCs	Portfolio B GCs	Portfolio C GCs	Total
	Yes	6	3	4	13
Listed	No	6	4	1	11
experience	Depended on govt	3	4	–	7
	Yes	22	27	9	58
No listed	No	13	12	1	26
experience	Depended on govt	4	1	–	5
	Total	54	51	15	120

We also find a correlation between sufficient liberty to maximise the productivity of the workforce, and sufficient freedom regarding the services offered and prices charged. We explored the latter issue in Chapter 4.[2] Table 5.17 shows the crosstabulations of these two sets of responses. It indicates that those thinking there was sufficient liberty on pricing and services were highly likely to take the same view on the workforce. Those taking negative views on the former question were also likely to take a negative view in relation to the workforce. The chi-square statistic is 21.771 ($df=4$), significant at $p<0.001$. Only 48 directors — 43% of the sample — supported the proposition that there was sufficient liberty to maximise the value of the corporation in both services and pricing, and labour utilisation. This result is important as it suggests that GC efficiency is compromised because of the proximity of the political sphere in which labour is one, but not the only, effective lobby group.

Table 5.17 Crosstabulation of Liberty on Pricing and Services and Freedom to Maximise Workforce Productivity

| | *Sufficient freedom to maximise workforce productivity?* | | | |
Services and pricing:	Yes	No	Depends on govt	Total
Sufficient freedom	48	10	8	66
Freedom in theory only	10	12	3	25
Insufficient freedom	8	13		21
Total	66	35	11	112

We asked directors what their opinion was regarding the competence and efficiency of the employees of the GC. The question asked was, 'Which of the following best describes the GC managers and staff?'. Directors could choose between the following options:

(a) Staff are generally as efficient as any in private sector employment.
(b) Staff are generally as efficient as any in public sector employment.
(c) Staff vary significantly — some are highly efficient; others are substandard.
(d) Staff seem generally below the standard appropriate for the business.

The purpose of the question was to gauge the extent to which any concessions obtained by labour affected the quality of the staff employed by the GC. For example, a commitment to union labour or to workplace contracts being negotiated at the enterprise level (rather than the individual level) may deter highly productive staff from accepting employment in the GC. Table 5.18 sets out the results. It indicates, fortunately, that no director selected the latter option, and over half the respondents chose the former option. Nonetheless more than a quarter of directors selected the third option, and fifteen per cent chose the former option, which may be thought to damn with faint praise. Table 5.18 reveals that there are no strong portfolio effects. However, when examining results by GC, views diverged markedly from organisation to organisation within portfolios. There are no significant associations with the director's experience in listed public companies.

Table 5.18 Efficiency of Staff Productivity (by Portfolio)

	Portfolio A GCs	Portfolio B GCs	Portfolio C GCs	Total
Staff are as efficient as any in the private sector	28	26	11	65
Staff are as efficient as any in the public sector	8	9	2	19
Staff vary significantly	17	15	2	34
Total	53	50	15	118

The final question asked was whether there was a labour or union representative on the board. Labour representatives are rare phenomena in the boards of English-speaking countries. Their presence in GCs would be an articulate demonstration of the greater influence that labour has in GCs than in BCs. Table 5.19 indicates how the responses are divided by portfolio. They are most prevalent in the miscellaneous corporations ($p<0.05$). There is a trend towards the appointment of more labour representatives — twelve of the 66 former directors said there was a labour representative on the board, compared to twenty of the 54 current directors ($p<0.05$). Curiously, there is an apparently off-setting trend — there is a correlation between directors who sit on boards with labour representatives and personal experience in a listed public company — 13 of the 31 directors with that experience reported that they sat on boards with labour representatives, vis-à-vis the 19 of 89 directors lacking that experience ($p<0.05$). Such a balancing of experience makes good intuitive sense if we believe that the biases of the two offset each other while extending the expertise and representativeness of the GC board. The results do not show any significant relation between the existence of a labour representative and the efficiency of staff or the liberty to maximise labour efficiency.

Table 5.19 Labour Representative on the Board (by Portfolio)

	Portfolio A GCs	Portfolio B GCs	Portfolio C GCs	Total
Representative present	14	10	8	32
No representative	40	41	7	88
Total	54	51	15	120

The Community Service Obligation

The CSO mechanism is a device which permits GCs to fulfil more explicitly 'public' functions which a firm driven only by profit maximisation imperatives would be unable to pursue. To recap earlier analyses, it works by allowing the government to require the GC to undertake action thought to be in the public interest, typically with the requirement that the government explicitly fund the marginal cost of the mandated obligation to the GC. It is an important safety valve for interest groups. It allows interest groups to compete for wealth transfers, but imposes the discipline that these be explicitly costed, and, thus, transparent in their application.

However, the CSO mechanism suffers from several problems. The first is that it may be evaded, through informal pressure or other forms of intervention by the Ministerial shareholder or other politicians. If pressure can be brought to bear on the GC to supply certain services, the use of a CSO is unnecessary. We have already seen that Ministers can and do wield significant influence on the management of the firm, and that this can certainly extend to services provided and prices charged.

Second, CSO funding can function as a cross-subsidy. That is, the CSO funding may exceed the marginal cost of the obligation undertaken, on the implicit understanding that the balance is used as a subsidy for some other form of activity demanded by an interest group but which is less justifiable as a publicly funded CSO. This is conceivable if estimation of marginal cost is difficult, which will often be the case. The GC is often a monopoly provider of services, so the existence of comparable market prices will not be readily available.

Third, a CSO will be insufficiently state contingent (Quiggin 2003). That is, the mandate imposed will not be differentiated for future changes in the state of the world. It may be both efficient and equitable to alter the content of the CSO in future states of the world, such as expanding the services provided, or altering prices. This places a great deal weight on the ability and willingness of both the government and the GC to be capable of ex post adaptation. Neither of these things should be assumed in light of the political incentives of the government, and the weak sensitivity of GC managers to the public interest.

We have seen in earlier empirical evidence, set out in Table 4.12, that CSOs are a surprisingly infrequent subject of communication between Ministers and the board of directors. Of the issues we surveyed directors on, the only subjects that portfolio Ministers raised *less* often were the pricing of services, corporate governance issues, and GC-department conflicts. The Treasurer, by contrast, raises the issue appreciably more

180 *Corporate Governance in Government Corporations*

often — only financial performance and major investment issues are raised more often.

We asked directors whether or not their GC had CSOs. Of the directors in Portfolios A and B, over 70% of directors indicated that they did. We then asked these directors to give their opinion on the pricing of the CSO. The question asked, 'what is the most accurate description of how CSOs were priced?' Four responses were offered:

(1) The GC overpriced the CSO.
(2) The GC set a competitive market price for the CSO.
(3) The GC was constrained to underprice the CSO.
(4) I don't feel I can answer this question.

The fourth option was included to reflect the possibility that some directors did not have the basis for an opinion on the subject. Table 5.20 sets out the responses divided by portfolio:

Table 5.20 Over- or Underpricing of CSOs (by Portfolio)

	Portfolio A GCs	Portfolio B GCs	Total
Overpriced	—	1	1
Competitive price	15	18	33
Underpriced	10	11	21
No answer	10	7	17
Total	35	37	72

Barely any directors believe that the CSOs are overpriced. If that is true, then it is unlikely that the CSO funding cross-subsidises other activities. Twenty-one of the 57 directors (evenly divided across the portfolios) who specifically stated an opinion, thought the CSO funding underpriced the goods, which may reflect a preference of the Ministers to use informal influence to avoid the CSO mechanism where possible and apply the CSO funding to other uses that yield higher payoffs. Thirty-three thought the price competitive. When examining the distribution of these responses across different GCs, opinions vary within the GC.

A Theoretical Examination of Stakeholders in Corporate Governance

We have so far limited most of our analysis to aspects of the role of interest groups in the practice of corporate governance in GCs. We have not yet considered the normative analysis of the case for such participation, so that we must reserve opinions regarding the appropriateness of the extent of the participation we have observed in practice. Our analysis below asks the question whether specific participation in corporate governance is the best means of protecting identifiable vulnerabilities of different constituencies associated with the GC.

Creditors

In the absence of a defined class of equity investors capable of participating even minimally in corporate governance, we may ask whether lenders to the GC should have any specific rights in corporate governance. The answer is negative. Often, GC's obtain their debt finance in part from governmental treasury corporations or similar governmental sources; in view of the governance entitlements in the hands of the government, no further rights appear to be needed. Where GCs significantly 'out-source' their finance requirements through public or private debt markets, the case for conferring additional governance entitlements is not very great. There is no reason creditors cannot protect themselves sufficiently against expropriation by contractual means, as is the norm in private lending. In general, one would expect that GCs, typically having monopolistic qualities to their business, have relatively low financial risk, which decreases further the case for additional governance entitlements.

Employees

Much of the advocacy of communitarian approaches to corporate governance implicitly predicates on labour interests. In some respects, however, the specific agenda of these scholars has been rather overtaken by the realities of many modern corporations. As Rajan and Zingales (2000) points out, the balance of power in the modern corporation has switched from the owners of capital to those employees capable of creating value through their investments of human capital in match with the other assets of the firm. However, this has been achieved independently of specific representation at the level of the board of directors, since it arises instead from the power associated with their ownership of their own human capital.

The case for granting additional rights in the governance of the GC to a wider class of labour interests is mixed. First, the GC is likely to be under either substantial governmental control or regulation which constrains substantially the scope for innovation and extensions into new business practices. Thus, the likelihood of creating substantial value through human capital investments is more limited than in entrepreneurial firms. As such, the existence of special vulnerability is likely to be substantially attenuated.

182   *Corporate Governance in Government Corporations*

On the other hand, to the extent that the GC is a monopoly, there may be limited market opportunities for the manager, enabling the manager the protection of walking away. There is some scope for opportunism, although as explained in the context of senior managers above, the incentive for senior managers or governments to engage in this form of opportunistic quasi-rent-seeking is very limited given their own weak property rights in the firm.

What we do know about the entitlements of employees in GCs and state owned enterprises, especially monopolies, generally is that their wages do tend to be higher on average than those paid in the private sector (Peoples 1998; Wachter *et al.* 2001). There are no consistent corresponding productivity improvements that have been linked with these higher wages. Although there are some risks associated with such comparisons, it is probably arguable that it may be undesirable to give labour further governance entitlements at board level because of the risk that these will be used to drive up wages and otherwise improve conditions.

That said, if we think about 'governance' in broader terms than just seats on the board, to include a corporation's systems of self-regulation, employee interests and values are ubiquitous. Corporations' self-regulatory processes include the procedures, policies and norms applicable to those who work for and deal with the corporation. These processes are adopted to decrease the risks of legal liability, but also to create an incentive compatible environment encouraging participants in the firm to add value to it, and finally, to implement those social values and concerns validated and internalised by the corporation (Parker 2002).

Employees' values are important in these contexts, since much of the self-regulatory system will be directed at them, and social values are most likely to be internalised when they resonate with those of the employees. It is clear that self-regulatory systems may sometimes be used as a means for the imposition of the values of the management. However, Christine Parker (2002) shows the potential for, and instances of the realisation of, more inclusive self-regulatory systems. Unlike the matter of employee representation on the board, it is impossible to oppose or criticise more inclusive internalisations of employee values in self-regulatory processes. It is however also impossible to be uniformly positive in one's own assessment of their welfare implications. Assessment is primarily context-specific. Moreover, where GCs are natural monopolies, it seems unlikely market forces will demonstrate which self-regulatory systems add value and which do not. We should therefore take an open-minded view of self-regulation that draws on employee values while watching for inefficiencies.

Customers

To what extent should customers of a GC be represented formally in its governance processes? As we have seen, the public interacts with GCs in two capacities — as residual claimants and as consumers of essential services. As such, the explicit representation of consumers in governance processes has an ostensible justification, especially where the GC is a monopoly. In these situations, the consumers are deprived of a market alternative, which deprives them of an important sanction — to withhold their business. The obvious problem, however, is one of collective action. How are customers to appoint an appropriate representative, and to ensure that the representative gives faithful service? To the extent that the government takes it upon itself to choose the representative, it has an incentive to select a representative from an influential interest group within the body of consumers. Such a representative may not share the preferences of the larger body of consumers, and will be likely to indulge his own interest group in interacting with the GC.

The other issue that also diminishes the case for representation of customers is the availability of the political process as a means by which the preferences of customers can be satisfied. Although it may be true that the management of GCs and its efficiency are highly unlikely to carry many votes in an election, that is arguably less true of the level and cost of GC services. Recent utility crises in California and New Zealand demonstrate that these service levels are a matter of much public interest and circumstances can cause them to carry significant votes. It is arguably preferable that the political process be used for representing the views of customers, compared to governance processes, as it allows greater transparency and visibility to the distribution of rents amongst interest groups, and it forces increased reliance on the use of CSOs. By contrast, absorbing that process into governance per se is likely to be less desirable. Subsidies become hidden, and the board's efficiency motivation is increasingly confused by distributional obligations.

As with employees, self-regulatory systems present a way of embodying the values and concerns of consumers without conferring explicit governance representation. One way is through a Corporate Justice Plan (Parker 2002) — a public document formed after a period of consulting consumers that confers a series of substantive and procedural rights — the service they are entitled to expect and the machinery for addressing complaints and wrongs. The SCI is a way of committing the GC to both a process of consultation and a timeline for implementation. Over time the SCI can be used to set goals for the Justice Plan, such as a decrease in the number of complaints made and the time taken to resolve them.

184   *Corporate Governance in Government Corporations*

Local Communities

Some GCs may have interactions with local communities that involve significant idiosyncratic investments by that community. An example might be a township that is the site of a regional electricity generating plant. That plant may be the dominant source of economic activity and investment in that town. Accordingly, the town may make significant efforts to invest in facilities and infrastructure that are idiosyncratic to the GC. As such, it is susceptible to opportunistic behaviour by the GC (Williamson 1985). This is arguably one of the situations that states a stronger case for some form of protection, because the political process may not provide much protection to the extent that there are only a relatively small number of voters in the rural seat.

However, it is unlikely that representation in corporate governance is the appropriate response to this problem. In the circumstances, unless the town was given a majority of seats on the board it is unclear how much the problem could be reduced by one or two nominee members. It would seem no less effective for the parliamentarians from the affected region to lobby the government in order to forestall action by the GC likely to harm the interests of the country town or to provide compensation for affected interests. If that action must be taken, lobbying is also appropriate to provide a series of remedial responses to the economic dislocation likely to occur, as part of policy on regional development. Simply because the action affects only one or two seats directly does not mean that such action has no political capital elsewhere. It can be taken up as a more general issue of rural politics.

Managers

As noted elsewhere, it is a tenet of modern corporate governance practice that a board needs to be in the hands of independent non-executive directors. That provides the necessary rigour for the board to monitor and control management, and so economise on the agency costs of management. That is also an article of faith in most Australian GCs where executive directors are extremely rare. It is worth considering whether there is a case for giving the GC's senior managers a greater degree of representation at the board level. We saw in Table 3.5 that most directors disagreed with the proposition that there should be more inside directors. However, the case for it is stronger than might first appear. The case for non-executive directors in BCs is a consequence in part of the impossibility of shareholders functioning in governance roles: some form of representational mechanism is essential. The situation is, however, quite

Stakeholders and Corporate Governance 185

different in a GC where Ministers have clear governance functions allocated to them, supported by their respective departments. In those circumstances, the role of the GC board, compared to the BC board, is likely to focus more on issues of performance (managerial and strategic issues) and less on issues of conformance (governance and compliance). As such, the case for increased use of executives is quite strong, since evidence supports the proposition that the presence of inside directors can be beneficial in some circumstances (Klein 1998).

Put more formally, to the extent we accept that increased use of executive directors increases agency costs of management, the advocacy of such a move must depend on the proposition that it would decrease the agency costs of governance by an equal or greater amount. How would this work? It works at two levels — the first is to recognise that the net agency costs of management associated with greater executive involvement are offset in part by the arguably greater capacity of managers to add value to board level decisions. The second point is that the agency costs of governance may be reduced substantially by the presence of managers who are likely to be less partisan than more representative appointments,[3] have more proficiency with corporate governance, and have stronger incentives than non-executives to be associated with a GC that is performing well. So, on balance, the strongest normative case for providing expanded representational opportunities is surprisingly associated with top executives.

Conclusion

Our analysis so far has revealed that stakeholders have a significant influence on the governance of GCs, as part of a larger process of interest group politics. Interest groups impact on governance both directly by their representation on boards and their lobbying of board members, as well as indirectly through their lobbying of Ministerial shareholders. Our evidence provides us with limited opportunities to specifically evaluate the direct effects of these interest groups, but there is evidence that some directors regard themselves as having insufficient freedom in relation to service levels and that there is political pressure on services. These factors are inconsistent with the guiding principles of corporatisation.

The mechanism designed to mediate between efficiency and the demands of different stakeholders is the CSO mechanism. However, as we have seen, in practice, CSOs are vulnerable at several levels. The first is that the extent of the Minister's informal power can circumvent the need to use them. The second is their vulnerability in changing situations. The third

186   *Corporate Governance in Government Corporations*

is the possibility that they can be used as a cross-subsidy for other activities, potentially upsetting the principle of competitive neutrality. Although not dispositive of the latter question, directors surveyed doubted the CSO cross-subsidises other activities of the GC.

The concluding theoretical analysis considers the argument that the scope for allowing stakeholders an explicit role in the formal corporate governance processes of the GC is actually quite limited even though self-regulatory processes can protect legitimate interests of these shareholders. The existence of investments in match that might support a stronger role in corporate governance are largely absent from GCs. This is compounded by the intense difficulties with the severe collective action problems associated with establishing proper processes for representing stakeholders. In the next chapter, we examine whether there are other roles that stakeholders and the GC's constituencies might possibly serve.

Notes

1. If the two categories, insufficient freedom and sufficient freedom only in theory — are combined, the chi-square is significant at $p<0.01$.
2. See Table 4.28.
3. However, to the extent that senior managers' tenure in GCs tends to be tied to the life of a government, managers may be just as partisan as some community appointments.

Chapter 6

Reforming Government Corporations

Whether one likes it or not, the state-owned enterprise, including the government corporation, remains an important part of the economic apparatus of virtually every country. That is especially true of jurisdictions which have yet to develop strong markets, and rely on greater levels of public ownership to overcome weak property rights. The balance between public and private ownership has of course shifted a great deal in the past two decades; however that shift is not completely unidirectional. Moreover, corporatised government enterprises can remain an important part of the landscape, since in the cases of partial privatisations (*e.g.*, Sidak 2002), the entity in question is poised half way between a BC and a GC. For these reasons, it is important to conclude this book with an examination of some of the means by which the integrity of corporate governance in GCs can be improved.

The mechanisms which enhance the integrity of corporate governance in BCs are often connected with the market. There are limited opportunities for markets in GCs. However, some opportunities for market governance can be built into the GC. This is obviously true of partially-privatised corporations, but other opportunities exist in this respect with wholly government-owned GCs, especially in relation to debt finance.

Other instruments useful for improving corporate governance fall into what might be described as the 'self-enforcing' category (Telser 1980). That is, the incentives created by the allocation of rights between the parties should encourage those rights to be optimally exercised. Recent scholarship emphasises the role of self-enforcing rights in corporate governance (Hart 1995).

Self-enforcing regimes can be difficult to create. In these circumstances, one depends more on the existence of administrative or hierarchical processes. The board of directors' power over senior managers is an example. In these cases, the crucial issues are the existence of the necessary prudential legal constraints that prevent managers from overreaching, the reinforcement of these by business ethics, and the

188   *Corporate Governance in Government Corporations*

selection of persons to participate in these processes with backgrounds and qualifications which increase the likelihood of the behaviours desired. The reforms discussed in this chapter draw from all three categories — market mechanisms, self-enforcing rights, and hierarchical processes. Initially, we focus on the role of finance and capital markets in GCs. We then turn to examine aspects of the contract between the managers and the GC, followed by the functioning of the board, and, finally, the governance functions of the Minister and the executive government.

Finance

Since the seminal research of Merton Miller and Franco Modigliani (1958), there has been significant interest in how the financing of a corporation impacts on the welfare of its shareholders. Research in this area has extended beyond the original focus on whether some mix of debt and equity was apt to minimise the firm's cost of capital, to analyse the larger question of the relation between finance, governance and agency costs.

For finance to matter, there must be some form of market imperfection or transaction cost. This follows from Miller and Modigliani's (1958) insight that debt and equity were simply different ways of dividing the cash flows of given assets: put simply, the pie was the same, only the slices were different. There are two imperfections of particular importance — the costs of financial distress and agency costs — each of which acts as a limit on the other. A company that becomes financially distressed necessarily incurs substantial costs. These are associated with the liquidation of the firm or the reorganisation of its claims. In addition, a financially distressed firm is likely to forfeit the economic surplus associated with 'firm-specific' investments, such as in human capital and specialised fixed assets which generate income through complementarities with other assets. Whereas generic assets can normally be sold at low or zero discounts to their value to a corporation, investments that are made 'in match' with other assets stand in the opposite situation and the surpluses associated with them ('quasi-rents') may disappear. Because the probability of financial distress increases with the amount of debt in the capital structure the expected costs of financial distress are likely to increase with leverage (Williamson 1996).

Agency costs (of management) work in the opposite direction. Jensen (1986) asserts that a principal source of agency costs is free cash flow — discretionary resources which are not precommitted. Free cash flow enables managers to consume excessive perquisites, to invest in projects which do not return their risk-adjusted cost of capital, and so on. Unlike equity, where returns paid to investors are discretionary, the use of debt finance bonds the firm to pay out free cash flow. Relatedly, debt is thought to create stronger incentives for managers because they are at greater risk of losing control of the firm, which they value highly. The trade-off between the two sources of costs is apparent in Figure 6.1. The curve, A, represents agency costs, and F represents the costs of financial distress. C is the combined cost of capital. Total cost of capital is minimised at c^*, at the ratio of debt to value of d^*/V.

Figure 6.1 Costs of Financial Distress and Agency Costs with respect to Leverage

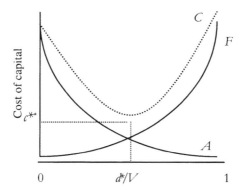

Debt as a proportion of total value

In applying this analysis to the GC, we must qualify both arguments for the effect of what has been called the 'soft budget constraint' problem. In describing the inefficiencies associated with enterprises in centrally-planned economies, Kornai (1992) noted that incentives were distorted by providing finance to ailing enterprises, such as for political and paternalistic reasons. The essential governance problem is how an investor, when making an initial decision to invest, can credibly commit not to provide finance when it is clear that the investment as a whole has a negative net present value. In a government context, for instance, obtaining this sort of commitment would discourage many enterprises if their proponents knew the finance 'tap' would be turned off ex post; it would provide a discipline on interest groups seeking government programs and politicians proposing them. The problem is that ex post, the investments that have already been made, being sunk, become irrelevant to a decision what to do *next* (Dewatripont and Roland 1999). It may be best to continue with projects that demonstrate that they were unworthy of finance ex ante.

190   *Corporate Governance in Government Corporations*

When we apply this theory to GCs, we can see how a given level of debt need not reduce agency costs as much as in a BC. This is because the budget constraint is soft — the likelihood that a government would permit a GC to become insolvent, and for there to be an auction of the assets, is quite low. Therefore, the disciplinary effect of the debt on reducing agency costs is reduced. This is enhanced when the government itself provides the loans, because these will be easier to reorganise than is true when the GC's debt is held by other creditors. It follows from this explanation that the costs of financial distress will also increase with leverage at a slower rate than in a BC. Figure 6.2 is representative:

Figure 6.2   Changes in Agency Costs and Costs of Financial Distress in a GC

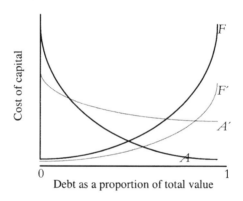

The total cost function, C', has not been drawn because the locus of its turning point is less clear given the flatter shape of A' and F'. C' could even be flat. Whether or not it is true that C' lies at all points above C, it is likely that $c^{*'}$ will lie above c^* (that is, the minimum cost of capital is lower for a GC than the minimum cost of capital for the most closely comparable BC), since the benefits associated with reduced agency costs will not cut in. Also complicating matters is the extent to which the agency costs of *governance* vary with the capital structure of the firm. This is not immediately clear. The most credible argument is that the agency costs of governance probably behave similarly to those of management — they probably diminish as debt rises. However, the agency costs of governance are very difficult to entangle from the soft budget constraint, since it is the government's capacity to soften the budget constraint that permits undesirable interventions to occur.

Reforming Government Corporations

That said, it is likely to be desirable for GCs to be subject to stronger discipline from the use of debt in its capital structure if this can be conjoined with harder budget constraints. First, it reduces the agency costs of management. Second, it may also reduce the agency costs associated with governance by Ministers if the budget constraint is difficult to change ex post. The stronger the incentives and the harder and less changeable the budget constraint on a GC, the harder it is for Ministers to interfere in the governance of GCs in suboptimal or politically motivated ways. The costs of such behaviour become higher, because the firm is more likely to experience a default. Third, more debt means less (state) equity, decreasing the drain on the public purse to fund the GC. The question becomes how the achievement of such outcomes is possible in the public sector?

We surveyed directors on issues associated with the hardness of their budget constraints. They were surveyed on the extent to which they agreed with the following propositions, based on a scale of 1–5, where 1 is strong disagreement, and 5 is strong agreement:

(1)　The scale of dividends and debt repayments disciplines the management to act effectively

(2)　The GC was confident the government would always bail it out if it became insolvent

Both proposals elicited varying responses. The mean response to question 1 was 3.45, which is significantly different from the mean of 3 (undecided) at $p<0.001$. The mean response to question 2 was 2.31, which is significantly different from the mean of 3 (undecided) at $p<0.001$. There is no significant portfolio effect for either question.

The responses arguably indicate that budget constraints in GCs are not soft. It is, however, important to be skeptical. First, we also asked directors if the provision of finance from the state treasury corporation was 'a major advantage compared to the cost of capital in the market'. The mean response to question 1 was 3.31, which is significantly different from the mean of 3 (undecided) at $p<0.01$. Such finance softens the budget constraint. Second, it may be the case that the government would not bail out the insolvent GC. But, more significantly, it is unlikely to permit it to get to that position. Third, the selection bias is likely to overestimate the hardness of the budget constraint in order to justify the value a director adds to the corporation.

It is possible and desirable to harden budget constraints. This can be done in two ways. The first is to make it harder to refinance a firm that is technically in default. This can be done by requiring that a GC obtain relatively more of its debt through normal capital markets, rather than from

192   *Corporate Governance in Government Corporations*

government. In this way, it is more difficult to refinance these loans by restructuring the term or the repayments. To refinance them, the lenders may have to be paid out, which will be less attractive for both management and government. In this way, debt has a greater disciplinary effect.

The second is to simulate the effects of default. The greatest incentive effect of debt is the fact that management loses control of the firm to the creditors if it cannot pay them as promised (Hart 1995). Therefore, even if it is the case that for public policy reasons, the government would never permit a creditor to foreclose on a security comprised of public infrastructure, it remains possible to simulate the effects of foreclosure *for GC management*. Thus, where government needs to refinance debt that management has defaulted on, the hands of government and the GC must be tied so that the CEO's tenure terminates forthwith. That therefore creates a stronger set of incentives for management, since his or her control becomes performance-contingent. Although this creates substantial risks in a competitive market environment, it does create essentially the same environment that private firms are likely to face.

This rule could also be applied to the directors as well, although if the firm is to remain a GC, the need for continuing 'corporate memory' indicates that only some proportion of the directors be sacked. In this case, which directors should be compulsorily terminated? One possibility is to terminate those closest to the end of their term. However, that rule will have little incentive effect when the director was appointed by a previous government given the high level of turnover. The alternative possibility is to terminate a randomly selected group. A concern is that such a rule might claim the best directors on the board. There is no obvious selection method. For example, giving the board the power to confer immunity from the random selection on one or two directors does not provide any guarantee that the best directors will survive. It is more likely simply to prolong the existence of those with the widest support base. For these reasons, it may be preferable simply to allow the Minister to make his own decisions in relation to termination, but with a proviso that some fraction of the board should remain for purposes of continuity and retaining corporate memory.

GCs should also be encouraged to develop plans for exchanging equity for debt. That is, they should be encouraged to repatriate over time the state's equity investment, and to satisfy new capital requirements from lenders, up to some target leverage set by comparison with similar private firms. This diminishes the free cash flow in the firm by substituting, for annual dividends, one-off capital reductions. This repatriates capital back to the state, where it may be used for other forms of social investment or to reduce the level of taxation. This is a form of partial 'privatisation' preferable in some respects to the sale of public assets — it creates cash

Reforming Government Corporations 193

flow by reducing the amount of the state's investment, and the disciplinary qualities of debt produce stronger incentives than those which are likely to be available by disseminating the rights of control to many diffused shareholders.

Another way to use the firm's capital structure to strengthen optimal incentives in the firm is to make use of puttable, subordinated debt ('PSD') (Skeel 2003). PSD involves the use of debt financed instruments the priority of which would rank below the GC's other debt. PSD is sold with an explicit put option that enables its holders to put it back to the GC at a specified price (which would be referable to the amount paid). The rationale for using PSD is that, first, it provides capital market monitoring. The value of the debt will constantly be analysed, since the holders will wish to exercise the put and sell to the GC where the debt's market value falls below the exercise price under the put option. Second, it strengthens the incentives to which the GC is exposed to maximise the value of the firm, because of the costs imposed on the GC should the holders decide, en masse, to put their securities back to the firm. Indirectly, this heavy cost hardens the firm's budget constraint.

The PSD proposal has its origins in proposals for the reform of the banking sector in the United States (Wall 1989). It was seen as a device to force the hand of regulators. One of its criticisms was the perception that it might contribute to 'runs' on the banking system given the tendency for problems in the banking system to occur on a systematic, non-random basis. As Skeel (2003, p. 113) points out, that criticism is less likely to be true of GCs.

Managers

Is it possible for the contracting process between managers and the GC to be finessed so that it improves the incentives of managers? In a BC, the usual answer is to incorporate incentive compensation into the contract so that the manager equates his effort at the margin with its effect on the value of the corporation. As we have seen, that is much harder in the GC because of the absence of a reliable index of the value of the firm that can be used to determine compensation. If one does not rely on incentive compensation, because of the absence of such indices, the only possible sources for incentives for the manager to manage well are public-spiritedness, personal ethics, and the effect on his market value as an executive. If one does rely on substitute measures for value, the risk, as we have seen, is that the manager will devote effort to maximising the substitute, but not the GC's value, so crowding out those forms of management behaviour that might

194   *Corporate Governance in Government Corporations*

increase value (King 2003). The additional problem is that the greater the stakes the CEO faces, so far as incentive compensation is concerned, the higher the chance that the CEO and the Minister collude. For example, the CEO may seek to persuade the Minister to exercise his governance powers in ways that allow the CEO to maximise his bonuses, but which do not increase social welfare (Dixit 2000). It is therefore not entirely clear which of these alternatives are preferable. Much may depend on the availability of proxies for value, which may be very limited in some GCs, but greater in others.

One possible means of improving the incentives of managers is to remunerate them for taking actions which, for example, harden their budget constraints. Examples include paying out higher dividends than those agreed in the SCI, or swapping debt for equity. The manager is being rewarded for a commitment to harden the budget constraint and minimise financial slack. One potential risk of such a proposal is a final period problem. That is, managers are prone to commit the firm to pay a high dividend or to swap debt for equity if they are in their final period, knowing that they can reap the benefits of higher compensation without bearing the future costs to the GC associated with paying out these cash flows.[1] This would appear to counsel the need for the bonuses paid for these pledges to be made in the form of deferred compensation (contingent on the GC continuing to achieve some defined target, whether that be solvency, or meeting some or all of its future profit targets). Of course, the tendency for GC management to be tied to the term of a party in government means that similar effects are possible in any event but compensation arrangements should preferably not exacerbate these.

The third possibility is to provide for financially defined grounds of termination for the GC CEO, rather than allowing this to be a source of discretion for the board or the Minister. The less discretionary the process is, the less susceptible it is to renegotiation with the Minister and the less likely the incidence of side-deals in order for the Minister to achieve political ends in return for prolonging the manager's tenure. If the CEO is eligible for termination, he would then have to compete with other candidates for the position.

Many of the other prudential constraints associated with modern corporate governance are surely relevant here, too. These include the need for aspects of senior managers' appointments to be subject to the scrutiny of a dedicated subcommittee of the board of directors, such as an executive compensation committee. We shall return later to some of these aspects when we examine the board of directors.

Contractual aspects of the CEO's appointment are affected by issues concerned with the operational discretion of management. Although corporatisation processes aim for a regime providing sufficient autonomy from government intervention, that autonomy must be limited to the extent that management could use it in a way that would increase the social costs of the GC's monopoly. Because some management actions may increase a manager's wealth, in light of his compensation contract with the GC, at the same time as they increase social costs, we must be conscious of the possibilities of these external effects from the contract's formal incentives. We shall return to study social costs of monopoly in more detail in the section on GC operations below.

The Board of Directors

Much of the analysis in this book has focused on issues connected with the board of directors, and the empirical evidence naturally has derived from that area, too. We have seen that the board of a GC operates in a manner quite different from the board of a BC. This is a consequence of various points of departure from the governance environment of the BC. The first is the difference between the shareholding structures, and the role that shareholders are capable of playing in governance. The second is the blurring of many of the characteristic affirmative and negative norms applying to the corporation. The concept of value maximisation (an affirmative norm), although it continues to be relevant, becomes somewhat diluted by complex issues regarding the social costs of monopoly and the existence of community service obligations. Likewise, traditional fiduciary prohibitions (a negative norm) have much trouble when applied to the ambiguities of political conflicts of interest. The third is the different profile of the board, regarding both effective tenure and the representational quality of many appointments to it.

The analysis below initially examines aspects of the appointment and selection of directors. We then consider the compensation entitlements of directors. Considered next are the appropriate roles and expectations of various key participants, specifically the chairman and committees of the board. The concluding issues considered are aspects of directors' duties, and the termination and tenure of directors.

Aspects of Appointment and the Structure of the Board

The process of making appointments to the board raises two pivotal questions — who should be responsible for appointments, and what sorts of persons should be appointed, to the GC board? The answers to these questions depend very much on the view one takes of the board and

196   *Corporate Governance in Government Corporations*

whether or not it is driven by efficiency or representational objectives. We have seen that this tension between values complicates governance processes, and that the means for reconciling them are imperfect. One way of reconciling them is to reform the structure of the board so that separate parts of it attend to different values.

A way of doing this is to establish what might be called an *executive* board, staffed by experts in corporate governance. The executive board would have much the same functions as the board of a BC: it would have principal responsibility for the monitoring and control of management and high-level input into strategic planning. This board is separate from an *advisory* board, consisting of community representatives and the principal users of the GC's services. The advisory board would be primarily responsible for monitoring the quality of service levels, evaluating the relation between the GC and shareholders, and advising the Minister on the delivery of CSOs. The existence of an advisory board would be mandatory for any GC with CSOs, and also for any other GCs providing essential services and infrastructure.

While the executive board would retain much the same powers as the board of the BC, what powers would continue to reside in the advisory board? Several powers would seem appropriate. The first is the right of its members to corporate information. Like BC directors, advisory board members would be subject to a fiduciary duty of confidence regarding the use to which they put that information and the persons to whom they disclose it. Information is needed in order to make appropriate judgments about the cost of different service levels and the imposition of CSOs, and to monitor performance in these areas. The second is for the advisory board to be able to require the attendance of the CEO and other senior managers in order to question managers in relation to issues of community concern, and to provide input into responding to the CSO's delivery. The third is a right of audience at meetings of the executive board. This is necessary as part of the monitoring process in order to evaluate how the executive board deals with issues raised by the advisory board.

Such a model may seem familiar from the dual-board structure characteristic of German corporations (Hopt 1998). However, there is an important difference — the executive board is not appointed by, nor does it account to, the advisory board. The model recommended is, ironically, most similar to the structure introduced by the Chinese Corporate Law (Schipani and Liu 2002).

This relocation achieves several things. First, it provides greater focus for both bodies by enhancing the sense of homogeneity in each body, and providing clearer and less inconsistent goals for each. Second, it diminishes the possibility of overreaching and political conflicts of interest that can occur when representative directors must deliberate or vote on matters relevant to their constituencies. Third, it allows for a potentially wider representation of community interests than the board of a GC will usually allow, given the need for at least some persons with corporate governance experience.

Once this division has been made the questions of the appropriate appointment processes and prerequisite qualifications become much clearer. If the executive board is seen, not as a representative institution, but as responsible for management performance, we no longer have to take the view that the Minister is entitled to a completely free hand in the appointment of directors. Rather, it is appropriate to attempt a more discriminating balance between the Minister's entitlement to take appropriate steps to ensure appropriate governance, and the autonomy of the board and management to manage. This can be done by providing the board with a greater degree of discretion in board appointments, contingent on the board being able to achieve targets set in the formal planning process undertaken between management and the GC. I expand on the details of such a process below in the section on the Minister's corporate governance role. For present purposes, the argument would be that where the GC has performed its financial targets, it could determine a short list of candidates that the Minister could make his selections from, via a nominations committee. Such committees are a commonplace phenomenon in modern BCs, and are being recognised as an appropriate means of preventing management from improperly dominating the process of selecting directors. Where the GC's financial targets have not been met, the Minister need not be bound by the selections of the nomination committee. We shall return to this issue below.

By contrast, the Minister should have a much broader entitlement to select the members of the advisory board, since they are representatives of the polity, as the Minister is. Therefore, those appointments may be made more broadly.

The more important question relates to what, if any, experience or qualifications should be mandated. Let us consider first the case of the executive board. There are competing arguments on whether or not there should be qualifications or pre-specified backgrounds for GC directors. One argument in favour is that directors with professional qualifications or extensive experience in corporate governance are capable of bringing important skills to the GC and to the board in its monitoring of management. Another argument in favour of the proposition is that more experienced and more professional directors have higher opportunity costs in serving on the board, and place greater reputational capital at hazard in serving on a GC board. Their higher opportunity costs mean that a threat to

198   *Corporate Governance in Government Corporations*

terminate their position has less weight and credibility. That limits at least some potentially inappropriate forms of Ministerial or managerial influence on the board. The director's greater reputational capital functions as a self-enforcing bond of their promises to act in the best interests of the GC and the public.

The argument against the most experienced directors is more subtle. As we saw in chapter 3, the remuneration for serving as a GC director is much lower than in other board positions on major companies. To the extent that these differentials are not satisfactorily explained by differences in litigation risk or other forms of liability, limiting qualifications and backgrounds may limit the GC board to a limited pool of appointments of lower quality. If GC appointments cannot compete on price, they must trade off quality.

We saw that in the Queensland sample, the extent of experience in corporate governance can be quite limited. A substantial proportion of GCs had no directors with experience in a listed company. Thus, there is a case for mandating some minimum number or proportion of appointments.

We have also seen arguments above that there is a case for allowing executives to sit on the board of directors. In particular, they may strengthen the performance focus of the board on issues of strategic planning. The appeal of executives is strong where GCs are present in rural areas and find it difficult to attract experienced directors; an insider may bring appreciably more competence than other available appointments. The optimal approach in relation to insiders is to permit them, but not to mandate them. Where they are present, it may be appropriate to prevent them voting on issues that involve the governance of management, such as issues of compensation, and the like.

The advisory board does not need prerequisite experience to be mandated. However, it may be appropriate to impose prerequisites regarding the sorts of groups and communities expected to be represented. For example, a utility GC might have a mandate for some particular balance between urban and rural service users. It is unlikely to be desirable to attempt to give every single group of stakeholders representation on the advisory board. For example, employees probably do not need representation on the board because they have their own industrial processes to work through terms and conditions. The general guideline is that the advisory board is best represented by individuals associated with large groups that have relatively high costs of collective action. Although there may be concerns with disciplining such a representative, that measure does correct the tendency for these groups to be disadvantaged in interest group politics in favour of other groups.

Reforming Government Corporations   199

Director Compensation

The historical means of compensating non-executive directors in both GCs and normal BCs has been the payment of a flat fee, usually supplemented by further payments for committee work, with a fee for each board committee a director takes part in.

There are several emerging trends in director compensation which are changing this profile somewhat. First, Korn/Ferry International (2000) indicate that there is a movement towards the payment of a single director's fee, without supplementary payments. Second, there is increasing acceptance of incentive payments or payment in stock for directors. In the United States, this is indeed quite common and has been rapidly on the rise — the Korn/Ferry survey for the United States in 1999 reports that 84% of corporations remunerate their directors partially in stock, a figure that is up from 62% five years ago. Australia has been much slower to embrace this trend. The Australian survey indicates that the comparable figure is 31%, although 74% of Korn/Ferry International's survey respondents thought that there would be an increased use of this form. The proportion of companies using a specific incentive scheme for non-executive directors is much lower — as small as 9%.

In order to gauge the magnitude of director compensation in GCs, we can see from the Korn/Ferry International (2000) survey, summarised in Table 6.1, that by comparison with other company types, GC directors' fees are low in mean and demonstrate low variance.

Table 6.1   Time and Remuneration of Non-executive Directors (by Company Type)

	Average days	Mean	Median	75th percentile
Listed public	21	52,760	47,000	64,250
Unlisted public	18	37,500	26,940	38,700
Private	15	37,560	25,000	47,500
Government-owned	23	27,700	29,000	33,500

Source: Korn/Ferry International (2000, p. 43). (Amounts in Australian dollars).

It indicates that the mean and 75th percentile are the lowest in absolute terms, and that the median, although slightly higher than the figures for private and unlisted public companies, is the lowest in dollars divided by the average number of days worked per year ($1261, compared to $1497 for private companies and $1667 for unlisted public companies). The low variance is apparent in the fact that the difference between the median (the

200 Corporate Governance in Government Corporations

50th percentile) and the 75th percentile is lower for GCs than any other company type.[2] There are similar trends in the remuneration of chairmen, where the mean and 75th percentile are somewhat higher than for private and unlisted public companies, but the time commitment is almost twice as high.

The fact that fees are low and have low variance is significant. It implies that the lowest quality directors are likely to be paid more than what they are worth, and the highest quality directors are likely to be paid less. This will diminish the average quality of the board, attenuate their performance incentives, and possibly render them more prone to furthering political or party agendas.

It may therefore be necessary to adjust compensation practices accordingly. Compensation must be sensitive to differences in opportunity costs of different appointees, presumably by negotiation with the Minister, and on the advice of a subcommittee of the board. If board remuneration is flat across the board, as it is in Australia, one is likely to deter the best directors and overcompensate the lowest quality ones. The most logical solution is not to increase compensation for all directors (since the least competent directors may not be undercompensated at all) but to pay negotiated loadings to reflect competencies and experience.

How does this recommendation square with our earlier comments in relation to the compensation of the CEO? There we said that incentive compensation could create substantial problems to the extent that there were disparities between the proxies for corporate performance and true value, and also where the GC was capable of collecting monopoly rents. There are similar problems in the GC for directors to the extent that significant incentive compensation payments are introduced for directors although the fractions are likely to be much lower than for directors. The point we have made here is that the general level of compensation needs to be higher in some cases, in order to expand the pool of available directors. This is more important than compensation needing to be significantly more responsive to corporate performance.

The Role of the Chairman

The role of the chairman of the board of directors bears a significant proportion of the weight of expectations that the board of directors performs its functions.[3] It is the chairman's responsibility, for example, to determine what material appears before the board, what business is considered, the order and manner of deliberation, and the enforcement of fiduciary obligations on voting or deliberating by interested directors. The chairman might also be expected to be responsible for seeing that directors

Reforming Government Corporations 201

continued to receive professional education and training, in light of the wide disparity in the levels of experience observed on GC boards. In addition, the chairman is the principal point of liaison between the various governance processes of the firm, and constituencies having dealings with those processes, of whom the Minister is most important.

We have already seen that there is agreement amongst GC directors with the proposition that persons with professional qualifications and experience chair boards. Thus, if qualifications are to be imposed for would-be directors, it could certainly be appropriate to do so for the chairman.

Second, and overlapping with later recommendations regarding Ministerial shareholders, it is necessary to articulate protocols for communication with the board that centre on the chairman. The Ministerial shareholders, for example, need to commit to routing all communications through the board via the chairman. Similar obligations should apply to other constituencies dealing with the board. We have seen in Table 5.1 that board members or managers are lobbied with frequency in relation to the extent and pricing of services. Table 5.2 shows that some directors acted on behalf of particular constituents at least on some occasions. In addition, in the examination of communications between the Ministerial shareholders and the board, it was not uncommon for Ministers to informally lobby board members. These practices show why it is important to develop ethics in this area, in order to limit irregular partisan use of the governance processes of the GC.

One way of responding to this problem is to incorporate these ethical norms into a revised version of fiduciary duties. One of the problems that we saw in earlier sections is that fiduciary duties don't respond very well to political conflicts of interest. It would be difficult to know how they should apply to someone who was undertaking to act for a lobby group. One way to respond is to incorporate an obligation to disclose the content of lobbying to the chairman, if the director is to be permitted to have any role in deliberations or voting. The obligation would be that the chairman be given a précis of the contact between the lobby group and the director, and the extent of any benefits conferred on the director in the present or previous situations. Provided that information is circulated to the Minister (unless the Minister is the lobbyist) and the other directors, the director may be permitted to continue to advocate that interest if to do so is not in breach of any other obligations. If, however, that information is not disclosed, a pecuniary penalty or a disqualification from office can be imposed on the director in default. That reinforces the ethic which focuses communication about a range of forms of conflicts on the chairman. It ought to lead to a higher level of information about the decisions before the board.

202　　　*Corporate Governance in Government Corporations*

Third, the chairman needs to take responsibility for issues associated with the training and development of GC directors.[4] As observed above, to the extent there are substantial expertise deficits in relation to governance, issues of continued training are important. It is important that this training is provided under the auspices of the board and the chairman, rather than under those of government departments or Ministerial shareholders. This ensures that the advice is independent and focused on the best interests of the GC. The Ministers may legitimately communicate their expectations. This is good practice as it ought to minimise cognitive dissonance between the board and the shareholders. But there may be differences in some respects between what the shareholders want, and what the directors are obliged to deliver. For example, we have mentioned that the Ministerial shareholders may want to intervene in governance in respects not countenanced by the GC legislation. If that is the case, then how directors react to an intimation to this effect by the Minister may be very important — directors may be accommodating or may resist. The crucial question, therefore, is how a chairman or how the government will differ in imparting information about how to respond to these issues.

We therefore asked directors, after investigating what sorts of education and guidance they had received, the following question, 'Who was responsible for providing this advice or guidance?', with options permitting them to choose between the Chairman, on the one hand, and a government department on the other. It was possible for directors to select both options, since the two are not mutually exclusive. Table 6.2 sets out the results.

Table 6.2　The Chairman and the Government as Sources of Advice

	Government provided advice	Govt did not provide advice	Total
Chairman provided advice	9	30	39
Chairman did not provide advice	<u>41</u>	<u>30</u>	<u>71</u>
Total	<u>50</u>	<u>60</u>	<u>110</u>

If this is broken down for current and former directors, it becomes apparent that the Chairman is performing the duty less and the government more. Of current directors, only 28% received advice from the Chairman, compared to 41% for past directors. For the government, those numbers are 53% and 37%. The Table also shows that it is rare for directors to receive advice from both sources.

It is also apparent that over a quarter of directors received advice, but did not get it from either the Chairman or the government. Where then did they get it? We anticipated such a situation, and provided space for directors to indicate the alternative supplier. The answers fall primarily into three categories. First, the director may seek out the information of his or her own motion. Thus, various directors indicate that they attended seminars by professional organisations. These seminars are uncontroversial. Second, the director may be supplied with information by one of the other non-executive directors. This occurred in various instances, and may be quite reasonable since corporate lawyers are not uncommonly appointed to boards. Provided this information is shared widely and is known to the chairman, it also occasions no great concern. Third, some directors' cited the CEO as their source of information (either directly or at his instance). This is problematic, since it is the function of the directors to monitor the CEO, and the CEO's own self-interest would be served by de-emphasising that function. The CEO might also encourage protocols that gave him more information rather than less. It is not a desirable phenomenon in general.

This serves to underline the importance of the chairman of the GC having principal responsibility for providing directors with education and advice regarding duties, ethics, and standards as a director. For these purposes, she should provide to the Ministerial shareholders a copy of a continuing education plan for the directors on the board, specifying the matters to be covered and the persons involved. These information opportunities should be provided to all directors. Where other directors take responsibility for continuing education, they should do so with the express permission of the chairman, and this should be noted in the continuing education plan. Chief Executive Officers of GCs should not provide education or guidance to directors regarding their responsibilities and duties. Advice provided to directors by the government should primarily be given as information about government policies and interacting with government, rather than as the principal source of information about duties and responsibilities.

Board Committees

Modern best practice in corporate governance has placed considerable emphasis on the establishment of permanent board committees performing a discrete set of key functions in the corporation. According to Korn/Ferry International (2000), 83% of Australian companies operate through formal committees. Committees bring their recommendations back to the board. The crucial questions have been to determine which committees are important for firms, and the persons who should make them up (and in particular the role of executive and non-executive directors). The observed type, size, and staffing of committees, and the frequency with which they

204 *Corporate Governance in Government Corporations*

meet, vary substantially from corporation to corporation (for an Australian survey, see Korn/Ferry International [2000]). Non-executives typically dominate the committees whose functions are at the heart of corporate governance, such as the executive compensation and audit committees. Executive directors are predictably more conspicuous on committees with executive functions such as finance and executive committees.

Academic studies of the specific committees that add value or improve firm performance are somewhat equivocal. There is evidence that executive membership is associated with superior performance (Klein 1998).

Commonwealth, South Australian and Tasmanian GCs are specifically required to establish an audit committee under the board's delegation powers.[5] While Victoria specifically grants GC boards the power to delegate functions to committees, other jurisdictions are silent on this point. Despite this, the resulting internal governance framework is often very similar across the board — most Queensland GCs (for example) have an audit committee, with remuneration, marketing, strategy, safety, quality and management, and finance committees also being common, particularly amongst the larger, more commercial company GCs.

Of board committees, two of the most important for governance purposes are the Audit and Executive Compensation Committees. Each of these is critically concerned with issues lying at the heart of the relation between management and the Minister, and the relation between the Minister and the people.

The importance of the Executive Compensation Committee is self-evident. We have seen how executive compensation is of prime importance because it determines the managers attracted to the firm and the nature of incentives to maximise its value. We saw in earlier chapters how performance incentives are complicated phenomena in GCs, given the absence of ideal proxies for value, and the existence of public interest objectives. The Executive Compensation Committee needs to be able to monitor these possibilities.

The Audit Committee is also self-evidently important. First, it has the major responsibility for financial accountability, and reporting on management's stewardship and Ministerial governance of the GC to parliament and to the public. In addition, as we have seen, GCs in Australia rely on explicit planning and accountability devices negotiated between the board and the Minister, such as the Statement of Corporate Intent and the Corporate Plan. Financial data has an important although non-exclusive role in these devices. Third, in the GC, the Audit Committee is closely related to the Executive Compensation Committee. As we have seen, performance incentives are likely to depend much more on financial data than in the BC, because security prices are unavailable as performance indicators. This

Reforming Government Corporations

places pressure on the reporting and verification of financial data, which in turn increases the importance of the Audit Committee.

Nomination Committees, although important in BCs, have little role in GCs at present, simply because the government dominates board appointments. However, there is an important role that nomination committees can play that we have touched on above. It relates to giving a state-contingent right to the board of greater independence. We return to the issue below, after first considering the Executive Compensation and Audit Committees in more detail.

In the companies making up the Queensland sample, directors with corporate governance experience from a listed public company are slightly more likely to sit on the Executive Compensation Committees (which consisted of three or four members with relatively little variation) than those without, but the difference is not significant. The chairman of the board was generally a member of the committee. We asked directors (both those sitting on the committee and those not) four questions, taking true or false format, in relation to the recommendations of the committee.

The first question asked was, 'On at least one occasion, the committee recommended an increase in the CEO's compensation'. Only seven out of 95 answered false. Five of these were in Portfolio A. No more than one person per GC answered false, suggesting that these responses may be unreliable.

The second question asked was, 'On at least one occasion, the committee recommended a decrease in the CEO's compensation'. Only ten out of 88 answered true. Five of these were in Portfolio B (and appear to be associated with two specific GCs). Nonetheless, of these ten responses, eight came from persons who are currently directors, a result which is significant at $p<0.05$. This suggests that committees may have become less inclined to rubber stamp increases in executive pay.

The third question was, 'On at least one occasion, the committee recommended that the CEO's compensation include a greater proportion of performance-based incentive compensation (*e.g.*, bonus payments)'. The results are set out in Table 6.3:

206   *Corporate Governance in Government Corporations*

Table 6.3   Increase in Performance-related Pay and Portfolio

	Portfolio A GCs	Portfolio B GCs	Portfolio C GCs	Total
Increase in performance pay recommended	35	16	10	61
Increase in performance pay not recommended	<u>7</u>	<u>20</u>	<u>2</u>	<u>29</u>
Total	<u>42</u>	<u>36</u>	<u>12</u>	<u>90</u>

The chi-square statistic for these results is statistically significant at $p<0.001$. It indicates that Portfolio B was least inclined to recommend performance-related pay. Directors with public company corporate governance experience do appear to be associated with greater recommendations for increased performance-related pay at the $p<0.05$ level of significance.

The fourth question was, 'The board always approved the recommendations of the committee'. Of 93 respondents, 76 responded affirmatively. It seems that on the whole, there is relatively little dissent from recommendations of the ECC.

Corporate governance in GCs is likely to be improved by standardising the constitution of the Executive Compensation Committees. It is desirable for the Executive Compensation Committee to have three or four members. Three is in line with the practices of listed public companies, but four is equally good if the chair does not have a casting vote since conclusions will need 3-1 majorities rather than just 2-1 majorities. At least one of the members of the Executive Compensation Committee should have corporate governance experience in a listed public company, in order to bring familiarity with experience in executive compensation in those companies. These members also seem to be associated with a greater reliance on performance pay. Finally, one of the members of the Executive Compensation Committee should be a member of the audit committee, in order to bring greater familiarity with the performance of the company in the accounts, and in view of the linkage between financial data and performance pay.

Like Executive Compensation Committees, Audit Committees are ubiquitous in the GCs in the sample. Over half of the sampled directors had sat on the committee. Again, directors with public corporate governance experience are more likely to sit on the Audit Committee, but those lacking that experience are still well-represented as well. Unlike the ECC, it is much more common for the chairman not to sit on the AC. Sixty-eight respondents said that the chairman was on the AC; 43 said he was not, and this is widely distributed across GCs. That said, the evidence indicates that this practice has decreased over time and it is now less common for the AC not to have the chairman on it. The practice is much less frequent in companies where directors have experience in the corporate governance of listed public companies.

We asked directors (both those sitting on the committee and those not) three questions, taking true or false format, in relation to the recommendations of the committee. The first question asked was, 'On at least one occasion, the committee recommended a new auditor'. Out of 110 respondents, 25 respondents answered true, roughly evenly divided amongst the portfolios. These responses seem frequently to be supported by other responses in the same GCs, so they appear to be reliable.

The second question was, 'On at least one occasion, the committee was told that the auditor intended to qualify the accounts unless changes were made.' Nineteen respondents answered that this was true. No true responses occurred in Portfolio C, whereas about 15% of Portfolio A and 25% of Portfolio B answered that the statement was true. There was one GC in which this answer was consistently supported by respondents.

The third question was, 'The board always approved the recommendations of the committee'. This was regarded as true by 88 directors, and false by 23 directors. There is only one GC in which more than two directors answered 'true' to this question, so some of this evidence may be unreliable.

One would make similar recommendations in relation to the Audit Committee as for the Executive Compensation Committee — they also should have three to four directors, chaired by the chairman of the board, with one person with experience as a listed public company director, and, in addition, one person with experience in financial accounting or auditing. We have already observed that one of the members of the ECC will be on the AC.

Directors' Duties

Directors' duties may serve two roles — one deontological, one teleological. These purposes might be thought to differ as between the BC and the GC. In the BC, and especially diffusely-held, manager-controlled BC, directors' duties are a crucial means of accountability. They impose a series of ex post sanctions which ought to deter certain forms of undesirable behaviour, such as gross negligence, expropriation, overreaching, and so on. The teleological value of them is particularly apparent in the limitations of other accountability mechanisms in the BC — the relative rarity of takeovers, the difficulty of displacement of directors in a proxy contest, and so on. The deontological motivation concerns their postulation of ethics in order to establish behavioural norms for fiduciaries that society regards as

208   *Corporate Governance in Government Corporations*

just and appropriate behaviour. This purpose is important in BCs; it is often revisited at times of corporate collapse and significant fiduciary misfeasance. However, the role of the law is in this respect not at all monopolistic. Corporate governance is much influenced by perceptions of best practice amongst professional bodies, as well as the contributions of business ethicists. Although the law doubtless sets the normative lowest common denominators, it is likely to have only a limited role beyond that domain.

In the GC, by contrast, the teleological value of directors' duties is likely to be lower than in the BC. That is because the opportunities for direct and effective intervention in governance are much greater in the GC. Ministerial shareholders can usually respond to derelictions of duty immediately and comprehensively, undaunted by many of the procedural and collective action problems that the shareholders of a BC face. Likewise, the existence of ex ante governance procedures, such as the Statement of Corporate Intent, means that there is less need to rely on ex post sanctions. By contrast, directors' duties may have a greater deontological value in articulating some of the complex ethical norms that may be expected of GCs. GCs remain a complex and unique organisational node, caught between the norms of public sector governance and corporate governance.

In the first instance, it is appropriate to note that the classic forms of fiduciary breach, such as misappropriation of assets and the like, remain equally inappropriate in a GC as in a BC. In these situations, directors' duties need little adaptation. However, as we have seen, there are many situations where they do require adaptation or at least serious re-examination. The major category is in relation to the existence of political conflicts of interest and the handling of lobbying of members of the board by Ministers or by other interest groups.

The second point, which we have already foreshadowed, is that one difficulty with fiduciary duties, in their traditional form, is that the rights, such as the right to sue or the right to affirm a voidable contract, all lie with the shareholder. However, if this is to apply to the GC, all those rights are conferred on the Ministerial shareholder. This is problematic for political conflicts of interest, since they centralise power in governmental hands, outside of constitutional and administrative safeguards. Are there any organising principles that may be developed in relation to the application of directors' duties to GCs?

As a preliminary matter, we should note that a proposal separating the functions of an executive board and a community advisory board allows directors to be selected for the former (where fiduciary duties will apply) based on the absence of substantial interests likely to occasion conflicts of interest. Such an ex ante measure decreases the pressure that is placed on directors' duties. A similar initial precaution may be taken at board level. Given other recommendations in this work for the role of a Nominations Committee of the board, one other role it may serve is to prepare a report that documents connections with interest groups and other sources of conflicts of interest. That report would be provided to a Minister before decisions were made to appoint a person to the board. Omitting only any confidential information, that report can then be placed on the public record given the public interest in the interaction of interest groups with GCs.

The first substantive question to be considered is whether or not we want to have legal principles that respond to political conflicts. Is this a matter that should lie within the remit of legal principles, or should it be left to alternative control devices, such as parliamentary accountability? We would argue that law has an important but complex role in responding to these issues. One cannot simply leave matters to the political process, because the most effective interest groups are likely to dominate in these contexts. Law can serve an important role by forcing disclosure in relation to interest group activity. These disclosures can lower the information costs of competing interest groups. Greater competition between interest groups might lead to greater efficiency (Becker 1983; *cf.* Przeworski 1991; Shleifer and Vishny 1993). It follows that the role of the law in relation to directors' duties must be less prohibitory, and more disclosural — thus differentiating it from the classic fiduciary duty. The problem with political conflicts is the difficulty of establishing causation — how does one show that an action taken by the GC, being a resolution of the GC directors, was specifically motivated by interest group lobbying?[6] Thus, a legal rule that prohibits transactions is harder to justify, although clearly there must be a sanction in order to provide an incentive to encourage disclosure. Causation problems, in addition to problems of valuation, render compensatory remedies such as damages even less suitable. What, then, should be the juridical operation of provisions directed to political conflicts?

The best remedies are ones oriented towards imposing a personal penalty on the director for a failure to comply with the disclosure obligation and any other prudential limitations imposed. The two plausible penalties are either disqualification (loss of office) or pecuniary sanctions. Disqualification is the better of the two remedies, because it can deprive an interest group of the future representation of that director. By contrast, pecuniary sanctions may simply be absorbed by the interest group as a part of the cost of lobbying. There is also a higher psychological penalty associated with dismissal, than with pecuniary sanctions.

I foreshadowed above one way these provisions might operate, in connection with the discussion of communication processes relating to the board. The legal rule would require a disclosure of information in relation to the extent to which individual directors have been lobbied and the nature of their associations with interested constituencies, as a precondition to any further deliberation. The information would be disclosed initially to the chairman, with copies to the other directors and Ministerial shareholders, and made available for public inspection. The question that remains is whether, on making the disclosure, the director should be entitled to deliberate and vote, to deliberate but abstain, or to absent himself after responding to all issues directed to him or her by the chair.

One possibility is a tiered approach which reflects some assessment of the degree of the conflict. The general principle is to permit a higher degree of participation in decisions that confer benefits on wider classes of recipients, and less participation in decisions that confer benefits on a more restricted class. Such a legal rule should make it relatively harder for well-organised and traditionally more effective interest groups to influence governance of GCs, without preventing directors from taking decisions that are genuinely motivated by a broader conception of the public interest. This principle can be usefully compared with the traditional fiduciary prohibition on pecuniary conflicts of interest. In the classic case where a fiduciary is the counterparty to a contract with the company, the beneficiary is as narrow as is conceivable — a single person, the fiduciary. That amply justifies a stringent prohibition. Where the fiduciary's interest is more indirect, as where he is simply one small shareholder of many in a public company, the case for a looser prohibition is stronger, although defining where the line should fall can be debated.

Figure 6.3 Representation of Political and Pecuniary Conflicts

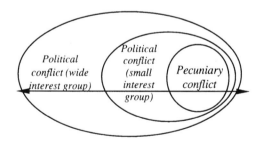

Large rent-seeking constituency; excludability difficult

Small rent-seeking constituency; no excludability problems

Reforming Government Corporations 211

Figure 6.3 represents this idea schematically by showing how pecuniary conflicts can be seen as a subset of a larger group of conflicts. These can be differentiated according to the size of the 'rent-seeking' interest group and the difficulties associated with excluding non-members from the benefit sought by an interest group. It follows, then, that a case for a new legal rule imposing sanctions for political conflicts is strongest in the case where the beneficiaries of any proposed action by the director come from a small, well-organised interest group, and weakest in the case of community-wide benefits. For example, determinations of the service levels delivered by the GC in the ordinary course of its business or under its community service obligations will often create a conflict of interest at some level for some of the directors. The same is true of conferring any benefit on a director which he or she enjoys in common with a wide and representative segment of the community. Some form of conflict of interest is likely to exist in these cases for one or more directors, either in a personal sense or in connection with associated interest groups. While it is appropriate for those directors to disclose their connections with interest groups ex ante, and reveal what lobbying they have received in individual instances, prohibiting deliberation would hamstring the board. To return to an earlier example, the country services transaction, falls into this category.

By contrast, other situations warrant a more demanding approach. An example is a labour union representative confronted by a board resolution in relation to workplace conditions. In these situations, there are substantial risks of rent-seeking where the representative participates in governance processes with a view to furthering the interests of the group. The interest group will already wield influence in the political sphere, which influence may be brought to bear indirectly on the governance processes through Ministerial intervention. There is no reason that further indulgence should be required. The broad distinction is that behaviour which has a claim to be public-regarding should be facilitated; behaviour which furthers an interest group should be limited.

How can these two cases be distinguished? The line can be drawn in different ways, but the essence of the difference is that the public-regarding set of behaviours is likely to relate to transactions that affect the 'public'. That is, they involve the open-ended communities who use or consume the goods and services produced by the GC, or who are affected by its operation. This distinguishes it from relatively 'closed' interest groups, such as employees. This distinction is also appropriate in the sense that the public as consumers of the GC's services, have a strong claim to representation in the GC's governance, especially in view of the natural monopoly status of many GCs and the absence of product market discipline.

212   *Corporate Governance in Government Corporations*

Other constituencies such as employees (absent a labour monopsony) lack a similarly strong claim.

To recapitulate the operation of the provision, the directors would be permitted to further presumptively public-regarding behaviours. That would be subject to an obligation to disclose to the chair, the other directors, the Ministers and the public the nature of any communications or lobbying directed to the director in relation to business that was expected to come before the board. The board would then have the right to make a decision in relation to whether or not the lobbied director can participate.[7] Failure to discharge the disclosure obligation should render the director liable to a pecuniary penalty.

In relation to private-interest-furthering behaviours, the same disclosure obligation would be imposed, but a director who is lobbied or who otherwise has a substantial political conflict of interest would be required to be absent from deliberations and abstain from voting. This obligation is not applicable to public-regarding behaviours.

Another basic legal principle requiring rethinking in GCs is the director's duty of care. In some respects, the duty of care is not all that relevant to GCs, since the vast majority of these cases arise in situations where the corporation is insolvent or otherwise undergoes a catastrophe. In these situations, the directors are sued in respect of some deficiency in information or procedure that is argued to have contributed to substantial loss. Given the relatively loose budget constraints of GCs, such cases are less likely (although this depends on standing rules, to which we turn next). Nonetheless, the duty may be invoked in connection with a change in government. A new government may wish to shake up the GC by commencing suits against some of its current directors; it may even be a tactic to encourage resignations. We therefore cannot overlook the content of the duty of care.

In principle, the duty of care should not be radically different as between BCs and GCs. However, it is important that the duty of care in the GC be adjusted to take into consideration the extent to which the GC's objectives and governance constraints diverge from those in a BC. So, for example, it is necessary to have regard to factors such as the following:

(1)   Ministerial imprimatur or direction regarding the impugned actions, procedures or processes.

(2)   The specification of formally recognised goals in official governance documents (for example, the Statement of Corporate Intent) that are inconsistent with value maximisation.

(3)   The existence of demonstrable public benefit, not internalised by the corporation, from the impugned actions.

Reforming Government Corporations 213

Australasian legislation has generally explicitly modified the duty of care to take some of these factors into consideration.[8] The final question to be addressed in this section is the question of standing — who should be entitled to sue? Technically, the GC has the benefit of a director's duties. In this sort of situation, the board would be thought to have the right to make the final decision in relation to prosecuting any action for breach of those duties. By contrast to the BC, the risk of self-interested decisions not to bring suit is much less in the GC, because of the central position of the Minister — he may have the capacity to make a directive, or replace the directors, for example. The Minister also presumably has the right to bring a derivative suit.

However, the Minister's advantage throws up a fundamental problem associated with directors' duties in the GC — the risk of a conflict of interest on the part of the Minister, creating a moral hazard problem for him in respect of prosecuting a breach. This is most acute in the context of political conflicts but it may occur in other contexts as well (for example, where a director, who is in breach of a more conventional type of duty, is an ally). In these situations, should there be a wider right of standing?

There are two possibilities — one is to seek judicial review of the Minister's actions, for example, seeking a mandatory injunction ordering the Minister to bring a derivative suit. The other is to widen rights of standing in order to allow other constituencies to initiate the equivalent of a derivative action. The former is not terribly promising; the right is conferred remotely from the underlying cause of action, and the Minister still has substantial discretionary powers to kill the suit. Wider rights of standing raise different considerations. One risk is the use of expanded entitlements for political self-seeking. The other is that litigation is expanded, doing away with the liberation from judicial review that the corporatisation process was thought to promise. These issues may not be insurmountable criticisms. Standing can be limited to those constituencies that can show substantial injury arising from the action they seek to impugn (Stearns 2001). In addition, the incentives to litigate in areas where wider standing might be thought to be needed most, namely political conflicts, will be limited. The main forms of remedies are disqualification and civil penalties, rather than undoing the transaction itself. The incentive to seek those remedies will be relatively limited, so a more liberal standing test need not be dispositive.

Termination and Tenure

We saw in Chapter 3 that qualitative and quantitative evidence point to a high level of director turnover. This turnover is not attributable to a failure

214   *Corporate Governance in Government Corporations*

to perform, or to the invocation of accountability mechanisms. It seems driven primarily by the desire that governments appoint directors that they prefer. The negative aspects of these characteristics have been discussed elsewhere.

We have already foreshadowed an approach which would limit the degree of control the Minister exercises over board appointments contingent on the achievement of SCI targets diminishing the scope for the Minister to make a clean sweep of the board. We will explain this in more detail later, but at the time directors are appointed, the Minister has a narrower choice of choosing between options articulated by a Nomination Committee when the corporation is achieving its financial targets. Similarly, Ministers would be unable to terminate directors at will prior to the end of their terms while the GC achieved its financial targets, although termination for other demonstrated causes (*e.g.*, forms of overreaching, infrequent attendance, other forms of non-compliance with standing orders) would remain appropriate. Such a method encourages, on the part of the Minister, greater attention to financial targets and their achievement, and on the part of the directors, a greater sense of security where they have performed their set targets.

Such a method can also usefully be combined with the structure of a 'staggered' board. In this approach, directors are appointed for a defined term of, say, three years. However, the end of those terms do not all occur at the same time, but are spaced out over time. In a board of six directors for instance, two might resign in any one year. In this situation, a new government confronted by a poorly performing GC would be able to appoint its own directors. However, if confronted by a GC that is doing well, relative to its defined targets, would be limited in the number of new appointments it could make as well as the persons from whose ranks those appointments could be made. The object is to preserve as much of a presumptively functional governance environment as possible.

The Minister's Governance Role

It is vital for the reform of corporate governance in GCs to focus on the accountability mechanisms associated with Ministers and their exercise of governance power over the GC. The norms and principles appropriate to the exercise of power by shareholders are much less applicable to GCs than the equivalent precepts for directors or managers. The object of the governance processes to which the Minister is subject must necessarily be to minimise the joint sum of agency costs of governance and management.

In this section, we consider a wide range of issues where governance principles can be included in the design of the GC. We start initially with the examination of the allocation of governance power within the executive government. We then analyse issues in relation to the role of goal setting and performance monitoring documents, and their integration into other governance processes. We then proceed to consider the function of the CSOs of the GC, and other tasks that the GC is directed to undertake or requirements it must observe that would not be expected to occur in a commercial environment where the Ministers were attempting to maximise the value of the firm. The final topics considered are the interaction between the GC and the department, and the Minister's interaction with interest groups.

The Allocation of Governance Power within the Executive Government

The allocation of power over the GC to the members of the executive government is a matter of considerable complexity. The possible allocations of power may vary in the number of members of the executive to whom power is given, the identities of those members, and the scope and means of exercise of that power given to each of them.

Typically, the statutory authority model, which might be thought a less 'advanced' form of internal reform of government than corporatisation, requires the chief executive of the authority to answer to a single minister. This is a model involving allocation of power to a single Minister, into whose portfolio the GC fits. The same principle is easily applied to a GC as well. In this situation, the scope of the power is complete, and the means of exercise uninteresting.

At the opposite extreme, the governance powers connected with the GC could be allocated widely across a number, or even all, of the members of the executive government. Such a regime is unlikely to be very effective, because of the diffusion of accountability. It is likely that power would, in this situation, be informally allocated to one member or a small number of members of the executive, so creating power without formal accountability.

The compromise is to allocate power to two (or some other small number of) members of executive government. This is the principal solution which has been adopted in Australasian GCs. In Australia, power is typically allocated to the Portfolio Minister and to another Minister with a focus that is wider and more responsive to 'whole of government' concerns. That is either a Minister with specific responsibilities for GCs, or the Treasurer reflecting general concerns with financial accountability. In New Zealand, the Ministers are a Minister responsible for GCs and the Treasurer.

216 *Corporate Governance in Government Corporations*

The merits of a double shareholder model, compared to a single shareholder model, are, first, that it limits the ability of any single Minister to engage in self-seeking behaviour. A single Minister may use his governance powers in a manner that increases, for example, his budget, his chances of re-election, the welfare of his department, and so on. Although some of these concerns will be shared by the entire government, others will not. In the latter instance, giving power to a second Minister may limit these forms of behaviour. Thus, strategic behaviour involving Ministers is less likely when there is a second Minister. A second Minister allows a fuller range of objectives and competencies to be brought to the task of governance. The portfolio Minister has greater operational competence at his disposal; the Treasurer may have greater concerns with financial control and accountability.

The deficiencies are best understood in terms of the economic problems of multiple principals. Because there *are* differences in the objectives of the different shareholders, the effect of dividing governance accountability between shareholders is to weaken the incentives of the agent to achieve the objectives specified by either of the principals (Dixit 1996, 2000). Each of the firm's two or more principals will pressure the agent (here, managers) to pursue that principal's goals, and will discourage her from pursuing other goals. In addition to limiting the agent's incentive to pursue any goal, the multiplication of objectives partially insures the agent against bad outcomes. This is because the principals have different perspectives when an agent does not achieve a particular goal, depending on whether they dictated it or not.

The multiple principal literature reaches several conclusions. The first and preferred solution is for the principals to agree a contractual compromise that maximises the parties' joint gains from the agents' efforts (Dixit 2000, pp. 17–18). Second, the firm in question should be structured, if possible, so that its principals have complementary rather than cross-cutting perspectives (p. 19). The more divergent the principals' interests are, the worse the problems described will be. Finally, where the multiple principals do have unavoidably diverse interests, lawmakers should try to segment the principals' interests (Dixit 2000, p. 19). One way to do this is to permit each principal to see outcomes only of the goal or goals in which he has an interest. The desirability of the double principal model is endogenous to the effectiveness of these different solutions.

As Skeel (2003) points out there are two features of the modern corporatisation governance processes that achieve these particular targets — the Statement of Corporate Intent, and the Community Service Obligation. The SCI functions as a contract-like agreement for the specification of the agreed compromise between the Ministers. The CSO allows the segmentation of principals' interests by fixing those goals that fall outside the commercial objectives of the GC. In this context, however, we should recall the evidence considered in Chapter 4 that important conflicts do appear to remain between the Ministers, and, most importantly, are frequently unresolved. These suggest, then, that the theoretical appeal of the SCI and CSO mechanisms are an imperfect solution to the multiple principal problem.

One alternative to the model in which both Ministers are conferred with governance powers is to confer the governance powers associated with shareholding on a single Minister most likely to internalise whole of government objectives. The other Minister with portfolio-specific concerns will interact with the GC outside the governance processes — via an essentially contractual interface as a customer and for other commercial interactions, and via a regulatory interface. The New Zealand model is closest to this power allocation. That Minister would retain the capacity to make directives, but only in relation to issues of operations and investments. Other directives related to governance would lie in the exclusive remit of the other Minister. This achieves a more effective segmentation of interests. In particular, it is consistent with the evidence that the Treasurer is most likely to focus on issues of financial performance and governance, whereas the Portfolio Minister is more likely to focus on issues of operation and investment.

Goal-setting and Corporate Plans

Using a performance contract such as the Statement of Corporate Intent is desirable. It can provide the performance targets for a system of incentive compensation, premised on achieving these targets. It can permit Ministers to reconcile conflicting objectives by means of a contractual compromise. It allows public interest objectives to be quantified more explicitly than injunctions of the most general form. In this section, we outline further uses in defining the entitlement to 'control', while outlining some of the limitations of the SCI and how they might be improved.

We saw in Chapter 4 that the role of the SCI in the GC differed in the degree of activism with which it was negotiated between the Minister and the board, and also in the consequences that were imposed for failing to meet targets in the SCI. One of the explanations for variation is that the Minister has only a weak incentive to negotiate appropriate targets and impose penalties for failing to achieve them. The Minister's property rights in the GC are weak, and compelling attention to financial goals may be inconsistent with the slack that the directors and managers need to pursue particular political aspirations of the Minister.

218   *Corporate Governance in Government Corporations*

It is therefore appropriate to see whether there are ways that both Ministers and managers self-enforce appropriate goals for the GC. One way to do this, which I have foreshadowed, is to allow the achievement of targets in the SCI to be used to define control of appointments to the board. Achievement of SCI goals would confer contingent control on the membership of the board. In other words, the board has a greater control over the persons who sit on it; if SCI goals are not achieved, that control reverts to the Minister. Both parties will want this control — the Minister in order to have persons he wishes to work with, the board to retain their positions and to maintain a certain degree of harmony.

The idea of contingent control is fundamental to the BC. In the BC, control over the property of the corporation is allocated to shareholders and their agents contingently on them paying the debts they contract for as and when they fall due (Hart 1995). If the corporation is insolvent, control reverts to creditors. Clearly, contingent control serves a powerful incentive function, encouraging the promisor to self-enforce the promise made. A similar idea can be used in GCs.

The Minister's desire to control the board and its appointments may be indulged where there is a failure of the GC to reach its annual SCI targets. The board's desire for more insulation from the Minister's intervention, and to keep their jobs, can be indulged where they have reached agreed targets. One possible approach to defining the contingency would be to set it as the failure of the GC to reach a specified accounting return on equity, with changes in accounting policy choices requiring agreement by the Minister and the board.

Such an approach requires that we define the respective degree of control the Minister and the board are permitted in deciding the future candidates for the board. Where the GC was 'in control' (it achieved its targets), the board could require the Minister to select candidates only from a list of nominees put forward by the directors, which would be settled by a Nominations Committee (to which the Minister could only make non-binding submissions). Where the GC was 'out of control', the Minister would have a much freer hand in selecting appointments (subject to any required qualifications), although it may still permit a Nominations Committee to make recommendations.

Arguably, this gives an incentive to the Minister to set unrealistically high targets that the GC never meets, in order to maximise his control over the board. However, this incentive is subject to conflicting political pressures. First, a Minister is responsible to parliament for setting SCI objectives and the governance of the GC — where he sets objectives the GC consistently misses, he is likely to face substantial criticism for running a slack operation. This will also expose his appointees to greater pressure.

Second, Ministers have an incentive to try to keep as many of their appointees on the board after his or her party loses government. However, they cannot do that, if, for the year that spans the run-up to an election, they set goals that the GC will miss, since a new Minister is then at liberty to neglect the determination of the nomination committee. Moreover, in many political environments, the timing of the next election may be unclear — for instance where a government lacks a parliamentary majority or seeks an electoral advantage by running prior to the end of the term.

One of the combined effects of these incentives is to encourage the Minister to set SCI targets which diminish towards the end of a government's term. Figure 6.4 illustrates such a problem on the basis of an assumption of three year parliamentary terms. Prior to the election year, the required return exceeds the highest return practically attainable, in the final year, it is below it.

Figure 6.4 Strategic Incentives with respect to Required Returns in SCIs

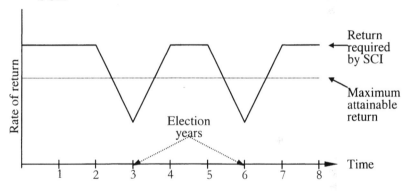

The incentive could be mitigated by a 'ratchet' rule, which allows the Minister to raise the required rate of return, but does not permit him to reduce it. The required rate of return could only be reduced by a new government — the very time when the government would like to *raise* it. This incidentally helps to reinforce the political pressure that should apply to the Minister not to permit the GC to work to less demanding standards. It would also discourage the board of a GC from attempting to trade-off return expectations in exchange for agreement to pursue electoral-support-maximising projects — a potentially major source of agency costs.

If the financial targets in the SCI are to be used for these purposes, this raises the related question whether or not there should be anything in the SCI other than financial targets. The better view is that the SCI should only

220   *Corporate Governance in Government Corporations*

contain verifiable targets, most of which are likely to be financial. Those verifiable targets form a better basis for contracting over other matters, such as the payment of bonuses linked to the SCI. The key things the SCI should contain are the target return on equity, the target dividend, and planned capital reductions for the financial year. The SCI could contain a limited group of other matters, such as the certification by an expert of the substantial completion of a project, or the adoption of a new collective bargain with labour before some date. Verifiability is the key to any document that is intended to serve the function of a performance contract (Hart 1995; Schwartz 1992). It follows that other matters that are less apt to be verifiable can remain in other documents, such as the Corporate Plan that many Australasian jurisdictions use. That document would then contain various commitments and policy statements.

It is also desirable for the GC to disclose in their accounts the reasons why SCI targets were not achieved, and how measures have been taken, either by the GC or at the instance of the Minister, to ensure that these failures do not recur in the next year. This facilitates public scrutiny of the consequences the Minister is seen to impose for non-achievement of the SCI.

Community Service Obligations and Policy Directives

The CSO is an important part of governance in GCs. As we have seen, it represents a partial solution to the problem of the disparity between the maximisation and public interest objectives of the GC. It also permits segmentation of the objectives of the Ministers. It is, however, attended by several problems. As Quiggin (2003) points out, the CSO does not respond very well to objectives which involve a range of tasks and elements, the optimal performance of which depends on the state of the world. For example, specifying that certain users should be entitled to receive, say, free utilities is relatively easy. By contrast, a broader objective, like maintaining the integrity of a telecommunications network, is extremely difficult. The 'optimal' performance of that task presumably depends on a number of variables, such as the cost and change of the technology, the number of persons residing in particular nodes of the network, and the opportunity costs of the money invested. This makes it difficult to specify the appropriate performance of the CSO, to cost the CSO ex ante, and to ascertain if the CSO has been fulfilled. The core difficulty is that the managers of the GC are likely to have private information regarding the revealed states of the world that influence the degree of optimal performance. There is thus a risk of opportunism in the performance of the CSO, especially where a fixed funding commitment is made ex ante. Shirking is one likely possibility.

An alternative risk of the CSO is that it is used to cross-subsidise activities in which the GC competes with private sector market participants. If this occurred, the CSO would violate competitive neutrality and drive out market competition. We have seen that directors don't think CSO funding overprices the service. Nonetheless, to the extent that CSOs help to fund some of the firm's fixed costs, the GC may still be in a position to diminish market competition. This is particularly true if governments subsidise particular services with the politically motivated intention that they appear to be well-patronised and thus successful (King 2003).

It is difficult for legal rules to do much to solve these problems, especially those relating to private information. It may be appropriate as part of the accountability processes associated with the GC for there to be ongoing performance audits of the benefits from the performance of the CSO. The principal risk is that a CSO becomes 'sticky' — once it is established, it becomes a fixture, which is difficult to shift.[9] Where this occurs, the GC and the government may have limited incentives to seek out more efficient means of delivering the service. Although the political realities may make some CSOs relatively immutable, it is necessary for these to be reviewed periodically in order to examine the distribution of benefits, the costs of delivering services, and alternative means (including those not involving the GC) of delivering the benefit to the community. The establishment of an Advisory Board is an important part of this process since it provides a feedback loop which includes persons who are supposed to benefit from the service as well as other representatives of groups who have incentives to establish superior claims to government funding. This adds both scrutiny and contestability to the delivery of the CSO.

Closely related to CSOs is the issue of Ministerial directives. CSOs are a species of operational directive. However, directives may also concern governance issues, such as in relation to financial controls or management compensation. A directive may also require that the GC follow a government policy which departments and other parts of government are subject to. The empirical evidence suggests that governmental policies rarely add value to the GC, and often are unnecessary and costly. Is it possible to limit the reserve powers of the Minister to issue directives to follow stated policies or other edicts?

Imposing a requirement that any directive binding a GC be funded specifically has appeal in theory, as it compels the costs of the directive to be disclosed publicly. However, the verification of marginal cost is very difficult for many policies, and the matter comes down to negotiation

222   *Corporate Governance in Government Corporations*

between the board and the Minister. An alternative approach is to provide a series of 'market-mimicking' bases for the judicial review of directives, with widely drawn rights of standing for both the GC and persons affected by the directive to invoke these principles. There are three possible grounds for such judicial review.

The first is an immunity from a directive relating to day-to-day or operational management. American securities regulation uses both tests to limit the capacity of shareholders seeking to propose resolutions for adoption by the vote of shareholders.[10] These matters are clearly within the discretion of management and the board.

The second is a test of 'equal protection'. This would immunise the GC from having to comply with policies on an ongoing basis which did not apply, or could not be applied, to private firms. An example would be a directive to use only union labour or to employ a certain number of employees with visual impairment. Such a principle establishes a legal basis for competitive neutrality.

The third is that Ministers would not be permitted to make directives where the directive would jeopardise capacity to achieve the return in the SCI. I have already suggested the possibility of predicating governance entitlements on the achievement of SCI targets. For such a regime to be effective, it is appropriate that a Minister be limited in making unfunded directives that would materially jeopardise the capacity of the GC to achieve a specified financial target.

Aspects of Government Departments

Many of the measures identified above would go some way to addressing the problems associated with strategic behaviour by departments, especially to the extent that there is Ministerial-departmental collusion, and many of the others are not likely to be susceptible to legal intervention. They depend on the culture of interaction, which is itself contingent on the personalities involved in the GC, the department, and the government.

One possible source of problems is the existence of offices within departments which serve advisory functions — for example, they are sources of expertise and guidance on governance or financial controls. Where these are part of the same department that serves regulatory or monitoring functions, there may be some difficulties in accommodating these advisory functions. Is it appropriate to combine these functions within the departments assisting shareholding Ministers? It can be done if two conditions hold. The first is that the GC's board has a broad range of discretion regarding its governance arrangements — that the advice from such an office is just advice, rather than direction. The second is that the

Reforming Government Corporations

GC is able to seek advice from a range of sources — the advisory office does not have a monopoly on providing that advice. We saw a similar issue in the context of developmental issues for GC officers — it is important for the chairman to remain the principal arbitrator of what advice the GC procures.

Interaction with Interest Groups

Many of the recommendations above concerning disclosure of lobbying of the board, the reforms of the CSO process, and so on, have in mind the regulation of the influence that interest groups can wield over GCs. That indirect effect is also achieved by such measures as hardening budget constraints and allowing the board a greater level of autonomy in the determination of its members when the GC has performed well. The goal is not to eliminate that influence but to render it more visible and more accountable. Thus, any influence of interest groups must be visible, and any subsidies afforded them be made as explicit as possible. This enables a more desirably competitive approach between interest groups. We have discussed the CSO mechanism above, since its role in the interaction between interest groups and the Minister is very clear. Note, however, that because Ministers can exert political pressure over GCs to render services, they may prefer *not* to use the CSO mechanism, both in order to apply the CSO funding elsewhere in their portfolios and in order to reduce the visibility of the subsidy. In order to counter that possible evasion of political accountability, it is desirable for GCs to demonstrate the relative profitability of different lines of business and also across different geographical areas, and second to justify changes in services and pricing by reporting on their impact on net income. Line of business reporting is highly desirable in order for there to be sufficient scrutiny of the justification for continuing with each line of business. Changes in services and pricing have similar justifications and respond to more short-term interest group pressures.

Ministerial Ethics

It will be apparent from the above analyses that one of the fundamental problems with corporatisation is that governments have so many sources of power over the GC. This enables explicit governance devices, such as the CSO, the SCI, and the conferral of management power on the board, to be circumvented by a government. It follows that the governance solutions recommended in this chapter are second-best solutions. They typically assume that savings in agency costs are possible by reallocating power away from the Ministerial shareholders to the board under some circumstances — despite the fact that the agency costs of management may increase in at least some of these situations.

It follows that ethical norms have an important role in contributing to governance in GCs. If Ministers can internalise norms that lend themselves to reducing agency costs of governance and increasing accountability, these norms will be highly desirable for GCs.

The central ethical norms that matter are a commitment to play by 'the rules' — to use the governance apparatus as it was meant to be used. These include such norms as:

(1) Communicating with the GC only through appropriate channels — the management in respect of operational issues, and the chairman in respect of governance issues — not through inappropriate means such as lobbying individual directors.

(2) Limiting intervention in management processes to the designated processes of directives and goal-setting.

(3) Cutting no deals with management that trade-off political aspirations for 'slack' in relation to operations and financial performance.

(4) Making appointments to the board that reflect performance and public interest representation, not politically *simpatico* motivations and aspirations.

The difficulty is in finding ways of reinforcing these ethics by rewarding Ministers who internalise these ethics, and punishing those who violate them. Political seniors in the government hierarchy are a possible source of reinforcement. In some cases, the most senior members of government may be willing to punish Ministerial shareholders who infringe these ethics — however this may not happen very often where the action has been taken for political and especially electoral advantage or in the interests of interest groups.

An alternative and more promising source of norm enforcement is the parliament itself. The Minister is accountable to the parliament for his use and misuse of his power in relation to governance of the GC. The role of the parliament may be critical to increasing the willingness of the more senior figures in the government to discipline wayward Ministers. Again, the motivations of the parliament may be questioned — matters may be reviewed for political advantage. Nonetheless, as a forum for Ministerial accountability, parliament's claims are clear.

Governing the Operations of the Government Corporation

So far in our analysis, we have primarily examined how governance practices and proposed reforms effect the agency costs of management and governance. The remaining objective for the governance systems of the GC — the minimisation of the social costs of monopoly — has only fleetingly engaged our attention. In this section, we examine some specific issues of governance where this issue is squarely raised.

The specific issue to be considered is how best to regulate and govern any desire by the GC to expand into a new line of business. This issue raises a number of complex problems. One the one hand, it is expected that the GC should make decisions to maximise their value. On the other hand, there are some substantial concerns arising where a GC exceeds its statutory mandate. The primary concern is the risk that the GC will use the monopoly rents that it earns to subsidise its operations in the new market. Even if total profits from all operations are reduced, this may not prove a disincentive to the GC's managers, given the imperfect incentives and property rights in GCs. Thus, a GC may undesirably undercut private competitors charging marginal cost. Thus, competition, and the social benefits arising from it may need to be protected against the GC (Sidak and Spulber 1996; Skeel 2003).

There are various options available to reduce these risks. The first is to regulate the prices the GC is permitted to charge in the competitive market. This, however, introduces the disadvantage that regulation has to be introduced not just for the monopolistic market but also for the competitive one, which seems unnecessary and wasteful.

The second is to prohibit the GC entering the market at all. A prohibition of this sort creates interpretive challenges, since it may not always be clear what is expansion and what isn't. A useful source of illustration is the question of whether or not the United States Postal Service should be permitted to handle express courier deliveries, in addition to its statutory mandate to handle letter mail. The statutory mandate enables a postal network to be established in rural and regional areas where it would be difficult to establish. However, the immunisation of that function from competition does create a situation where the USPS could potentially undercut participants in the competitive market for express courier delivery. It is by no means clear in this situation where the letter mail should finish, and where courier deliveries should begin. That said, prohibition may be the simplest and best answer in the clearest of cases — where the new business is unrelated to the old one. In these cases, efficiency explanations for the expansion (*e.g.*, economies of scale) will be least persuasive, and the interpretive problems are at their weakest. For those reasons, Skeel (2003)

226 *Corporate Governance in Government Corporations*

favours this approach, which he notes is reminiscent of the now obsolete doctrine of *ultra vires* in corporate law.

The third, which is more of a compromise, is to allow the GC to expand, but to require it to institute governance practices that will make it clear whether and to what extent the GC's monopolistic business is subsidising its entry into the competitive market. Transparency at that level is difficult to achieve by simply mandating reporting practices, because of the risk of distortion. One solution favoured to respond to that problem is for the GC's expansion to be 'channeled' through the medium of a new subsidiary (Skeel 2003). Although some issues of accounting practice (particularly regarding transfer pricing) remain, this practice is designed to allow a clearer sense of the profitability of the new line of business. If, for example, that subsidiary was turning a loss, it would be clear that the monopolistic business was cross-subsidising its viability; other transfers of funds between the parent and subsidiary would also be apparent. Again, a similar interpretive problem arises regarding the meaning of what constitutes expansion or a new business. By inference from the use of a prohibition on business expansion, it would seem that this is the preferred option for businesses that are related to the monopolistic business.

Conclusion

State-owned enterprises have been with us for centuries, and will continue to be around in the foreseeable future. They continue to manage substantial assets, often in important parts of the economy. The depressed conditions of world equity markets in the early years of the new millennium suggest that a fresh wave of privatisations is not imminent, and that those that do occur are likely to be done on a pragmatic, case-by-case basis in Western economies. Emerging economies will continue with economic reform of SOEs as best they can, vexed by fragile economies, weak market institutions, and short political attention spans.

We have seen that governance themes in SOEs and GCs recur in every generation. GCs offer promise as a means of increasing the efficiency of the delivery of public goods and other essential services, while still providing the interface by which government can respond to public interest concerns directly. The problem is not that GCs are inefficient, in a narrow X-efficiency sense of the relationship between inputs and outputs. The case against state ownership in some situations, such as the post-war nationalisations in the United Kingdom was obviously profound, but other analyses of efficiency have been ambiguous and confounded by different objectives. Rather, the problem lies, first, in the difficulty of enforcing an ex ante commitment by the state to create an environment in which it restricts its functions to governance. Second, it is difficult to create the requisite system of incentives for management to add value to the corporation without encouraging either wasteful behaviour or costly monopolistic behaviour. Usually the state-owned assets are simply too large for politicians and governments not to be tempted to overreach the conditions originally declared.

This has been true even in the Australasian corporatisation model, in which these problems have been recognised. The empirical evidence in this paper demonstrates this quite clearly. Management remains substantially politicised. Ministerial shareholders continue to be involved in management often intervening and interfering in ways that are not esteemed to be helpful, and which reflect political considerations rather than efficiency or even public interest ones. Customers and other lobby groups interact with the GC through the medium of the political process rather than the market, inconsistently with the purpose of corporatisation.

This is not, to be sure, a plea for privatisation. The evidence is only of the costs of one form of ownership; it does not tell us anything about the costs of some other form of ownership. Recent events in BCs, such as extravagant compensation packages for executives and the frauds connected with these, are evidence of the agency costs of management in BCs, and the imperfection of the incentives that they are subject to.

The principal insight of this book and this chapter, as a guide to possible reforms, is to begin with the idea that governance structures are not self-enforcing. They can, however, be made more so by way of contingent allocations of control. At the same time, legal rules can assist to clarify the involvement of interest groups with the governance processes of the firm, and ethical principles can establish the roles and interactions we can expect of participants in GC governance. A recurring theme in this book is that simply appropriating the governance processes, laws, and ethics of BCs is unlikely to be optimal. For that reason, alone, the idea that corporatisation is substantively intermediate between privatisation and a government department is dangerous if it is used as a basis for deducing governance processes. Governance is discontinuous. It makes sense to try to design governance appropriate to the form, rather than to emulate the incentive structure of other alternatives. As Williamson has argued, selective intervention is rarely possible. This need be fatal neither to the viability of GCs, nor continued research on their governance. By contrast, the capacity to recognise GCs and their governance as a subject of research in its own right liberates us from the comparative static analysis of the past, and opens up a dynamic new field for the future.

228   *Corporate Governance in Government Corporations*

Notes

1. An example is where the GC pays out higher dividends by cribbing on maintenance expenditure.
2. Table 6.1 also indicates another notable property of GC directors' fees. GC directors fees are unlike the fees for other company types in that the mean is less than the median, indicating that the highest directors' fees are relatively low.
3. *AWA v Daniels* (1992) 7 ACSR 759.
4. Guidelines for Canadian GCs identify the chairman is usually responsible for this function (Minister of Finance and the President of the Treasury Board 1996).
5. SA: s. 31; ACT: s. 16(1)(a); Cth: ss. 32 (Commonwealth authorities), 44 (Commonwealth companies).
6. Similar problems are experienced in conventional directors' duties. In strict equitable doctrine, transactions tainted by a conflict of interest are all voidable. However, the existence of an improper purpose for a permissible action, such as defensive action in a takeover is much harder to judge by that standard, because of variable penetration of that motive amongst all of the directors, the lower incidence of moral hazard in an action responding to a takeover initiated externally, and the equivocal merits of defensive action designed to solicit competing bids, for example.
7. To similar effect, see *Corporations Act* 2001 (Cth Aust) s. 195.
8. See the discussion of this issue: *supra*, p. 31.
9. This is a particular issue when CSOs involve sunk costs, especially where investments in match are made by the government in connection with the CSO. In these cases, a market that may have been contestable will be transformed into a bilateral monopoly.
10. See 17 CFR § 240.14a-8 (1999).

Bibliography

Ahern, M., Goss, W., Innes, A. (1989), *Management of the Queensland Public Sector in the 1990s* Centre for Australian Public Sector Management, Research Paper No 5.

Alatas, S.F. (1997), *Democracy and Authoritarianism in Indonesia and Malaysia — The Rise of the Post-Colonial State*, Macmillan Press, London.

Alchian, A (1965), 'Some Economics of Property Rights', *Il Politico*, **30**, 816–829.

Alonso-Zaldivar, R., Meun, J. and Brooks, N.R. (2002), 'Ex-Enron Trader Admits Rigging Energy Market', *Los Angeles Times*, October 18.

American Law Institute (1982), Principles of Corporate Governance and Structure: Restatement and Recommendation, Tentative Draft No. 1.

Armour, J. and Whincop, M.J. (2003), 'The Proprietary Structure of Corporate Law', unpublished working paper.

Ayres, I. and Gertner, R. (1992), 'Strategic Contractual Inefficiency and the Optimal Choice of Legal Rules', *Yale Law Journal*, **101**, 729–773.

Bacon, J. (1993), *Corporate Boards and Corporate Governance*, Conference Board, New York.

Baird, D., Gertner, R. and Picker, R. (1994), *Game Theory and the Law*, Harvard University Press, Cambridge.

Baker, M.P. and Gompers, P. (1999), 'An Analysis of Executive Compensation, Ownership, and Control in Closely Held Firms', unpublished working paper.

Balfour, M. and Crise, C. (1993), 'A Privatisation Test: The Czech Republic, Slovakia and Poland', *Fordham International Law Journal*, (1993), **17**, 84–125.

Bebchuk, L.A. and Roe, M.J. (1999), 'A Theory of Path Dependence in Corporate Ownership and Governance', *Stanford Law Review*, **52**, 127–170.

Becker, G.S. (1983), 'A Theory of Competition Among Pressure Groups for Political Influence', *Quarterly Journal of Economics*, **98**, 371–400.

Berle, A.A and Means, G.C. (1932), *The Modern Corporation and Private Property*, MacMillan, New York.

Blair, M.M. and Stout, L.A. (1999), 'A Team Production Theory of Corporate Law', *Virginia Law Review*, **85**, 247–328.

230   *Corporate Governance in Government Corporations*

Blanchard, O. and Shleifer, A. (2000), 'Federalism With and Without Political Centralization: China Versus Russia', Massachusetts Institute of Technology Department of Economics Working Paper 00-15.

Blasi, J.R., Kroumova, M. and Kruse, D. (1997), *Kremlin Capitalism – The Privatization of the Russian Economy*, Cornell UP, Ithaca.

Blaszczyk B. and Dabrowski, M. (1993), *The Privatisation Process in 1989-1992: Expectations, Results and Dilemmas*, Centre for Research into Communist Economies, London.

Boubakri, N. and Cosset, J.-C. (1998), 'The Financial and Operating Performance of Newly Privatized Firms: Evidence for Developing Countries', *Journal of Finance*, **53**, 1081–1110.

Boubakri, N., Cosset, J.-C. and Guedhami, O. (2001), 'Liberalization, Corporate Governance and the Performance of Newly Privatized Firms', unpublished working paper, available at http://papers.ssrn.com/sol3 /papers.cfm?abstract_id=270642

Bratton, W.W., Jr. (1989), 'The "Nexus of Contracts" Corporation: A Critical Appraisal', *Cornell Law Review*, **74**, 407–465.

Broadman, H.G. (2001), 'Lessons from Corporatization and Corporate Governance Reform in Russia and China', unpublished conference paper.

Brown, A.J. (2003), 'Halfway House or Revolving Door? Corporatisation and Political Cycles in Western Democracy' in M.J. Whincop (ed.), *From Bureaucracy to Business Enterprise: Legal and Policy Issues in the Transformation of Government Services*, Ashgate, Aldershot.

Buchanan, J. and Tullock, G. (1965), *The Calculus of Consent*, Duke University Press, Durham.

Business Week (2001), 'California's Bitter Bailout', 5 March, 44.

Butlin, N.G., Barnard A. and Pincus, J.J. (1982), *Government and capitalism: public and private choice in twentieth century Australia*, Allen and Unwin, Sydney.

Cao, L. (1995), 'The Cat that Catches Mice: China's Challenge to the Dominant Privatization Model', *Brooklyn Journal of International Law*, **21**, 97-178.

Chandler, M.A. (1983), 'The Politics of Public Enterprise', in J.R.S. Prichard (ed.), *Crown Corporations in Canada*, Butterworths, Toronto.

Chang, R. (ed) (1997), *Incommensurability, Incomparability, and Practical Reason*, Harvard University Press, Cambridge.

Chorney, H. (1998), 'The Future of Crown Corporations: Government Ownership, Regulation or Market Control: A Keynesian Approach', in J.R. Allan (ed.), *Public Enterprise in an Era of Change*, Canadian Plains Research Center, University of Regina.

Coffee, J.C., Jr. (1990), 'Unstable Coalitions: Corporate Governance as a Multi-Player Game', *Georgetown Law Journal*, **78**, 1495–1549.

Bibliography

Collier, B. and Pitkin, S. (1999) (eds), *Corporatisation and Privatisation in Australia*, CCH, Sydney.

Curnow, G.R. and Saunders, C.A. (1983) (eds), *Quangos: The Australian Experience*, Hale and Ironmonger, Sydney.

Davies, M.R. (1998), 'Civil Servants, Managerialism and Democracy in the UK', International Review of Administrative Sciences, **64**, 119–129.

Davis, G. (1993) (ed), *Public Sector Reform under the First Goss Government: A Documentary Sourcebook* Royal Institute of Public Administration Australia/Centre for Australian Public Sector Management, Brisbane.

De Alessi, L. (1969), 'Implications of Property Rights for Government Investment Choices', *American Economic Review*, **59**, 13–24.

De Alessi, L. (1973), 'Property Rights, Transaction Costs, and X-Efficiency: An Essay in Economic Theory', *American Economic Review*, **63**, 64–81.

De Angelo, H. (1981), 'Competition and Unanimity', *American Economic Review*, **71**, 18–27.

De Lacy, K. (1993), 'The Corporatisation of Government Owned Enterprises in Queensland', in G. Davis (ed), *Public Sector Reform under the First Goss Government: A Documentary Sourcebook* Royal Institute of Public Administration Australia/Centre for Australian Public Sector Management, Brisbane.

Demsetz, H. (1967), 'Towards a Theory of Property Rights', *American Economic Review,* **57**, 347–359.

Deutsch, C.H. (2003), 'The Revolution that Wasn't: 10 Years Later, Corporate Oversight is Still Dismal', *New York Times*, January 26, BU2, BU12.

Dewatripont, M. and Roland, G. (1999), 'Soft Budget Constraints, Transition and Financial Systems', working paper.

Dirmeyer, J. Tulley, F. and Block, W. (2002); 'Should Airlines be Subsidized in an Emergency? The Libertarian View', *Journal of Social, Political and Economic Studies*, **27**, 65–81.

Dixit, A.K. (1996), *The Making of Economic Policy: A Transaction-Cost Perspective,* MIT Press, London.

Dixit, A.K. (2000), 'Incentives and Organizations in the Public Sector: An Interpretive Review', unpublished manuscript.

Dixit, A.K. and Nalebuff B.J. (1991), *Thinking Strategically: The Competitive Edge in Business, Politics, and Everyday Life*, W.W. Norton, New York.

Domberger, S., Meadowcroft, S. and Thompson, D. (1986), 'Competitive Tendering and Refuse Collection', *Fiscal Studies*, **7**, 69–87.

232   *Corporate Governance in Government Corporations*

D'Souza, J., Megginson, W.L. and Nash, R. (2000), 'Determinants of Performance Improvements in Privatized Firms: The Role of Restructuring and Corporate Governance', paper presented at 2001 American Finance Association 2001 annual meeting.

Duncan, I. and Bollard, A. (1992), *Corporatization & Privatisation: Lessons from New Zealand*, Oxford University Press.

Dunleavy, P. (1991), *Democracy, Bureaucracy and Public Choice: Economic Explanations in Political Science*, Harvester Wheatsheaf, Sydney.

Easterbrook, F.H. and Fischel, D.R. (1991), *The Economic Structure of Corporate Law*, Harvard University Press, Cambridge.

Ehrlich, I., Gallais-Hamonno, G., Liu, Z., and Lutter, R. (1994), 'Productivity Growth and Firm Ownership: An Empirical Investigation', *Journal of Political Economy*, **102**, 1006–1038.

Eisenberg, M.A. (1989), 'The Structure of Corporation Law', *Columbia Law Review*, **89**, 1461–1526.

Encel, S. (1968), 'The Concept of the State in Australian Politics', in C.A.H. Hughes (ed), *Readings in Australian Government*, University of Queensland Press, Brisbane.

Fama, E.F. and Jensen. M.C. (1983a), 'Separation of Ownership and Control', *Journal of Law & Economics*, **26**, 301–325.

Forsyth, P. (1992) 'Public Enterprise: A Success Story of Microeconomic Reform?', *CEPR Discussion Paper No. 278*, Australian National University, Canberra.

Froomkin, A.M. (1995), 'Reinventing the Government Corporation', *University of Illinois Law Review,* **1995**, 543–634.

Frydman, R., Gray, C.W., Hessel, M., and Rapaczynski, A. (1999), 'When Does Privatization Work? The Impact of Private Ownership on Corporate Performance in Transition Economies', *Quarterly Journal of Economics*, **114**, 1153–1191.

Frydman, R. and Rapacyznski, A. (1994), *Privatization in Eastern Europe: Is the State Withering Away?*, Central European University Press, London.

Gibbon, H. (1997), 'A Seller's Manual: Guidelines for Selling State-Owned Enterprises' in *Privatisation Yearbook*, Privatisation International, London.

Gillan, S.L. and Starks, L.T. (1998), A Survey of Shareholder Activism: Motivation and Empirical Evidence, *Contemporary Finance Digest*, **2**, 10–34.

Gilson, R.J. (1996), 'Corporate Governance and Economic Efficiency: When Do Institutions Matter', Washington University Law Quarterly, **74**, 327–345.

Bibliography

Gilson, R.J. and Roe, M.J. (1993), 'Understanding the Japanese Keiretsu: Overlaps Between Corporate Governance and Industrial Organization', *Yale Law Journal*, **102**, 871-906.

Goodrich, C. (ed.) (1967), *The Government and the Economy, 1973–1861*, Bobbs-Merrill, Indianapolis.

Graham, C. and Prosser, T. (1991), *Privatising Public Entities: Constitutions, the State and Regulation in Comparative Perspective*, Clarendon Press, Oxford.

Hancock, W.K. (1930), *Australia*, Benn, London.

Hansmann, H. and Kraakman, R. (2000), 'The End Of History For Corporate Law', *Georgetown Law Journal*, **89**, 439–468.

Harper, J.T. (2001), 'Short-term Effects of Privatization on Operating Performance in the Czech Republic', *Journal of Financial Research*, **24**, 119–131.

Hart, O. (1995), *Firms, Contracts, and Financial Structure*, Clarendon Press, Oxford.

Hellman, J. (1998), 'Winners Take All: The Politics of Partial Reform in Postcommunist Transitions', *World Politics*, **50**, 203–234.

Hendricks, W. (1977), 'Regulation and Labor Earnings', *Bell Journal of Economics and Management Science*, **8**, 483–496.

Hilmer, F., Rayner, M., and Taperell, G. (1992), *National Competition Policy*, Report by the Independent Committee of Inquiry, AGPS, Canberra.

Hirshhorn, R., (1984), 'Government Enterprise and Organizational Efficiency', *Economic Council of Canada*, unpublished paper.

Hlaváček, J. and Mejstřick, M. (1997), 'The Initial Economic Environment for Privatization', in M. Mejstřick (ed), *The Privatization Process in East-Central Europe: evolutionary process of Czech Privatization*, Kluwer, Boston.

Holmstrom, B. and Milgrom, P. 'Multitask Principal-Agent Analyses: Incentive contracts, asset ownership, and job design', *Journal of Law, Economics, and Organization* 7, 24–52.

Hopkins, T.D. (1998), 'The Czech Republic's Privatization Experience', in D.S. Iatridis and J.G. Hopps (eds), *Privatization in Central and Eastern Europe — Perspectives and Approaches*, Praeger, London.

Hopt, K.J. (1998), 'The German Two-Tier Board: Experience, Theories, Reforms', in K. Hopt, *Comparative Corporate Governance — The State of The Art And Emerging Research*, Clarendon Press, Oxford.

Jefferson, G.H., Rawski, T.G., Zheng, Y. (1996), 'Chinese Industrial Productivity: Trends, Measurement Issues, and Recent Developments', *Journal of Comparative Economics*, **23**. 146–180.

Jefferson, G.H. and Rawski, T.G. (2001), 'Enterprise Reform in Chinese Industry', in R. Garnuat and Y. Huang (eds.), *Growth Without Miracles*

234   *Corporate Governance in Government Corporations*

— *Readings on the Chinese Economy in the Era of Reform*, Oxford University Press, Oxford.

Jensen, M.C. (1986), 'Agency Costs of Free Cash Flow, Corporate Finance, and Takeovers,' *American Economic Review*, **76**, 323–329.

Jensen, M.C. and Meckling, W.H. (1976), 'Theory of the Firm: Managerial Behavior, Agency Costs, and Ownership Structure', *Journal of Financial Economics,* **3**, 305–360.

Jensen, M.C. and Murphy, K.J. (1990), 'Performance Pay and Top-Management Incentives', *Journal of Political Economy,* **98,** 225–261.

Johnstone, C. (2002), 'State's Profits set to Slump', *Courier Mail*, 9 April, 1.

Jones, S., Megginson, W.L., Nash R.C., and Netter, J.M. (1999), 'Share Issue Privatizations as Financial Means to Political and Economic Ends', *Journal of Financial Economics*, **53**, 217–253.

Kapstein, E.B. and Milanovic, B. (1999), 'Dividing the Spoils: Pensions, Privatizations and Reform in Russia's Transition', working paper.

Kelly-Escobar, J. (1982), 'Comparing state enterprises across international boundaries: the Corporación Venezolanda de Guayana and the Companhía Vale do Rio Doce', in L.P. Jones (ed.), *Public Enterprise in Less Developed Countries*, Cambridge University Press, Cambridge, MA.

Kikeri, S., Nellis, J., and Shirley, M.M. (1992), *Privatization: The Lessons of Experience*, World Bank, Washington, DC.

King, S. (2003), 'Corporatisation and the Behaviour of Government Owned Corporations' in M.J. Whincop (ed.), *From Bureaucracy to Business Enterprise: Legal and Policy Issues in the Transformation of Government Services*, Ashgate, Aldershot.

Klein, A. (1998), 'Firm Performance and Board Committee Structure', *Journal of Law and Economics*, **41**, 275–303.

Klein, B., Crawford, R.G. and Alchian, A.A., (1978), 'Vertical Integration, Appropriable Rents, and the Competitive Contracting Process', *Journal of Law & Economics,* **21**, 297–326.

Klich, J. (1998), 'The Concept of Mass Privatization in Poland: Theoretical and Practical Considerations', in D.S. Iatridis and J.G. Hopps (eds), *Privatization in Central and Eastern Europe — Perspectives and Approaches*, Praeger, London.

Korn/Ferry International (2000), *Boards of Directors Study in Australia and New Zealand 2000.*

Kornai, J. (1992), *The Socialist System: The Political Economy of Communism*, Princeton University Press, Princeton.

Kraakman, R. (1984), 'Corporate Liability Strategies and the Costs of Legal Controls', *Yale Law Journal*, **93**, 857–898.

Bibliography

Kuznetsov, A. and Kuznetsova, O. (1999), 'The State as a Shareholder: Responsibilities and Objectives', *Europe-Asia Studies*, **51**, 433–446.

Langford, J.W. (1979), 'Crown Corporations as Instruments of Policy', in G.B. Doern and P. Aucoin (eds), *Public Policy in Canada: Organization, Process and Management*, McGill-Queen's University Press, Montreal.

Lardy, N.R. (1998), 'China's Unfinished Economic Experiment', in J.A. Dorn (ed.), *China in the New Millennium: Market Reforms and Social Development*, Cato Institute, Washington, D.C.

Levac, M. and Wooldridge, P. (1997), 'The Fiscal Impact of Privatization in Canada', *Bank of Canada Review*, **1997**, 25–39.

Li, W. (1997), 'The Impact of Economic Reform on the Performance of Chinese State Enterprises, 1980–1989', *Journal of Political Economy* **105**, 1080–1106.

Lin, C. (2000), 'Corporate Governance of State-Owned Enterprises in China', working paper, Asian Development Bank.

Lipsey, R.G., and Lancaster, K. (1956), 'The General Theory of Second Best', *Review of Economic Studies*, **24**, 11–32.

Longstreth, F.H. (1989), 'From Corporatism to Dualism? Thatcherism and the Climacteric of British Trade Unions in the 1980s', *Political Studies*, **36**, 413–432.

López-de-Silanes, F. (1997), 'Determinants of Privatization Prices', *Quarterly Journal of Economics*, **112**, 965–1025.

Macey, J.R. (1991), 'An Economic Analysis of the Various Rationales for Making Shareholders the Exclusive Beneficiaries of Corporate Fiduciary Duties, *Stetson Law Review*, **21**, 23–41.

Macey, J.R. and Miller, G.P. (1995), 'Corporate Governance and Commercial Banking: A Comparative Examination of Germany, Japan and the United States', *Stanford Law Review*, **48**, 73–112.

McCarthy, D.J., Naumov, A.I., and Puffer, S.M. (2000), 'Russia's Retreat to Statization and the Implications for Business', *Journal of World Business*, 35, 256–274.

McCraw, T.K. (1981), *Regulation in Perspective: Historical Essays*, Harvard University Press, Boston.

McMinn, W.G. (1979), *A Constitutional History of Australia*, Oxford University Press.

Megginson, W.L., Nash R.C., and van Randenborgh, M. (1994), 'The Financial and Operating Performance of Newly Privatized Firms: An International Empirical Analysis', *Journal of Finance*, **49**, 403–452.

Megginson, W.L. and Netter, J.M. (2001), 'From State to Market: A Survey of Empirical Studies on Privatization', *Journal of Economic Literature*, **39**, 321–389.

236   *Corporate Governance in Government Corporations*

Milne, R.S. and Mauzy, D.K. (1999), *Malaysian Politics under Mahathir*, Routledge, London.

Minister of Finance and the President of the Treasury Board (1996), 'Corporate Governance in Crown Corporations and Other Public Enterprises — Guidelines', Treasury Board of Canada Secretariat, Ottawa.

Mitchell, L.E. (ed.) (1996), *Progressive Corporate Law*, Westview, Boulder.

Mládek, J. (1997), 'Initialization of Privatization through Restitution and Small Privatization', in M. Mejstřík (ed.), *The Privatization Process in East-Central Europe: Evolutionary Process of Czech Privatization*, Kluwer, Boston.

Modigliani, F. and Miller, M.H. (1958), 'The Cost of Capital, Corporation Investment, and the Theory of Investment', *American Economic Review*, **48**, 261–297.

Morton, E. (1999), 'Economic Reform of GBEs', in B. Collier and S. Pitkin (eds), *Corporatisation and Privatisation in Australia*, CCH Australia, North Ryde.

Muzikar, K. and Drevinek, K. (2002), 'Historical Overview of Privatization', *Focus Europe*, **2002**, Summer, 54–55.

Niskanen, W. (1968), 'The peculiar economics of bureaucracy', *American Economic Review* **58(2)**, 293–305.

Niskanen, W. (1971), *Bureaucracy and Representative Government*, Aldine, Chicago.

Olson, M. (1971), *The Logic of Collective Action: Public Goods and the Theory of Groups*, 2nd ed., Harvard University Press, Cambridge.

Olson, M. (2000), *Power and Prosperity: Outgrowing Communist and Capitalist Dictatorships*, Basic Books, New York.

Otsuka, K., Liu, D. and Murakami, N. (1998), *Industrial Reform in China Past Performance and Future Prospects*, Clarendon Press, Oxford.

Pagoulatos, G. (2001), 'The Enemy Within: Intragovernmental Politics and Organizational Failure in Greek Privatization', *Public Administration*, **79**, 125–138.

Parker, C.E. (2002), *The Open Corporation: Effective Self-Regulation and Democracy*, Cambridge University Press.

Parkes, H. (1892), *Fifty Years in the Making of Australian History*, Longmans Green, London.

Patience, A. and Head, B. (1979), 'Australian politics in the 1970s', in Patience and Head (eds), *From Whitlam to Fraser: reform and reaction in Australian politics*, Oxford University Press, Melbourne.

Patterson, R.H. (1996), 'How the Chicago School Hijacked New Zealand Competition Law and Policy', *Competition Law & Policy*, **17**, 160-192.

Peltzman, S. (1976), 'Toward a More General Theory of Economic Regulation', *Journal of Law & Economics*, **19**, 211–240.

Peoples, J. (1998), 'Deregulation and the Labor Market', *Journal of Economic Perspectives*, **12**, 111–130.

Perotti, E.C. and Guney, S.E. (1993), 'The Structure of Privatization Plans', *Financial Management*, **22**, 84–98.

Perry, T. and Zenner, M. (2000), 'CEO Compensation in the 1990s: Shareholder Alignment or Shareholder Expropriation?', *Wake Forest Law Review*, **35**, 123–152.

Pinto, B., Belka, M. and Krajewski, S. (1993), 'Transforming State Enterprises in Poland: Evidence on Adjustment by Manufacturing Firms', *Brookings Papers on Economic Activity*, 213–261.

Poznanski, K.Z. (1993), 'An Interpretation of Communist Decay: The Role of Evolutionary Mechanisms', *Communist and Post-Communist Studies*, **26**, 3-24.

Prichard, J.R.S. (ed.), (1983), *Crown Corporations in Canada*, Butterworths, Toronto.

Przeworski, A. (1991), *Democracy and the Market*, Cambridge University Press, New York.

Queensland Government (1993), *Corporatisation in Queensland — Policy Guidelines: A Queensland Government White Paper.*

Quiggin, J. (2003), 'Governance of Public Corporations: Profits and the Public Benefit' in M.J. Whincop (ed.), *From Bureaucracy to Business Enterprise: Legal and Policy Issues in the Transformation of Government Services*, Ashgate, Aldershot.

Rajan, R.G. and Zingales, L. (2000), 'The Governance of the New Enterprise', in Vives, X. (ed.), *Corporate Governance Theoretical and Empirical Perspectives*, Cambridge University Press, Cambridge.

Rajan, R.G. and Zingales, L. (2001), 'The Firm as a Dedicated Hierarchy: A Theory of the Origins and Growth of Firms', *Quarterly Journal of Economics,* **116**, 805-851.

Rawski, T.G. (1996), 'Implications of China's Reform Experience', in A.G. Walder (ed.), *China's Transitional Economy*, Oxford University Press, Oxford.

Rodan, G., Hewison, K. and Robison, R. (1997), *The Political Economy of South-East Asia — An Introduction*, Oxford University Press, Melbourne.

Roe, M.J. (1993), 'Some Differences in Corporate Structure in Germany, Japan, and the United States', *Yale Law Journal*, **102**, 1927–2000.

Romano, R. (1993), 'Public Pension Fund Activism in Corporate Governance Reconsidered', Columbia Law Review, **93**, 795–853.

Romano, R. (1996), 'Corporate Law and Corporate Governance', *Industrial & Corporate Change*, **5**, 277–339.

238   *Corporate Governance in Government Corporations*

Romano, R. (1999), 'Less is More: Making Shareholder Activism a Valued Mechanism of Corporate Governance', *Yale Journal on Regulation*, **18**, 174–251.

Sappington, D. and Sidak, J.G. (1999) 'Incentives for Anticompetitive Behavior by Public Enterprises', Working Paper 99-11, AEU–Brookings Joint Center for Regulatory Studies.

Sappington, D.M.E. and Sidak, J.G. (1999), 'Incentives for Anticompetitive Behavior by Public Enterprises', unpublished draft.

Schipani, C.A. and Liu, J. (2002), 'Corporate Governance in China: Then and Now', *Columbia Business Law Review*, **2002**, 1–69.

Schmitz, P.W. (2000), 'Partial Privatization and Incomplete Contracts: The Proper Scope of Government Reconsidered', *FinanzArchiv*, **57**, 394–411.

Schnitzer, M.C. (1987), *Contemporary Government and Business Relations* (3rd ed), Houghton Mifflin, Boston.

Schwab, S.J. and Thomas, R.S. (1998), 'Realigning Corporate Governance: Shareholder Activism by Labor Unions', *Michigan Law Review*, **96**, 1018–1094.

Schwartz, A. (1992), 'Relational Contracts in the Courts: An Analysis of Incomplete Agreements and Judicial Strategies', *Journal of Legal Studies*, **21**, 271–318.

Shapiro, C. and Willig, R.D. (1990), 'Economic Rationales for the Scope of Privatization' in E.N Suleiman and J. Waterbury (eds), *The Political Economy of Public Sector Reform and Privatization*, Westview, Boulder.

Shen, R. (2000), *China's Economic Reform An Experiment in Pragmatic Socialism*, Praeger, London.

Shirley, M.M. (1999), 'Bureaucrats in Business: The Roles of Privatization Versus Corporatization in State-Owned Enterprise Reform', *World Development*, **27**, 115–136.

Shirley, M. and Xu, L.C. (1998), 'Information, Incentives, and Commitment: An Empirical Analysis of Contracts Between Government and State Enterprises', *Journal of Law, Economics, and Organizations*, **14**, 358–378.

Shleifer, A. and Treisman, D. (1997), 'The Economics and Politics of Transition to an Open Market Economy', OECD Development Center Working Paper.

Shleifer, A. and Vishny, R. (1993), 'Corruption', *Quarterly Journal of Economics*, **108**, 599–617.

Sidak, J.G. (2002), 'Acquisitions by Partially Privitized Firms: The Case of Deutsche Telekom and Voicestream', *Federal Communications Law Journal*, **54**, 1-29.

Sidak, J.G. and Spulber, D.F. (1996), *Protecting Competition from the Postal Monopoly*, AEI Press, Washington DC.

Bibliography

Skeel, D.A., Jr. (1998), 'The Law and Finance of Bank and Insurance Insolvency Regulation', *Texas Law Review,* 76, 723–780.

Skeel, D.A., Jr. (2003), 'Virtual Privatization', in M.J. Whincop (ed.), *From Bureaucracy to Business Enterprise: Legal and Policy Issues in the Transformation of Government Services,* Ashgate, Aldershot.

Spann, R. (1977), 'Public versus Private Provision of Government Services', in Borcherding (ed.), *Budgets and Bureaucrats: The Sources of Government Growth,* Duke University Press, North Carolina.

Stearns, M.L. (2003), 'A Private-Rights Standing Model to Promote Public-Regarding Behaviour by Government Owned Corporations' in M.J. Whincop (ed.), *From Bureaucracy to Business Enterprise: Legal and Policy Issues in the Transformation of Government Services,* Ashgate, Aldershot.

Stevens, D.F. (1993), *Corporate Autonomy and Institutional Control: The Crown Corporation as a Problem in Organization Design,* McGill-Queen's University Press, Montreal.

Stigler, G. (1971), 'The Theory of Economic Regulation', *Bell Journal of Economics,* **2,** 3–21.

Stiglitz, J.E. (2002), *Globalization and its Discontents,* W.W. Norton, New York.

Sunstein, C.R. (1987), 'Constitutionalism After the New Deal', *Harvard Law Review,* **101,** 421–510.

Swann, D. (1988), *The Retreat of the State: Deregulation and Privatization in the UK and US,* Harvester/Wheatsheaf, New York.

Telser, L.G. (1980), 'A Theory of Self-Enforcing Agreements', *Journal of Business,* **53,** 27–44.

Tiebout, C.M. (1956), 'A Pure Theory of Public Expenditures', *Journal of Political Economy,* **64,** 416–424.

Tivey, L.J. (1966), *Nationalisation in British Industry,* Jonathan Cape, London.

Treasury Board of Canada Secretariat (2001), *Crown Corporations and Other Corporate Interests of Canada 2001,* Canadian Government Publishing, Ottawa.

Trebilcock, M.J. and Prichard, J.R.S (1983), 'Crown Corporations in Canada' in J.R.S. Prichard (ed.), *Crown Corporations in Canada,* Butterworths, Toronto.

Tupper, A. (1998), 'The Changing Political Environment of Canadian Crown Corporations', in J.R. Allan (ed.), *Public Enterprise in an Era of Change,* Canadian Plains Research Center, University of Regina.

von Nessen, P. and Reynolds, A. (1999), 'The Government Owned Corporations and State Owned Corporations Statutes', in Collier, B. and

240 *Corporate Governance in Government Corporations*

S. Pitkin (eds), *Corporatisation and Privatisation in Australia*, CCH, Sydney.

Wachter, M., Hirsch, B. and Kleindorfer, P.R. (2001), 'Difficulties of Deregulation When Wage Cuts are the Major Cost', in M.A. Crew, and P.R Kleindorfer (eds), *Future Directions in Postal Reform*, Kluwer, Boston.

Walker, M.A. (1998), 'Who Benefits from Privatization', in J.R. Allan (ed.), *Public Enterprise in an Era of Change*, Canadian Plains Research Center, University of Regina.

Wall, L.D. (1989), 'A Plan for Reducing Future Deposit Insurance Losses: Puttable Subordinated Debt', *Economic Review of the Federal Reserve Bank of Atlanta*.

Wang, X., Xu, L.C. and Zhu, T. (2001), *State-owned Enterprises Going Public: The Case of China*, HKUST Social Science Working Paper.

Weisman, J. (1997), 'Congress Looks West for Lesson in Utility Deregulation', *Congressional Quarterly Weekly Report*, Feb 15, 55, 7, 412–420.

Weisskopf, T.E. (1998), 'Economic Perspectives on Privatization in Russia: 1990–1994', in Iatridis, D.S. and Hopps, J.G. (eds), *Privatization in Central and Eastern Europe – Perspectives and Approaches*, Praeger, London.

Wettenhall, R. (1966), 'The Recoup Concept in Public Enterprise', *Public Administration (London)*, Vol 44; also in (1987) *Public enterprise and national development: Selected Essays*, Royal Australian Institute of Public Administration, Canberra, 45.

Wettenhall, R. (1966), 'The Recoup Concept in Public Enterprise', *Public Administration (London)*, **44**, 391–413.

Wettenhall, R. (1987), *Public enterprise and national development: Selected Essays*, Royal Australian Institute of Public Administration, Canberra.

Whincop, M.J. (1996), 'A Theoretical and Policy Critique of the Modern Reformulation of Directors' Duties of Care', *Australian Journal of Corporate Law*, **6**, 72–92.

Whincop, M.J. (1999), 'Painting the Corporate Cathedral: The Protection of Entitlements in Corporate Law', *Oxford Journal of Legal Studies*, **19**, 19-50.

Whincop, M.J. (2001), *An Economic and Jurisprudential Genealogy of Corporate Law*, Ashgate, Aldershot.

Whincop, M.J. (2002a), 'Another Side of Accountability: The Fiduciary Concept and Rent-seeking in the Governance of Government Corporations', *University of New South Wales Law Journal*, **25**, 379–407.

Whincop, M.J. (2002b), 'Contracting Around The Conflict Rule: An Empirical Analysis Of A Penalty Default', *Journal of Corporate Law Studies*, **2**, 1–23.

Winiecki, J. (1997), 'Introduction: Seven Year's Experience' in J. Winiecki (ed.), *Institutional Barriers to Poland's Economic Development*, Routledge, London.

Williamson, O.E. (1984), 'Corporate Governance', *Yale Law Journal*, **93**, 1197–1230.

Williamson, O.E. (1985), *The Economic Institutions of Capitalism*, Free Press, New York.

Williamson, O.E. (1996), *The Mechanisms of Governance*, OUP, New York.

World Bank (1997), *China's Management of Enterprise Assets: The State as Shareholder*, World Bank, Washington D.C.

Zeckhauser, R.J. and Horn, M. (1989), 'The Control and Performance of State-Owned Enterprises', in P.W. MacAvoy, W.T. Stanbury, G. Yarrow and R.J. Zeckhauser (eds), *Privatization and State-Owned Enterprises,* Kluwer, Boston.

Zhuang, J. and Xu, C. (1996). 'Profit-Sharing and Financial Performance in the Chinese State Enterprises: Evidence from Panel Data', *Economics of Planning*, **29**, 205–222.

Zingales, L. (1998), 'Corporate Governance', in P. Newman (ed.), *The Palgrave Dictionary of Economics and the Law*, Macmillan, London.

Index

agency costs
  calculation 57-9
  GCs 6, 11, 13, 22, 24, 26, 30, 31, 42, 43, 47, 53, 56, 63, 114-19, 188-90
  Ministers' discretion 120-1
agents, perquisite consumption 64
airlines, quasi-nationalisation 1
Australia
  corporatisation 14, 33, 36
  GCs 30-7
  privatisation 29-30
  SOEs 27, 28-30
  see also Queensland

BCs (Business Corporations)
  board of directors 68-9
  CEOs 65
  dividends 66
  GCs, comparison 5-9, 10-11, 18, 65-8
  governance 5, 6-7, 23
  managers 65, 67-8
  shareholders 6-7, 65, 113
board of directors
  BCs 68-9
  GCs 69-71, 195-214
    appointments 78-9, 116, 195-8
    board structure 196-7
    chairman's role 200-3
    committees 203-7
    duties 207-13
    experience 79-82
    fiduciary duties 72, 89-94
    liability 85-6
    perceived quality 86-7
    politicisation 113
    remuneration 84-5, 199-200
    reputational effects 87-8

  tenure and termination 94-109, 213-14
  governance problems 68-9
business corporations *see* BCs

Canada
  GCs 40-2
  privatisation 42
capitalism, *laissez-faire* 38
CEOs (Chief Executive Officers)
  BCs 65
  GCs, remuneration 74-8
China
  privatisation 44, 51-6
  SOEs 51-6
community service obligations *see* CSOs
corporate governance *see* governance
corporatisation
  Australia 14, 33, 36
  GCs 3, 14-18
  model 14-18
  New Zealand 14
  and privatisation 57
  Queensland 20
  SOEs 23
  US 14
creditors, GCs 181
CSOs (Community Service Obligations), GCs 8, 11-12, 17, 36, 116-18, 120, 179-80, 220-2
customers, GCs 183
Czech Republic, privatisation 49-51

data, GCs 19-20
dividends
  BCs 66
  GCs 66-7

244 *Corporate Governance in Government Corporations*

employees, GCs 181-2
Europe, Eastern, privatisation 43-4
executives, GCs 73-8
extant corporatisation model, GCs
14-18

FGCs (Federal Government
Corporations), US 39-40
finance, GCs 188-93
firm, theory of 64

GCs (Government Corporations)
agency costs 6, 11, 13, 22, 24, 26,
30, 31, 42, 43, 47, 53, 56, 57, 58,
59, 63, 114-21, 188-90
Australia 30-7
BCs, comparison 5-9, 10-11, 18,
65-8
board of directors 69-71, 78-110
appointments 78-9, 116, 195-8
chairman's role 200-3
committees 203-7
duties 207-13
experience 79-82
fiduciary duties 72-3, 89-94
liability 85-6
qualifications 81-3
qualities 86-7
remuneration 84-6, 199-200
reputational effects 87-8
tenure and termination 94-109,
213-14
Canada 40-2
CEOs, remuneration 74-8
corporatisation 3, 14-18
creditors 181
CSOs 8, 11-12, 17, 36, 116-18,
120, 179-80, 220-2
customers 183
data 19-20
dividends 66-7
employees 181-2
executives 73-8
remuneration 73-5

extant corporatisation model 14-
18
finance 188-93
governance 6-13, 225-7
government
departments 10, 146-52, 222-3
policy 9, 152-8
relationship 9-10, 113
reserved powers 16-17
institutional investors 10
interest groups 10, 163-78, 223
investment 67
local communities 184
managers 184-5, 193-5
Ministers' role 114-46, 214-24
appointments 122-4
ethics 223-4
goal setting 129-33, 217-20
governance 133-45, 215-17
interventions 16, 124-9
models 14-18
monopoly 7, 9, 12
New Zealand 14
Queensland 5, 6, 19-20
SCIs 183, 219-20
stakeholders 8, 180-5
studies 3-4
and Treasury 148-52
UK 26-7, 43
and value 8, 66
see also SOEs
governance
aim 2-3
BCs 5, 6-7, 23
board of directors, problems 68-9
GCs 6-13, 225-7
and investment 64-5
legal rules 71-3
problems 64-5
Queensland 19, 36-7
self-enforcing regimes 187-8
and shareholders 162-86
SOEs 23, 56-60
and stakeholders 162-86

Index 245

studies 3
government corporations *see* GCs

institutions, and GCs 10
interest groups
  GCs 10, 163-78, 223
    labour policies 174-8
    lobbying activities 166-74
    and privatisation 163-4
investment
  GCs 67
  and governance 64-5
  SOEs 27

legal rules, governance 71-3
local communities, GCs 184

managers
  BCs 65, 67-8
  GCs 184-5, 193-5
markets, equilibria 4
monopoly, GCs 7, 9, 12
Morrison, Herbert 24

New Zealand
  corporatisation 14
  GCs 14
  privatisation 27-8
  SOEs 27-8, 35

perquisite consumption, agents 64
Poland, privatisation 47-9
privatisation
  Australia 29-30
  Canada 42
  China 44, 51-6
  and corporatisation 57
  Czech Republic 49-51
  drawbacks 2
  Eastern Europe 43-4
  and interest groups 163-4
  New Zealand 27-8
  Poland 47-9
  Queensland 29-30

Russia 44-7
Slovak Republic 49-51
SOEs 23
UK 26, 42
see also GCs; SOEs
public choice theory 1

Queensland
  corporatisation 20
  GCs 5, 6
    governance 19, 36-7
    research data 19-20
  government system 20
  privatisation 29-30
  SCI 33-6, 116

rent-seeking 2, 5, 21 n.3, 67, 160
  n.73, 164, 165, 182, 210, 211
Russia
  privatisation 44-7
  SOEs 45-6

SCI (Statement of Corporate Intent)
  GCs 183, 219-20
  and Ministers 129-33, 219-20
  Queensland 33-6, 116
shareholders
  BCs 6-7, 65, 113
  and governance 162-86
Sherman Act (1890) 38
Slovak Republic, privatisation 49-51
SOEs (State Owned Enterprises) 22
  Australia 27, 28-30
  China 51-6
  corporatisation 23
  governance 23, 56-60
  investment 27
  New Zealand 27-8, 35
  privatisation 23
  Russia 45-6
  UK 24-7, 67
    governance 25-6
  US 37-40, 67-8
  see also GCs

stakeholders
GCs 8, 180-5
creditors 181
customers 183-4
employees 181-2
local communities 184
managers 184-5
and governance 162-86
Statement of Corporate Intent *see* SCI

UK
GCs 26-7, 43

privatisation 26, 42
SOEs 24-7, 67
US
corporatisation 14
FGCs 39-40
SOEs 27, 37-40, 67-8

value, and GCs 8, 66

Williamson, Oliver 13

Bullying in Youth Sports Training

Based on an extensive national research project with global relevance, this pioneering volume draws on unique data on bullying in youth sports training collected from both athletes and coaches using a variety of methodological approaches. Nery, Neto, Rosado and Smith use this research to establish a baseline of the prevalence of bullying among young male athletes, offering evidence-based strategies for prevention and providing a solid theoretical basis for the development of anti-bullying intervention programmes.

Bullying in Youth Sports Training explores how often bullying occurs, how long it lasts, where and when bullying takes place, the coping strategies used by victims, and the individual roles of victims, bystanders and bullies. It provides new insights into theories of youth sports bullying and highlights the particular characteristics specific to bullying in sport. The backgrounds of bullies and victims are also explored, as well as the consequences and practical implications of sustained bullying. The book provides both theoretical and practical approaches to bullying in youth sports training, providing anti-bullying guidelines based on the results of the research.

The book is essential reading for scholars and students in child development and sport sciences as well as sports coaches and professionals in mental health, education and social work.

Miguel Nery is a clinical psychologist and psychodynamic psychotherapist. He is currently a researcher at the Motor Behaviour Laboratory in the Faculty of Human Kinetics, Lisbon University, Portugal. He is responsible for a Portuguese Government funded intervention project about bullying in sport, Red Card to Bullying.

Carlos Neto is Full Professor at the Faculty of Human Kinetics, Lisbon University, Portugal. He is a member of the Motor Behaviour Laboratory.

António Rosado is Full Professor at the Faculty of Human Kinetics, Lisbon University, Portugal. He is a member of the Sport and Exercise Psychology Laboratory.

Peter K. Smith is Emeritus Professor of Psychology at Goldsmiths College, University of London, UK. He is editor of *Making an Impact on School Bullying: Interventions and Recommendations* (Routledge, 2019).